'Out Of The Dark Woods

The Messages Behin

MW00791883

This book is published on a non-profit basis (all proceeds will go the Oasis Trust) for review and analytical purposes (to describe the sources of inspiration of the copyrighted material). It necessarily relies upon the limited use of partial quotations from the songs of Bob Dylan, which are reproduced on a large number of websites worldwide. It is strongly recommended that this book (to be read in context with the full lyric) be read alongside the official 'Bob Dylan Lyrics' book, available from Mr Dylan's own website, www.bobdylan.com. Quotations are kept to a minimum, no breach of copyright is intended and all the rights to the lyrics' material are retained by Mr Dylan and his publishers.

As Mr Dylan himself recently said, 'Everybody knows by now that there's a gazillion books on me either out or coming out in the near future. So I'm encouraging anybody who's ever met me, heard me or even seen me, to get in on the action and scribble their own book. You never know, somebody might have a great book in them.' [1]

This book largely draws (unless otherwise indicated) upon scripture quotations taken from the New American Standard Bible®, Copyright © 1995 by The Lockman Foundation. Used by permission. Verses from The Holy Bible, New International Version®, NIV/ANIV® Copyright © 1973, 1978, 1984, 2011 by Biblica, Inc.™ are used by permission. All rights reserved worldwide. Scripture quotations marked 'NKJV' ™ are taken from the New King James Version®. Copyright © 1982 by Thomas Nelson, Inc, and used by permission. All rights reserved.

Thanks are due to D Perrem and M Bradford for editorial work, and, as always, to my wife Gloria.

Contents

"Christ is no religion. We're not talking about religion… Jesus Christ is the Way, the Truth and the Life. I follow God, so if my followers are following me, indirectly they're gonna be following God too, because I don't sing any song that hasn't been given to me by the Lord to sing." (Bob Dylan to Bruce Heiman, December 7, 1979).

"Christianity is not Christ and Christ is not Christianity. Christianity is making Christ the Lord of your life. You're talking about your life now, you're not talking about just part of it, you're not talking about a certain hour every day. You're talking about making Christ the Lord and the Master of your life, the King of your life. And you're also talking about Christ, the resurrected Christ, you're not talking about some dead man who had a bunch of good ideas and was nailed to a tree. Who died with those ideas. You're talking about a resurrected Christ who is Lord of your life. We're talking about that type of Christianity." (Bob Dylan to Karen Hughes, Dayton, Ohio, 21 May, 1980).

"I truly had a born-again experience, if you want to call it that. It's an over-used term, but it's something that people can relate to. It happened in 1978. I always knew there was a God or a creator of the universe and a creator of the mountains and the seas and all that kind of thing, but I wasn't conscious of Jesus and what that had to do with the supreme Creator… I've made my statement and I don't think I could make it any better than in some of those songs. Once I've said what I need to say in a song, that's it. I don't want to repeat myself." (Bob Dylan to Robert Hilburn, Los Angeles, California, 19 November, 1980).

"The answers to those questions, they've got to be in those songs I've written. Someplace, if you know where to look, I think you'll find the answers to those questions. It's right there in the songs. Better than I could say it." (Bob Dylan to Dave Herman, London, July 2, 1981).

"I'll tell you one thing, if you're talking just on a scriptural type of thing, there's no way I could write anything that would be scripturally incorrect. I mean, I'm not going to put forth ideas that aren't scripturally true. I might reverse them, or make them come out a different way, but

I'm not going to say anything that's just totally 'wrong'; that there's not a law for." (Bob Dylan to Bill Flanagan, New York, March 1985).

Bob Dylan: "Angels... The Pope says this about angels. He says they exist. And that they're spiritual beings." Sam Shepard: "Have you had any direct experience with angels?" Dylan: "Yeah. Yeah, I have." (California, August 1986, 'Esquire', July 1987).

"Peace, love and harmony are greatly important indeed, but so is forgiveness, and we've got to have that too." (Bob Dylan, New York City, January 1988).

"Gospel music is about the love of God, and commercial music is about sex... Religion has nothing to do with faith." (Bob Dylan to Kathryn Baker, Beverly Hills, August 1988).

On being 'born-again': "If that's what was laid on me there must have been a reason for it." (Bob Dylan to Edna Gundersen, September 1989).

"I believe in everything that the Bible says." (Bob Dylan, Hungary, June 1991).

"A person without faith is like a walking corpse." (Bob Dylan to Gary Hill, San Diego, October 1993).

"'Work while the day lasts, because the night... cometh when no man can work.' I don't recall where I heard it. I like preaching, I hear a lot of preaching, and I probably just heard it somewhere. Maybe it's in Psalms, it beats me." (Bob Dylan to Jon Pareles, California, September 1997; the scripture quoted is from St John's gospel, chapter 9, verse 4.)

"I know God is my shield and he won't lead me astray." (Bob Dylan, ''Til I Fell In Love With You', 'Time Out Of Mind', 1997).

'I went to church on Sunday...' (Bob Dylan, 'Cold Irons Bound', 1997).

'Well I'm sitting in church in an old wooden chair. I knew nobody would look for me there…' (Bob Dylan, 'Marching To The City', 1997).

"Those old songs are my lexicon and my prayer book… All my beliefs come out of those old songs, literally, anything from 'Let Me Rest on That Peaceful Mountain' to 'Keep On The Sunny Side.' You can find all my philosophy in those old songs. I believe in a God of time and space, but if people ask me about that, my impulse is to point them back toward those songs. I believe in Hank Williams singing 'I Saw The Light.' I've seen the light, too." (Bob Dylan to Jon Pareles, September 28, 1997. 'Keep On The Sunny Side' - 'Let us trust in our Saviour always, to keep us every one in his care. Keep on the sunny side always on the sunny side, keep on the sunny side of life' - The Carter Family).

'This world can't stand long, be ready, don't wait too late, we should know it can't stand long, for it is too full of hate. For a long time this world has stood, gets more wicked every day, the Maker who created it, surely won't let it stand this way… This world been destroyed before, 'cause it was too full of sin, for that very reason, it's going to be destroyed again… If we only give our hearts to God, let him lead you by the hand, nothing in this world to fear, he'll lead you cross the burning sand.' ('This World Can't Stand Long' sung by Bob Dylan, March 10, 2000, Anaheim, California).

'Pass me not, O gentle Saviour, hear my humble cry. While on others thou art calling do not pass me by. Saviour, Saviour, hear my humble cry. While on others thou art calling, do not pass me by. Let me at the throne of mercy, find my sweet relief, while I kneel in deep contrition, heal my unbelief.' (Bob Dylan, 'Pass Me Not, O Gentle Saviour', Bismarck, North Dakota, March 29, 2000, lyrics personalized by Dylan).

'I'm gonna baptize you in fire, so you can sin no more…' (Bob Dylan, 'Bye And Bye', 'Love And Theft', 2001).

'I'm preaching the Word of God.' (Bob Dylan, 'High Water (For Charley Patton)', 'Love And Theft', 2001).

'I went to the church house, every day I go an extra mile… Well, I'm crying to the Lord - I'm tryin' to be meek and mild.' (Bob Dylan, 'Cry Awhile', 'Love And Theft', 2001).

'Look up, look up - seek your Maker - 'fore Gabriel blows his horn.' (Bob Dylan, 'Sugar Baby', 'Love And Theft' 2001).

"I'm not that big on birthdays. It's kind of a pagan holiday, after all." (Bob Dylan, The Times Magazine, 8 September 2001).

'I let my Saviour in and he saved my soul from sin, Hallelujah, I'm ready to go… Sinner don't wait, before it's too late, he's a wonderful Saviour to know, Well, I fell down on my knees and he answered all my pleas, Hallelujah, I'm ready to go…' (Bob Dylan, 'Hallelujah, I'm Ready To Go', Brussels, Belgium, 28 April, 2002).

'I hear a voice calling, it must be our Lord. He's calling from heaven on high. I hear a voice calling, I've gained the reward, in the land where we never shall die. He died and he paid a dear price for me, he died on the hill so that I should go free, and I'll follow his footsteps up the narrow way, and be ready to meet him when he calls on that day. He died on the cross, that old rugged cross, so we would be saved from our sins and not lost. And I'll follow his footsteps up the narrow way, and be ready to meet him when he calls on that day.' (Bob Dylan, 'A Voice From On High', Omaha, Nebraska, August 21, 2002).

'Rock of Ages, cleft for me, let me hide myself in thee. Let the water and the blood, from thy wounded side which flowed. Rock of Ages, cleft for me, let me hide myself in thee. While I draw this fleeting breath, when mine eyes shall close in death. When I rise to worlds unknown, and behold thee on the throne. Rock of Ages, cleft for me, let me hide myself in thee.' (Bob Dylan, 'Rock Of Ages', April 4, 2004, Omaha, Nebraska, lyrics personalized by Dylan.) Austin Scaggs: "What's the last song you'd like to hear before you die?' Dylan: "How about 'Rock Of Ages'?" (October 26, 2004.)

'I've been to St Herman's church, said my religious vows...' (Bob Dylan, 'Thunder On The Mountain', 'Modern Times', 2006).

'Everybody saying this is a day only the Lord could make...' (Bob Dylan, 'The Levees Gonna Break', 'Modern Times', 2006).

'In the human heart an evil spirit can dwell.' (Bob Dylan, 'Ain't Talkin'', 'Modern Times', 2006).

'While I was praying, somebody touched me, must've been the hand of the Lord...' (Bob Dylan, 'Somebody Touched Me', Calgary, Albert, Canada, August 28, 2008).

"Pray the Sinner's Prayer - what's the Sinner's Prayer?" "That's the one that begins with 'Father, forgive me for I have sinned.'"... "Are you a mystical person?" "Absolutely"... "In the song 'I Feel A Change Coming On' the character says..." "- Wait a minute, Bill. I'm not a playwright. The people in my songs are all me."... "A lot of performers give God credit for their music. How do you suppose God feels about that?" "...It sounds like people just giving credit where credit is due." (Bill Flanagan to Bob Dylan, April 2009).

'In this world of sin, where meek souls will receive him still, the dear Christ enters in...' (Bob Dylan, 'O Little Town Of Bethlehem', 'Christmas In The Heart', 2009).

Bill Flanagan: "There's something almost defiant in the way you sing, 'The hopes and fears of all the years are met in thee tonight.' I don't want to put you on the spot, but you sure deliver that song like a true believer." Bob Dylan: "Well, I am a true believer." (Bill Flanagan's 'Christmas In The Heart' Interview, 2009).

'Jesus is coming, coming back to gather his jewels. Yeah, Jesus is coming, coming back to gather his jewels... Storms on the ocean, storms out on the mountain too, Oh Lord, I've got no friend but you... Gonna put my best friend forward, stop being influenced by fools.' (Bob Dylan, 'Gonna Change My Way Of Thinking', live in Beijing April 6, Shanghai

April 8, 2011 and continuing to be sung through to the London Feis Festival, June 11, 2011 - the time of final editing of this book).

There can be absolutely no doubt that in 1978 Bob Dylan had a profound spiritual experience that radically changed him, his concert set lists and in particular the music of his next three albums. As his current concert announcement says, "He emerged to find Jesus." The quotations above show that Dylan never went back on his newfound faith and the personal relationship with God that it brought. Rather he went forward, bringing in the Jewish heritage that his experience of God had re-vitalised, practicing both faiths, in harmony with each other, in what is sometimes called Messianic Judaism. For many Jews, 'Jewish Christian' is a contradiction in terms, an unnecessary complication of language evoking memories of centuries of persecution by Gentile 'Christians'. The term 'Messianic' or 'Messianic Jew' will be used, because for a Jew to find faith in Y'shua, the Jewish Messiah, is a natural forward movement and not a sharp right turn. Evidence of a major depressive episode in the 1990's will be examined, believed to be responsible for the 7 year creative gap between 'Under The Red Sky' and 'Time Out Of Mind'.

This book will demonstrate what recent events have made clearer - that Dylan has an on-going love for God, a clear-cut spirituality with the ups and downs inevitable in any journey of faith. It will demonstrate Dylan's use of allegory, and show how much Dylan draws from the books of the Old and New Testaments for his lyrical inspiration, as well as a variety of other sources, from Roman poets to Japanese novelists. The book has been written to mark the 50th anniversary of his recording contract with Columbia Records, and look back at a career of an astonishing 56 albums at the time of writing. It is recommended that the Bob Dylan 'Lyrics' book be read in company with this book, in order to understand the quotations used. Copyright prohibits verbatim reproduction; quotations are only used as far as is necessary for the educational and review purposes that this book sets out to accomplish. All profits will go to The Oasis Trust, a charity supporting homeless people. Oasis provides homeless young people with safe accommodation, support and opportunities to develop essential life skills, gain emotional support and be resettled into independence.

Chapter 1

No Rabbi In Hibbing

As with most Jewish people, Dylan was raised with a good understanding of the God of Israel and the spiritual heritage of his chosen people. He recalls the arrival of a rabbi at his hometown of Hibbing, Minnesota, almost as if it were a God-sent provision, just in time to prepare him for his bar-mitzvah, the official marking of a Jewish boy's entry to formal adult status in their community. 'Suddenly a Rabbi showed up, under strange circumstances...' [2] The other version is that Mrs Zimmerman drove her son from Hibbing to Duluth, where Rabbi Isaac Neuman taught him Hebrew. [3]

Wherever his Hebrew schooling occurred, Dylan grew up with a good generic North American understanding of Christianity. This is clear from a line in one of his very earliest songs, 'Long Ago And Far Away' (1961). 'To preach of peace and brotherhood, of what might be the cost? A man who did that long ago, they hung him on a cross.' The sacrifice made by Christ figured prominently in the civil-rights movement leaders' minds, an image that strongly influenced Dylan in his earliest compositions.

The inclusion of other specifically Christian songs on his first album, entitled 'Bob Dylan', in 1962, confirms this. For example, 'Gospel plow': 'Mary wore three links of chain, every link was Jesus' name, keep your hand on that plow, hold on.' This is derived from Jesus' teaching in Luke's gospel chapter 9. [i] The inference is that there is a need to persevere in the spiritual endeavour being undertaken.

---

[i] Luke 9:57-62: 'A certain man said to him, "Lord, I will follow you wheresoever you go." And Jesus said to him, "Foxes have holes, and birds of the air have nests; but the Son of man has nowhere to lay his head." And he said to another, "Follow me." But he said, "Lord, suffer me first to go and bury my father." Jesus said to him, "Let the dead bury their dead; but go and preach the kingdom of God." And another also said, "Lord, I will follow you; but let me first go bid them farewell, which are at home at my house." And Jesus said to him, "No man having put his hand to the plough, and looking back, is fit for the kingdom of God."

Similarly, the album's 'In My Time Of Dying' carried a religious theme. The song originated as a gospel blues piece, recorded by Willie Johnson during the Great Depression and entitled 'Jesus Make Up My Dying Bed'. Dylan sings, 'So I can die easy, Jesus gonna make up, Jesus gonna make up, Jesus gonna make up my dying bed. Well, meet me, Jesus, meet me, meet me in the middle of the air; if these wings should fail me, Lord, won't you meet me with another pair.' This is a reference to St Paul's first letter to the church at Thessalonica, chapter 4:13-17. [ii]

The album also included a song by the Texan blues singer 'Blind' Lemon Jefferson (1893-1929), 'See That My Grave Is Kept Clean'. This had the lyric 'and my heart stopped beating and my hands turned cold, now I believe what the Bible told... There's just one last favour I'll ask of you... See that my grave is kept clean.' The song takes it as read that when people die, they will all 'believe what the Bible tells'. The problem is that for some by then it may be too late. Dylan's inaugural album also featured the traditional song, 'Man Of Constant Sorrow' ('I'll see you on God's golden shore'), covered by the bluegrass gospel singers Carter and Ralph Stanley. (Dylan was to return to this reference in his 1997 outtake 'Red River Shore'. 'I heard about a guy who lived a long time ago, a man full of sorrow and strife, that if anyone around him died or was dead, he knew how to bring them back to life.')

The Hebrew prophet Isaiah (53:3) described a figure who 'was despised and forsaken of men, a man of sorrows, and acquainted with grief'; and he is widely believed to have been prophesying about Jesus of Nazareth,

---

[ii] 1 Thessalonians 4:13-17: 'But we do not want you to be uninformed, brethren, about those who are asleep *[have died]*, so that you will not grieve as do the rest who have no hope. For if we believe that Jesus died and rose again, even so God will bring with him those who have fallen asleep in Jesus *[died having faith towards Christ]*. For this we say to you by the word of the Lord, that we who are alive and remain until the coming of the Lord will not precede those who have fallen asleep. For the Lord himself will descend from heaven with a shout, with the voice of the archangel and with the trumpet of God, and the dead in Christ will rise first. Then we who are alive and remain will be caught up together with them in the clouds to meet the Lord in the air, and so we shall always be with the Lord.'

who was despised and rejected at his trial and crucifixion. Dylan included the song 'Man Of Constant Sorrow' twelve times in his stage show between 1988 and 1990.

The 2010 release 'The Bootleg Series Volume 9 - The Witmark Demos 1962-1964' carries outtakes of original Dylan material in the form of 'I'd Hate To Be You On That Dreadful Day', a reference to the traditional image of St Peter standing at heaven's gates (permitting or denying entry). The song finishes with the line 'Should'a listened when you heard the word down there', a salutary warning indeed. Similarly 'What'cha Gonna Do?' asks some questions that have a particularly scriptural ring to them. 'Tell me what you're gonna do when... The devil calls your cards... Your water turns to wine... You can't play God no more... Oh Lord, what shall you do?'

All this simply underlines the well-known fact that one of Dylan's most formative early musical influences was gospel music. For example, 'The Carter Family' (of 'Will The Circle Be Unbroken' fame); a husband, wife and sister-in-law singing group from Virginia who recorded material including gospel music between the 1920's and the 1950's. For Dylan, the words of the Bible, both the Jewish scripture (the Old Testament) and the predominantly Jewish writers of the New Testament were part of his sources of lyrical inspiration. A recording artist who released a debut album covering such blatantly scriptural material today, would almost certainly be thought of as being in some way religious.

But it was to be the 1960's protest movement, with its associations with folk music, which would propel Dylan towards fame, not any type of religious musical orientation. With a helping hand from one of America's leading folk artists, Joan Baez, who included Dylan in her stage shows, Dylan quickly gained national prominence in his own right. There were not many black people living in rural Minnesota at that time, but the anti-racist cause would naturally appeal to one whose Jewish ancestors had known oppression and discrimination for millennia. Songs like 'The Death Of Emmett Till' (1963) expressed Dylan's concern for justice in the face of racist violence. 'If we gave all we could give, we could make this great land of ours a greater place to live.' 'Only A Pawn

In Their Game' (from the 1963 album 'The Times They Are A Changin'') lamented the racially motivated murder of the civil rights campaigner Medgar Ever. ('A bullet from the back of a bush took Medgar Evers' blood.') Dylan's concern for social justice was expressed in his taking part in the civil rights protest rally in Greenwood, Mississippi in June 1963.

While his first album was not a huge seller, the commercial faith that Columbia Records had shown in him was re-paid many times over by the success of his second album, 'The Freewheelin' Bob Dylan' (1963). This contained the classic anti-nuclear protest 'A Hard Rain's A-Gonna Fall' where Dylan sang he would 'reflect it from the mountain so all souls can see it, then I'll stand on the ocean until I start sinkin', but I'll know my song well before I start singin', and it's a hard rain's a-gonna fall.' With the Soviet empire threatening to place nuclear missiles in communist Cuba, in easy reach of the USA's southern shores, the song struck a chord with the American public, some of whom were already building nuclear shelters in their back gardens.

Dylan's third album 'The Times They Are A-Changin'' (released in 1964) contained the classic anti-war track 'With God On Our Side'. Dylan sang, 'In many a dark hour, I've been thinking about this, that Jesus Christ was betrayed by a kiss, but I can't think for you, you'll have to decide, whether Judas Iscariot had God on his side.' Judas Iscariot's betrayal of Christ was foretold in the Old Testament Jewish scriptures. [iii]

While the promotion into the public eye that Joan Baez gave him undoubtedly helped, by 1964 Dylan was established as a publicly recognised performer in own right, and his songs (now all of his own

---

[iii] Psalm 55:12-14: 'If an enemy were insulting me, I could endure it; if a foe were raising himself against me, I could hide from him. But it is you, a man like myself, my companion, my close friend, with whom I once enjoyed sweet fellowship as we walked with the throng at the house of God.' Here King David is speaking about his advisor Ahithophel, who betrayed him in advising David's rebellious son Absalom (2 Samuel chapter 17), seen as a prophetic prefiguration of the betrayal that David's descendant Jesus would receive at the hands of one of his closest companions, Judas Iscariot.

composing) were to become anthems of the political era, earning him the title of 'spokesman for a generation'. Songs such as 'The Times They Are A Changin'' spoke for themselves. Tracks like 'The Lonesome Death Of Hattie Carroll' (a black woman who died after being assaulted by a white Southerner who was let off very lightly by the local court) established Dylan's claim to be first and foremost a poet who could also sing and compose music, and also a social activist, a role that had a wide public appeal in the post-Vietnam war era.

In his fourth album, 'Another Side Of Bob Dylan', also released in 1964, he cleverly balanced such offerings with songs like 'It Ain't Me, Babe', stating 'it ain't me your looking for.' He gave interviews that leant somewhat imaginatively towards the surreal ('I was with the carnival on and off for six years... I was mainliner on the Ferris wheel'), [4] and thus maintaining an aura of mystique. This was made all the stronger by his later reluctance to be interviewed or pinned down on the issue of his beliefs, even to some of those closest to him; he famously remarked to Joan Baez that he had written 'Masters Of War' 'for the money'. As the future would prove, there was more than one 'side' to Bob Dylan.

His recordings continued, producing classics like 'Mr Tambourine Man' on 'Bringing It All Back Home' (1965), and 'Like A Rolling Stone' from 'Highway 61 Revisited' (1965). The income streams from such material, covered by many other artists, kept the business managers at Columbia Records happy, and classics like 'Blonde On Blonde' (1966) kept the music critics and Dylan's public happy. Another 'side' of Dylan's outstanding musical creativity was revealed in 1967 and 1969, when he released the country music-influenced albums 'John Wesley Harding' and 'Nashville Skyline'.

Still the genius ran through, as classic songs like 'All Along The Watchtower' on 'John Wesley Harding' showed. It contained references to the Old Testament book of Isaiah chapter 21. Dylan's lyric was, 'All along the watchtower, princes kept the view', as compared with 'Watch in the watchtower, eat, drink; arise ye princes', of Isaiah 21:15 (KJV). Dylan's 'Two riders were approaching', can be compared with 'Here cometh a chariot of men, with a couple of horsemen', of Isaiah 21:9

(KJV). On this album Dylan recorded the opening track, 'Girl From The North Country', with Johnny Cash, one of America's leading country music stars and a committed Christian.

Dylan has stated that Johnny Cash was a major influence in his musical development. "I've heard Cash since I was a kid... I love him." [5] At his "Johnny Cash at San Quentin" concert, Cash (introducing a song co-written by Dylan) described Dylan as "the greatest writer of our time". By 1969, Cash was the best-selling artist alive, outperforming even the Beatles. The ABC TV network gave Cash his own weekly television show, airing from the Grand Ole Opry, from which Cash had been banned only four years earlier for an alcohol-fuelled kicking-in of the stage lights.

Cash played many gospel numbers, and one night told the crowd, "I am a Christian." This was an announcement that his commercially minded music industry masters did not welcome. Alcoholism they could deal with. Even kicking stage lights earned a certain amount of publicity. But Christianity was apparently a step too far. The ABC network allegedly sent one of their producers to tell Cash not to talk about religion during the broadcasts. Cash replied, "You're producing the wrong man here, because gospel music is part of what I am and part of what I do. If you don't like it, you can always edit it." Cash would later describe the industry fall-out from his declaration of faith as 'severe'.

"I don't compromise my religion," Cash later said. "If I'm with someone who doesn't want to talk about it, I don't talk about it. I don't impose myself on anybody in any way, including religion. When you're imposing, you're offending, I feel. Although I am evangelical [*a Christian who believes in personal conversion and the inerrant truth of the Bible*], and I'll give the message to anyone that wants to hear it, or anybody that is willing to listen, but if they let me know that they don't want to hear it, they ain't never going to hear it from me. If I think they don't want to hear it, then I will not bring it up... Telling others is part of our faith all right, but the way we live it speaks louder than we can say it." Cash said, "The gospel of Christ must always be an open door with a welcome sign for all." [6]

Dylan would soon learn for himself the lesson that Christianity was not good for your career in the music business. Fortunately for him when that day came he would, like Cash, be an artist of sufficient world renown to withstand the repercussions.

But Dylan had not yet arrived at that point on his spiritual journey. And by now his creative output was fluctuating in intensity, with albums such as 'Self Portrait' and 'New Morning' (both 1970) and the film soundtrack to 'Pat Garrett and Billy the Kid' (1973) being fairly uneventful as regards hit records. The exception was the latter album's 'Knocking On Heaven's Door', which went to number one in the singles charts, a rarity for an artist known for album success with tracks significantly longer than 2-3 minutes, as beloved by commercial radio stations.

The film soundtrack was followed in 1973 by the album 'Dylan', which did contain numbers that would go on to be widely regarded as classics, such as 'Can't Help Falling In Love', and a return to a concern for the less socially privileged in 'The Ballad Of Ira Hayes'. This was a song about a Pima Indian who joined the US marines in World War II and raised the US flag at Iwo Jima in the Pacific, an act captured on film in what became an iconic US photograph. A war hero, Hayes' struggle with alcoholism and the plight of his own people were documented in a song written by Peter La Farge and recorded by both Bob Dylan and Johnny Cash.

By this time Dylan's marriage to his first wife Sara Lownds was starting to become rocky. 'Planet Waves' released in 1974, did contain a classic though. 'Forever Young' is a Jewish father's blessing to his children, and a song of which Dylan would remark, "I wrote 'Forever Young' in Tucson. I wrote it thinking about one of my boys and not wanting to be too sentimental. The lines just came to me. They were done in a minute, and that's how the song came out. I certainly didn't intend to write it - I was going for something else. The song wrote itself. Some songs are like that." This illustrates the intrinsically spiritual nature of music. He had previously told 'Sing Out!' magazine that when it came to writing song lyrics, the words just came to him. "The songs are there. They exist all by themselves just waiting for someone to write them down." [7]

When 'Blood On The Tracks' was released in 1975, the scars of domestic conflict were plain for all to see, in songs such as 'If You See Her, Say Hello' ('She might be in Tangiers'). Jakob Dylan has commented that the album is a reflection of the trauma his parents were experiencing at the time. [8] 'Desire', released in 1976, seemed to mark a patching up domestically, with Dylan's wife being present for the recording of 'Sara' ('Don't ever leave me, don't ever go…'). Delivered straight from the heart, with Sara reportedly standing outside the recording booth, it is said to have been well received. Dylan's concern for the marginalised once again comes across, in the song co-written with Jacques Levy, entitled 'Hurricane'. This was a plea for justice for one Ruben Carter, a black boxer who had been convicted, many felt unjustly, for murder. Dylan visited Carter in prison, and held a benefits concert to raise money for the legal costs of his appeal. He was eventually re-convicted.

The pain of his eventual divorce (finalised in June 1977) from Sara was apparent in Dylan's next album, 'Street Legal'. Songs such as 'Baby Stop Crying' ('It's tearing up my mind'), 'True Love Tends To Forget' ('Every day of the year's like playin' Russian roulette' and 'This weekend in hell is making me sweat') and 'Where Are You Tonight? (Journey Through Dark Heat)' tell their own story.

There was also an indication that, despite his emotional pain, Dylan was beginning to look more outside of himself. In the 'Street Legal' number 'Señor' (the Spanish word for 'Lord'), Dylan sings 'Can you tell me where we're heading, Lincoln County Road or Armageddon?', and 'There are hearts here as hard as leather, well give me a minute and let me get it together.' These are biblical images of some strength. Armageddon, literally 'Mount of Megiddo', is the place of the final battle before the world's ending (Revelation 16:16). A 'hard heart' was the reason for Pharaoh's refusal to let the people of Israel leave Egypt under Moses' leadership (Exodus chapters 7 and 8). A hardened heart was also the problem Jesus' own disciples had in their refusal to reconcile, in their minds, his ability to miraculously multiply bread and fish with his ability to walk on water during a storm on Lake Galilee. [iv]

As an album, 'Street Legal' sat on the cusp of the spiritual revelations that were to follow. The mental and emotional pain of his divorce from his first wife Sarah is written into songs such as 'We Better Talk Things Over' - 'The vows that we kept are now broken and swept, 'neath the bed where we slept', and 'Why should we go on watching each other through a telescope? Eventually we'll hang ourselves on all this tangled rope.'

The loss of wife and children was a low point in his life, but not so low as, to Dylan, be a reason for motivating spiritual change, and by the following year Dylan seems to have recovered. As Dylan would later say to Robert Hilburn (of 'The Los Angeles Times') in November 1980, "The funny thing is a lot of people think that Jesus comes into a person's life only when they are either down and out, or are miserable, or just old and withering away. That's not the way it was for me. I was doing fine. I had come a long way in just the year we were on the road. I was relatively content, but a very close friend of mine mentioned a couple of things to me and one of them was Jesus."

[iv] Mark 6:49-52: 'When they saw him walking on the sea, they supposed that it was a ghost, and cried out; for they all saw him and were terrified. But immediately he spoke with them and said to them, "Take courage; it is I, do not be afraid." Then he got into the boat with them, and the wind stopped; and they were utterly astonished, for they had not gained any insight from the incident of the loaves, for their hearts were hardened.'

Chapter 2

Boarding The Slow Train

Whatever the reason for Dylan's spiritual experience, there seems to have been some point of personal need. He was playing in San Diego in November 1978, when 'Towards the end of the show someone out in the crowd... knew I wasn't feeling too well. I think they could see that. And they threw a silver cross on the stage. Now usually, I don't pick things up in front of the stage. Once in a while, I do. Sometimes I don't. But I looked down at that cross. I said, "I gotta pick that up." So I picked up the cross and put it in my pocket... And I brought it backstage and I brought it with me to the next town, which was out in Arizona... I was feeling even worse than I'd felt when I was in San Diego. I said, "Well, I need something tonight." I didn't know what it was. I was used to all kinds of things. I said, "I need something tonight that I didn't have before." And I looked in my pocket and I had this cross.' [9]

By this stage in his career Dylan had taken to employing black female backing singers in his stage performances. These women were not especially familiar with Dylan's musical history or even particularly his standing in the commercial world; consequently they were much less in awe of him and more ready to speak their minds to him than any white equivalent might have dared to. They also had a background in the black gospel music traditions, and many of them had a vibrant personal faith in a living God. Dylan dated some of them, and they helped him through his post-divorce pain. They also pointed him to Jesus Christ; the person whom Dylan had begun his career singing about.

One of them, Mary Alice Artes, was attending a Vineyard Fellowship [v] Church in Tarzana, in the San Fernando Valley, Los Angeles, California. Artes was Dylan's girlfriend at the time, and her involvement with the church caused her to 're-dedicate' her life to the Lord (and stop living

---

[v] 'The Vineyard' is a non-denominational church movement that grew out of a spiritual ministry to artists and musicians that started in California in the mid-1970's. It is now international.

with Dylan). The church had pastors who were musicians themselves; one of their most famous ministers, John Wimber, was himself a keyboard player with 'The Righteous Brothers'. Vineyard pastor Ken Gulliksen says Mary Alice Artes approached him one Sunday in January 1979, after a service in a rented church building in Reseda, and said she wanted somebody to speak with her boyfriend at home.

Gulliksen related: "At the end of the meeting she came up to me and said that she wanted to re-dedicate her life to the Lord. That morning she did re-dedicate her life to the Lord." Then she asked if a couple of the pastors would come and talk to her boyfriend, who, they were to find, was Bob Dylan. Two of Pastor Ken's colleagues, Paul Edmond and Larry Myers, went with Artes to an apartment in the Los Angeles suburb of Brentwood. According to Pastor Ken, who received a report back, Bob told them his life was empty. The pastors replied that God was the 'only ultimate success' and Bob indicated that he wanted what Pastor Ken calls a 'lifestyle relationship' with God. "He was apparently ready to ask for God's forgiveness for sin", said Pastor Ken. [10] Larry Myers spoke to Bob about Jesus Christ, and talked about the Bible, from Genesis through to the book of Revelation, explaining who Jesus was and his place in God's plan of salvation.

This, in Dylan's own words, was what happened. "Jesus did appear to me as King of kings, and Lord of lords. There was a presence in the room that couldn't have been anybody but Jesus. Jesus put his hand on me. It was a physical thing. I felt it. I felt it all over me. I felt my whole body tremble. The glory of the Lord knocked me down and picked me up. Being born again is a hard thing. You ever seen a mother give birth to a child? Well it's painful. We don't like to lose those old attitudes and hang-ups." [11]

What Dylan seems to have experienced was the power of God's Holy Spirit coming to him in answer to prayers offered in the name of Jesus, from others who had themselves arrived at a personal experience of (and relationship with) Jesus Christ as the resurrected Son of God. This is the basis of true Christian faith and is commonly referred to as being 'born again', or 'born from above' (heaven), as described by Jesus in John's gospel (John 3:3). It is this deep inner personal experience of forgiveness and starting afresh spiritually that was behind the transformation in the life of one of the world's premier recording artists. The man known to the world as a Jew was now seen performing with a cross around his neck.

He also began to put new lines into his song 'Tangled Up In Blue'. When the singer meets his girl again in a topless bar, whom in the original version 'opened up a book of poems and handed it to me, written by an Italian poet from the thirteenth century', she was now found to be quoting from the Bible. Firstly from the gospel of Matthew and finally arriving at a verse from the Old Testament prophet Jeremiah, a verse which found its way on to the inner sleeve of the 'Saved' album. 'Behold, the days come, says the Lord, that I will make a new covenant with the house of Israel, and the house of Judah.' (Jeremiah 31:31).

One of the Tarzana Vineyard Church's other pastors, Bill Dwyer, later commented that the approach they took with Dylan was to simply 'encourage him to grow in the Lord, not to run off and become an evangelist, but to really let the Lord work in his life.' [12] Dylan enrolled, at the expense of his tour schedule, in the Vineyard Church's three-month programme of full-time Bible study ('School of Discipleship'), from January to April 1979. A fellow Jewish member of the church, Al Kasha, hosted some of the church's evening Bible studies in his home and recalls that Dylan would stay on hours after it had finished, into the small hours of the morning, asking questions about the Bible and discussing the teaching.

Dylan directed his newfound spiritual energy into musical creativity. [13] Band member Billy Cross (guitarist), sitting next to Bob on the tour bus, noticed that Dylan seemed to be writing a faith-based song that he, with the railway parlance of a Northern Minnesotan, had called 'Slow Train Coming'. The result was the title track of Dylan's first 'Christian' album: 'Slow Train Coming'. In the song 'Precious Angel', Dylan thanked his then girlfriend who helped lead him to a personal faith in the Jewish Messiah. 'How was I to know you'd be the one, to show me I was blinded, to show me I was wrong, how weak was the foundation I was standing upon.' He sets his new terms of reference out unequivocally; 'You either got faith or you got unbelief, and there ain't no neutral ground.' The song is intensely personal, 'My so-called friends have all fallen under a spell.' Dylan would later say that his conversion had cost him friends but not any 'real friends'. [14] The track 'I believe in you' recounts, 'They ask me how I feel, and if my love is real; they look at me and frown, they'd like to drive me from this town, they don't want me around...'

The album closed with 'When He Returns', in which the deeply meaningful and heartfelt plea is given, 'Surrender your crown, on this blood-stained ground.' This recalls the scene in heaven depicted in Revelation 4:10-11 where 'the twenty-four elders fall down before him who sits on the throne, and worship him who lives forever and ever. They lay their crowns before the throne and say, "You are worthy, our Lord and God, to receive glory and honor and power, for you created all things, and by your will they were created and have their being."' The blood referred to in the song is the blood that Christ shed on the cross, making Calvary holy ground for all who will come to offer themselves to him and receive his spiritual life.

Dylan's zeal for his newfound faith was quickly to spill over into his concert appearances. The material from 'Slow Train Coming', his first album recorded as a Jewish Christian, was presented in a series of 14 shows at the Warfield Fox Theatre in San Francisco, not the friendliest choice of location for a concert that was to put forward his new faith-based material. Shows started on November 1st 1979, and band member Spooner Oldham (keyboardist) recalls that around half the crowd booed the show. Some of the audience walked out in disgust, saying that if they'd wanted a religious meeting they could have gone to a church for free. The San Francisco Chronicle reviewer Joel Selvin slated the new gospel-type show, under the now infamous headline, 'Dylan's God-Awful Gospel'.

Dylan later recalled, "In the review in the paper, the man did not understand any of the concepts behind any part of the show, and he wrote an anti-Bob Dylan thing. He probably never liked me anyway, but just said that he did. A lot of them guys say stuff like, "Well, he changed our lives before, how come he can't do it now?" Just an excuse, really. Their expectations are so high, nobody can fulfil them. They can't fulfil their own expectations, so they expect other people to do it for them. I don't mind being put down, but intense personal hatred is another thing. It was like an opening-night critic burying a show on Broadway." [15]

On all but the first of the 14 nights a local faith based organisation, 'Jews for Jesus' (a group of Messianic Jews), were outside to meet them, answer questions about Dylan's change in musical direction and offer them a hastily put together leaflet explaining what Dylan's new faith stood for. This was a move initiated by Dylan himself, according to the local 'Jews for Jesus' leader Mitch Glaser. Fans were not the only people interested in gaining an understanding of Dylan's spiritual position. Glaser recalls how one evening none other than Bill Graham, Dylan's manager and a fellow-Jew, came out to ask just how long it was likely to be before Dylan slowed down the intensity of his desire to bring Graham himself into a new place of faith. [16]

When asked about the negative audience response to his new Christian material, Dylan said, "They want the old stuff, but the old stuff's not going to save anybody, and I'm not going to save anybody, and neither is anybody else they follow going to save them. You can boo all night, and it's not going to work. I can understand why they're rebellious about it, because up until the time the Lord came into my life, I was rebellious. I knew nothing about all this, and was just as rebellious, and didn't think that much about it either way. I never did care much for those preachers who asked for donations all the time, and talked about the world to come, you know. I was always grown up and it's right here and now, and until Jesus came real to me in that way, I couldn't understand it." [17]

Dylan's response to the criticisms was to proclaim his new message all the more strongly, with a particular emphasis on the apocalyptic content of the New Testament's book of Revelation, which contains the Apostle John's prophetic vision of the end of the world. This had been highlighted in a book that was popular at the time by the author Hal Lindsey, 'The Late Great Planet Earth'. Dylan would address his concert audiences in this way: 'Do you know about the spirit of the anti-Christ? Does anyone here know about that? There is only one gospel. The Bible says that anybody who preaches anything other than that one gospel, let him be accursed.' *[Galatians 1:8]*. (Voice from audience: 'Rock and Roll!') 'If you want rock and roll, you can go down and rock and roll, you can go down and see Kiss *[a heavy metal rock band]*, and you can rock and roll all the way down into the pit *[hell]*. It doesn't matter how much money you got, there's only two kinds of people. There's saved people, and there's lost people. Sometime down the line, you remember you heard it here, that Jesus is Lord. Satan's called 'the god of this world' *[2 Corinthians 4:4]*, and it's such a wonderful feeling when you've been delivered *[set free]* from that. I'm curious to know, how many of you do know or don't know that Satan has been defeated on the cross? I suppose you've been reading the newspapers and watching the TV, and you see how much trouble that the world is in. Madmen running loose everywhere. Course, we know that the world is going to be destroyed *[at the end of the world]*. Christ will set up his kingdom for a thousand years in Jerusalem *[Revelation chapter 20]*, where we know that the lion will lie down with the lamb *[Isaiah 11:6]*. We know this is true. I read the Bible a lot. It tells you specific things, in the book of Daniel and the book of Revelation.' [18]

Political events at that time (before the break-up of the Soviet Union) seemed to lend themselves to such an apocalyptic interpretation. Dylan's emphasis on this may have made him appear more right-field in his faith than he really was, but there was simply no denying his love for, and heartfelt commitment to, the Jewish Messiah, Y'shua (Jesus) from Nazareth. His music brooked no other option. All nine tracks on the 1979 album 'Slow Train Coming' spoke about faith in Christ. At first the music critics were kind to him, awarding him a Grammy (Best Male Vocalist) for 'Gotta Serve Somebody'; such kindness was not to last long.

The Bible had become even more integral to Dylan's message. "For me, there is no right and there is no left. There's truth and there's untruth, you know? There's honesty and there's hypocrisy. Look in the Bible, you don't see nothing about right or left. Other people might have other ideas about things, but I don't, because I'm not that smart. I hate to keep beating people over the head with the Bible, but that's the only instrument I know, the only thing that stays true... Don't forget, Jesus said that it's harder for a rich man to enter the kingdom of heaven than it is for a camel to enter the eye of a needle. I mean, is that conservative? I don't know; I've heard a lot of preachers say how God wants everybody to be wealthy and healthy. Well, it doesn't say that in the Bible. You can twist anybody's words, but that's only for fools and people who follow fools. If you're entangled in the snares of this world, which everybody is..." [19]

As time went on, the degree of indulgence the recording industry was to show to one of its best known and most highly regarded artists would be severely strained. Dylan's second Christian album, released after the highly successful live album 'Budokan', was simply called 'Saved'. With a cover portraying the hand of God pointing from heaven towards an individual, this was even more blatant than 'Slow Train Coming' in promoting his faith in the Messiah. Songs like 'A Satisfied Mind' (...'I'll leave this old world with a satisfied mind') announced his state of peace with God and with himself, a peace that, the Bible had much earlier promised, would 'pass all understanding.' (Philippians 4:7).

The title track 'Saved' announced in a no-holds-barred proclamation that he had 'been saved, by the blood of the Lamb'. This is a reference to the first letter of the Apostle Peter (1: 18-19). 'For you know that it was not with perishable things such as silver or gold that you were redeemed from the empty way of life handed down to you from your forefathers, but with the precious blood of Christ, a lamb without blemish or defect.' Jesus' offering of himself on a cross is seen as superseding the Jewish Passover sacrifice of lambs as offerings for sin.

'Covenant Women' (like 'Precious Angel' did on 'Slow Train Coming') honoured Dylan's one-time girlfriend Mary Alice Artes, who was instrumental in leading him to a place of personal trust in Christ. 'What Can I Do For You?' is a heartfelt prayer of Dylan's to his newfound Saviour. In it Dylan offers his life in its entirety to Messiah as his servant, words which were echoed in 2006 in a line from 'Thunder On The Mountain.' 'Remember this, I'm your servant both night and day.'

In 'Solid Rock' Dylan sings, 'For me he was chastised, for me he was hated, for me he was rejected by a world that he created.' This is a reference to Isaiah 53:4-5: 'Surely he has borne our grief, and carried our sorrows: yet we did esteem him stricken, smitten of God, and afflicted. But he was wounded for our transgressions, he was bruised for our iniquities, the chastisement of our peace was upon him; and with his stripes we are healed.' The song title recalls Jesus' teaching about life's foundations in a parable found in Luke 6:47-49. [vi]

'Pressing On' evokes the words of another famous Jew who was rejected by his own people. The Apostle Paul recorded in his letter to the Philippian church (3:13-14), 'Brethren, I do not regard myself as having laid hold of it yet; but one thing I do: forgetting what lies behind and reaching forward to what lies ahead, I press on toward the goal for the prize of the upward call of God in Christ Jesus.' This song was so powerfully presented that it would occasionally lead into spontaneous worship, with Dylan, hands raised toward heaven, withdrawing from front and center-stage and thereby making it clear that he was merely a vehicle for the worship and not the recipient of it.

Then came 'In The Garden', a song about Jesus' arrest in the Garden of Gethsemane (Matthew's gospel chapter 26, Mark's gospel chapter 14 and Luke's gospel chapter 22), which, in typical Jewish rabbinic style, asks questions to evoke answers from the listener. 'When they came for him in the garden, did they know? Did they know that he was the Son of God, did they know that he was Lord?' This was followed by 'Saving Grace' in which Dylan sings, 'The wicked knows no peace and you just

---

[vi] Luke 6:47-49: "Everyone who comes to me and hears my words and acts on them, I will show you whom he is like. He is like a man building a house, who dug deep and laid a foundation on the rock; and when a flood occurred, the torrent burst against that house and could not shake it, because it had been well built. But the one who has heard and has not acted accordingly, is like a man who built a house on the ground without any foundation; and the torrent burst against it and immediately it collapsed, and the ruin of that house was great."

25

can't fake it, there's only one road and it leads to Calvary.' The song is a declaration of thanks for the unmerited favour ('grace') that is freely available to all men and women in Jesus' offering of himself on the cross at Calvary, outside the city gates of Jerusalem.

The album closed with 'Are you ready?' - a blatant challenge to the listener. 'Are you ready to meet Jesus? Are you where you want to be? Will he know you when he sees you, or will he say, "Depart from me"?' This is a reference to Jesus' teaching in Matthew chapter 25, recording the words of those who thought they had performed enough by way of religious duties to qualify for entry to heaven, but who lacked the necessary underlying relationship with the God they claimed to be serving. [vii]

As a musical statement of spirituality the album rocked. Unfortunately, spirituality doesn't sell many records, and as a commercial venture the album bombed. It was a testimony of Dylan's iconic musical and artistic talents that he was allowed by CBS to record a third overtly Christian album in 'Shot of Love'.

The title track hinted at some things that love for Christ had overshadowed. 'Don't need a shot of heroin to kill my disease… I need a shot of love.' For those critics who had detected a measure of anger in some of the lyrical statements, e.g. 'My so-called friends have all fallen under a spell…' ('Precious Angel' on 'Slow Train Coming'), the album

---

[vii] Dylan's words echo Jesus' account of what Jesus will say on his return (his second coming): 'Then he will also say to those on his left, "Depart from me, accursed ones, into the eternal fire which has been prepared for the devil and his angels; for I was hungry, and you gave me nothing to eat; I was thirsty, and you gave me nothing to drink; I was a stranger, and you did not invite me in; naked, and you did not clothe me; sick, and in prison, and you did not visit me." Then they themselves also will answer, "Lord, when did we see you hungry, or thirsty, or a stranger, or naked, or sick, or in prison, and did not take care of you?" Then he will answer them, "Truly I say to you, to the extent that you did not do it to one of the least of these, you did not do it to me." These will go away into eternal punishment, but the righteous into eternal life.' (Matthew 25:41-46).

focused on one of the central attributes of God, namely that he is love personified. 1 John 4:15-16: 'Whoever, confesses that Jesus is the Son of God, God abides in him, and he in God. We have come to know and have believed the love which God has for us. God is love, and the one who abides in love abides in God, and God abides in him.'

Dylan was still defending his spiritual position. 'Property Of Jesus' (track number 3) rails: 'Laugh at him behind his back… Remind him of what he used to be… But he's the property of Jesus, resent him to the bone, you've got something better, you've got a heart of stone.'

This type of riposte to the criticism he had been receiving from fellow rock artists featured on the track 'Dead Man': "Satan got you by the heel, there's a bird's nest in your hair. Do you have any faith at all; do you have any love to share?" This is a rhetorical question seemingly answered in the negative. The lyric reflects the line in the book of Genesis where God addresses Satan, personified in a snake's body, that (consequential to his role in Adam and Eve's sin) he would 'put enmity between you and the woman, and between your seed and her seed.' *[Christians believe that the use of the singular in 'her seed' points to the passage referencing one person, namely Christ.]* 'He shall bruise you on the head, and you shall bruise him on the heel.' The 'bird's nest' is a reference to the famous Chinese proverb that states that while you cannot stop birds flying over your head, you can certainly prevent them from making a nest in your hair!

Self-examination (a spiritual exercise where one reflects upon the measure of one's love for God) figures in the track 'Heart Of Mine' - 'So malicious and so full of guile, give you an inch and you'll take a mile.' 'Watered Down Love' has a similar theme. 'Love that's pure hopes all things, believes all things, won't pull no strings…' This is taken from the Bible's famous description of God's love (1 Corinthians chapter 13), and verse 7. 'Love… bears all things, believes all things, hopes all things, endures all things.'

The album closed with the beautiful and haunting 'Every Grain Of Sand'. 'Onward in my journey, I come to understand, that every hair is numbered, like every grain of sand.' This is a reference to Matthew 10: 29-31: "Are not two sparrows sold for a penny? Yet not one of them will fall to the ground apart from the will of your Father. And even the very hairs of your head are all numbered. So don't be afraid; you are worth more than many sparrows." Hosea 1:10 refers to grains of sand on the seashore as being beyond man's ability to count. God, however, knows their number.

To many commentators it seemed that Bob Dylan had 'got religion'. This was not Dylan's view. "A religion which says you have to do certain things to get to God - they're probably talking about that kind of religion, which is a religion which is by works; you can enter into Kingdom by what you do, what you wear, what you say, how many times a day you pray, how many good deeds you may do. If that's what they mean by religion, that type of religion will not get you into the Kingdom, that's true. However there is a Master Creator, a Supreme Being in the universe." [20]

'Shot Of Love' was to be Dylan's last overtly Christian album. The San Francisco Chronicle music reviewer Joel Selvin surmised later that record industry pressure had closed down a further religious offering. Selvin said, 'If I was a real cynical person, I might suggest that there were a lot of Jewish people in positions of power at Columbia Records who had absolutely no interest in promoting Bob Dylan's Christian propaganda, and did not relate to it anyway.' [21]

Chapter 3

'Yonder Comes Sin'

"The 'Slow Train' record was out and I had the songs to the next record and then I had some songs that never were recorded." [22]

Dylan's 'Christian period' was not one that his record company Columbia/CBS enthusiastically supported. His previous album 'Shot of Love' had indicated the hostility he was experiencing. 'They look at me and frown, they'd like to drive me from this town, they don't want me around...' ('I Believe In You').

Marc Bolan and Yardbird's manager Simon Napier-Bell recalls overhearing CBS executive Dick Katz make the industry's point to Dylan in a typically forthright manner over the phone. "I've told you, Bob - no f**king religion! If you can't agree to that, the deal's off... Look, I'm telling you. There'll be no f**king religion - not Christian, not Jewish, not Muslim. Nothing. For God's sake, man - you were born Jewish, which makes your religion money, doesn't it? So stick with it, for Christ's sake. I'm giving you 20 million bucks - it's like baptizing you, like sending you to heaven. So what are you f**king moaning about? You want 20 million bucks from us? Well, you gotta do what we tell you. And what we're telling you is - No Torah! No Bible! No Koran! No Jesus! No God! No Allah! No f**king religion! It's going in the contract!" [23]

With or without the support of Columbia Records, an impartial review of the situation in 1982 could well have concluded that Dylan had got as far as he was going to get with his 'full-on' style of declaring spiritual truth. Banging one's head against a brick wall can get tiring after a while! But whatever the reason for Dylan stopping such an overt approach to declaring his faith, it was certainly not for want of suitable material. There was a good size album's worth of songs many of which did not see the official light of day, but which did however appear as a bootleg under the title, 'Yonder Comes Sin'.

This contained some classic tracks, such as 'Caribbean Wind', later to appear on the album 'Biograph' (released in 1985). Written during a visit to the West Indies (on waking from a strange dream in the hot St Vincent sun),[24] the song is a brilliant example of the allegorical direction that Dylan would take from his next album, 'Infidels', onwards. (The title 'Infidels' itself might well have reflected upon certain recording industry executives.) Allegory is a time-honoured and well-recognised way of communicating spiritual truth. Jesus had taught in parables; stories that got around people's prejudices by posing as a simple tale rather than a formal lesson in spirituality. Some of the greatest Christian writers chose allegory as a method of passing on spiritual truth. C.S. Lewis wrote 'The Lion, The Witch And The Wardrobe' (where the lion Aslan represents Christ) in this style, as did J.R.R. Tolkien in 'The Lord Of The Rings'. [viii]

The Caribbean wind (well known to Dylan who kept a sail boat, *The Water Pearl'* at Bequia, St Vincent, in the Caribbean) was what enabled the slave boats to carry their human cargo to New Orleans. Slavery is how the Bible portrays the human condition of sin; fundamentally an attitude of indifference or rebellion towards God. Sin is a condition that we have no power to remedy in and of our own selves. In the song these winds fan 'the flames in the furnace of desire' (the desire for riches and power, and presumably also all other manner of lust contrary to God-given principles), and bring 'everything that's near to me nearer to the fire' (and the ultimate judgement of God). The song opens by describing a woman from 'Paradise Lost', (Milton's poem describing the strategy Satan employed to deceive mankind, and especially Eve, into sinning, and the redemptive action of God in Christ's victory over sin and death).

The woman 'told about Jesus', and leads Dylan to what is presumably a night club 'where men bathed in perfume' on what is described as a 'gay night.' (Tuesday is a popular night for Miami clubs to promote a homosexual theme and these men are practicing 'the hoax of free

---

[viii] The wizard Gandalf dies and is then raised back to life; Aragorn is the prophesied king but in a hidden state as a lowly ranger, his real status known only to a few.

speech'; substitute 'love' for 'speech' and you have a connection to the activity that fuelled the AIDS epidemic amongst gay men.) The woman is able to look into Dylan's soul, but 'her heart was a snare'. Dylan is helped to get out of the situation by his hearing (presumably spiritually) his name being called ('I had to be moving on'), and by his ability to see, (also presumably spiritually), 'the devil pound tin', and 'a house in the country being torn from within'. As Jesus had said in Luke 11:17-18, 'A house divided against itself falls. If Satan also is divided against himself, how will his kingdom stand?' Dylan also hears his 'ancestors calling from the land far beyond'. Dylan was starting to celebrate being able to join his new spiritual adventure with the faith of his forefathers (men like the patriarch Abraham who had Messianic faith), a faith that would lead him too, towards heaven 'far beyond'.

The Bootleg's title track 'Yonder Comes Sin' is a masterpiece of Dylan's art, and it is a great shame that it has not yet been published. The song personifies sin in some of the various ways it manifests itself, not always overtly, but there all the same, bubbling away beneath the surface. 'Sin' may be defined fundamentally as an attitude rather than as a list of wrongdoings; one of indifference and/or rebellion toward God. It is primarily a state of being rather than a set of actions or omissions. The Bible states that all of humanity is born in the spiritual condition of sin that separates us from God, but one that can be bridged and overcome by personal trust in the offering that Jesus made on the cross.

'Yonder Comes Sin' begins with a woman who wants to talk to Dylan, because she has 'many things to say'. After decades in the music business, Dylan must have just about heard it all, and would have been used to sycophants and assorted chancers seeking to bend his ear in their own direction. The woman wants God's Spirit to be 'speaking through' her, but she has a 'lust for comfort' that is getting in the way. Dylan, with maturity far beyond his spiritual years, can discern those who have a superficial interest in the spiritual realm but are too firmly planted in the material realm to embrace it. They are being pulled in two directions, and often their sin-driven human nature (what the Bible terms as 'the flesh') wins out over their spiritual interest. He can read in her eyes exactly what her heart is not telling. The eyes are termed the windows of the soul, and the prophet Jeremiah had said, 'The heart is deceitful above all things, and desperately wicked; who can know it?' (Jeremiah 17:9). It is cut off from God in a state of sin and has to be brought to God to be given a new start, under the direction of God's Holy Spirit. There is an 'old evil burden' upon her, pulling her down, and seeking to 'grind her 'neath the wheel'. The 'evil burden' here is sin, and its pervasive power makes our natures grist for the devil's mill.

The song now switches to portray some of the ways in which sin works. It walks as men do, it talks as angels do, it is as 'proud' as a 'peacock', and can move more swiftly than an 'eagle'. Pride was the downfall of the angelic being that became the devil, through the use of free will to go his own way in rebelling against the Creator's will. It makes its appearance in the heart of the human condition, quick to infect all it is near to (as Dylan would later express in 'Disease Of Conceit' on 'Oh Mercy'). Where have her 'feet been to?' and what have her 'hands been into?' the chorus enquires. This is a call to self-examination of our lives and motives. The song asks if we can 'take it on the chin?' - call a spade a spade, and face up honestly to where we are spiritually?

The song then switches to the sin of racial prejudice. Dylan had married one of his black backing vocalists, Carolyn Dennis, on June 4 1986 and despite that being kept secret he had, no doubt, begun indirectly to be on the receiving end of prejudice through association. His 'woman' is perceived as 'foreign' and her eyes are coloured differently to Dylan's, but she has the same colour blood and bones as everyone else.

His enquirer may seem on the outside to be interested in 'seeking them eternal spiritual things', but her artificial '50 dollar smile confirms' Dylan's suspicions that she is 'trying to buy her way into the dreams of them, whose bodies will be food for worms'. She cannot discern the fallen human state ('food for worms') from the phony, star-filled world of people's dreams. Her spiritual interest is, in this case, just another way of trying to access what the person is really seeking; the fleeting fame and glamour that the world associates with the music industry's leading players.

Sin is always 'ready' and 'willing'; it seeks to dominate by 'standing on the chairs and table'. It is always close at hand, ready to control if given half a chance. Dylan then relates a spiritual picture he has, in which he sees 'six white horses'. His enquirer replies that she cannot see any, and asks Dylan to 'point them out', at which Dylan decides that it is time to leave. He is seeing with spiritual eyes and his companion cannot; her presence is now to him sufficiently negative that he is looking for an exit. He doesn't just see things that others can't; he hears them (spiritually speaking) as well. His 'brother's blood' calls out to him 'from the grave'; his enquirer can't discern it, but the voice is clear to him. Her misplaced sense of spiritual confidence causes Dylan to 'stand in jeopardy', fearful for the eventual consequences of her superficiality. When Cain slew Abel (Genesis 4:8), the Bible tells that Abel's blood cried out to God from the grave. Dylan's natural younger brother David was alive and well; presumably he is speaking of a spiritual brother. [ix]

The song then relates the condition of those in his female enquirer's shoes; 'vomiting' back up spiritual things they have received, into the 'ditches' in which they find themselves. Sin will always impair and degrade the human condition; it may provide a temporary sense of 'riches' but they will soon be 'vomited up', and leave us spiritually homeless, as Mary and Joseph are said to have been in Bethlehem where there was allegedly 'no room' for them. [x]

Dylan then provides a great line about the Old Testament prophet Jeremiah, who preached to the people of Israel prior to their deportation to Babylon in the fifth century before Christ. Jeremiah's message was one exhorting the Jewish people of Judah (southern Israel) to turn back to God (repent), before it was too late 'to turn from hell'. 'Thus says the Lord of hosts, the God of Israel, "Amend your ways and your doings, and I will cause you to dwell in this place."' (Jeremiah 7:3, KJV). He was opposed by various false prophets who wrongly reassured the

---

[ix] In Christ, all men and women are brothers and sisters.

[x] The Greek word is 'guest room', the context being Joseph's family home. See Dr Bradford's 'The Jesus Discovery'. ISBN 9780956479808

people that all was well, or as Dylan's line put it, 'The critics all gave him such bad reviews; put him down at the bottom of a well.' The people had not listened to Jeremiah, and the Babylonian King Nebuchadnezzar had invaded. Jeremiah had foretold that would be God's judgement on the people's sin.

In fact, Jeremiah was called a traitor by the advisors to Zedekiah, the King of Judah; they had punished Jeremiah by putting him into the mud at the bottom of an empty well within the prison of Malchiah the son of Hammelech. (Jeremiah 38:6 - the king subsequently released him.) Prominent American music critics had reacted harshly to some of Dylan's Christian music; this could easily have had a depressing effect on Dylan and 'put him down in the bottom of a well' too.

But Jeremiah was not deterred. He kept on prophesying right up until the people of Jerusalem were placed in chains by the Babylonian army. As Dylan put it, no one was around to 'say "Bon voyage"', or shatter any bottles of champagne'! When the Babylonians invaded, they did indeed take the Jewish inhabitants away in chains. And like Jeremiah, Dylan would 'keep talking anyway'; he would just subtly change the style of communication.

Next, sin is portrayed as a slave owner cracking his whip. Sin's deceitfulness is also mentioned, for example, knifing somebody from behind while making innocent small talk 'about the weather'. Backstabbing from within the music business must have been something that the new and spiritually different Dylan was becoming accustomed to. He was finding out first-hand the cost of his commitment; even artistic 'survival' was more costly than expected, particularly given his new moral code. He was at least attempting to get on with his enemies (as Jesus had taught 'Love your enemies, and do good to those who hate you.' Luke 6:27) whilst maintaining his 'self- respect'. What would be the cost to Dylan of his faith? Loss of 'so-called friends', as related in the 1979 song 'Precious Angel'? Being leant on by the music business to compromise his beliefs? When the road got very rough, even just getting on with your enemies is pretty good going.

Dylan laments that his hearer is accepting the bad as though it were good. Young children, relatively uncorrupted by the world's negative influences, know the difference between right and wrong. As they get older, those distinctions become blurred, and compromise becomes the universal moral currency.

Sin is described as trying to look younger and cooler than it really is, with the rhyme 'tasting like peaches, hanging on like leaches'. Sin, ages old and dirty, can appeal to both male and female independently and be sweet as the juice of any forbidden fruit. The book of Hebrews (12:1-2) speaks of sin's power to attach itself to us. 'Let us also lay aside every weight, and sin which clings so closely, and let us run with perseverance the race that is set before us, looking to Jesus the pioneer and perfecter of our faith.' Temptation to sin comes in whatever guise will appeal to us the most.

Dylan then speaks to people who are ignoring truth simply to get richer, and who will sing about life's injustices whilst bringing a 'curse' on themselves by (presumably) doing nothing about it. This may be another reference to the music industry's refusal to sponsor further forays into Christian music; the albums had too narrow an audience scope and were probably becoming financially unrewarding. Truth may be truth, but profit is profit. Dylan compares their situation with that of Macbeth, who had sought power through occult means (the advice of three witches) rather than from God. Men's kingdoms cannot stand, and 'corruptible crowns' are really not that worthwhile having, especially if procuring one means, in Dylan's lyric, 'a deal with Mr Death'. Ultimately, only God's kingdom can endure for eternity, and the devil will try to drive a hard bargain.

'Who can understand sin?' asks Dylan. The devil is described in scripture as 'the prince of the power of the air', [xi] and Dylan calls sin the ruler of 'the airways' and 'the planet', reminiscent of the biblical terms

---

[xi] Ephesians 2:2: 'The prince of the power of the air, the spirit that now works in the children of disobedience.'

'the air' and 'the world'. Much of humanity is in rebellion to God, and the Bible uses the term 'the world' [xii] to mean that part of God's creation in rebellion against him. Dylan knows from experience what it is to ignore God; to do what you please, and 'not think about it too much'. [25]

The Law (the moral code) is contrasted in scripture with God's grace. The former is a 'good works' orientation, which cannot change our hearts, but the real purpose of the Law of Moses was to demonstrate to mankind their inability to keep it in and of their own efforts. Thus they were in need of a saviour; a crowning act of unearned favour from a gracious God. Dylan is lifting off the 'engine cover' so we can get a good look at the real source of our problems - our own selfish and the sinful nature within.

Sin is really only interested in owning people so that it can kill them. A relationship with the slave master called sin only leads to one place - death. The Apostle Paul states, 'The wages of sin is death; but the gift of God is eternal life through Jesus Christ our Lord.' (Romans 6:23, KJV). 'Yonder Comes Sin' truly is a great song, song with passion and the certainty of true faith. Was Dylan a true believer? It certainly seems so.

The album continued with a number that often figured in Dylan's live shows of the time, 'Ain't Gonna Go To Hell For Anybody', in which Dylan is extremely honest about his personal ability to influence for good or ill. He is quite clear that he is able to 'manipulate people as well as anybody', through 'holding' and 'controlling', 'teasing' and 'squeezing' them. He can 'make believe' that he is 'in love' with just about anyone, and can then set about busting, burning, blaming and leaving them. But, he sings, he has 'been down that road' and he knows which direction it leads in, and he is most certainly not going to 'go to hell for anybody'. The song is almost a public confession of sin that

---

[xii] 1 John 2:15-1: 'Do not love the world nor the things in the world. If anyone loves the world, the love of the Father is not in him. For all that is in the world, the lust of the flesh and the lust of the eyes and the boastful pride of life, is not from the Father, but is from the world. The world is passing away, and also its lusts; but the one who does the will of God lives forever.'

Dylan has now turned away from under the leading of a new master, Y'shua from Nazareth.

The second verse continues in the same vein: Dylan can 'deceive people as well as anybody', because he knows 'all the angles', as well as 'how to make the jangles'. He is adept too at twisting the truth, 'finding and blinding', 'wining and dining'. But these old skills no longer suit Dylan's 'purposes', it isn't his goal to 'gain the whole world and give up his soul'. Jesus had said to his disciples, "If any man will come after me, let him deny himself, and take up his cross *[die to your own ways and live to new ways of behaviour]*, and follow me *[as my disciple]*. For whosoever will save his life *[live it for himself only]* shall lose it: and whosoever will lose his life *[into my care]* for my sake shall find it. For what is a man profited, if he shall gain the whole world, and lose his own soul? Or what shall a man give in exchange for his soul?" (Matthew 16:24-26).

Dylan employs a graphic warning in verse 3 with a vivid picture of an eternally arising smoke and a 'one-way ticket to burn', to a place that God intended 'for the devil, and for all of those that love evil'. In the Jewish scripture that Y'shua taught from, hell was named Gehenna ('Valley of Hinnom'), after the rubbish dump of Jerusalem. This was a deep, narrow ravine outside the city where all sorts of unwanted debris was put, with a never ending source of fuel for the fire that burned at the bottom and which prevented the rock fissure from becoming full. Jesus had taught (Matthew 25:41) that the eternal equivalent had been prepared for 'the devil and his angels'. Dylan breaks off the horror of its description, to emphasize the permanency of that state of being for the eternal human spirits that may also end up there, for eternity.

The fourth verse of 'Ain't Gonna Go To Hell For Anybody' finds Dylan confessing that he is quite capable of misleading people, he knows 'all the dices', and he has paid for them too; he is as good as anyone at influencing people, he 'can do it', he 'can easily see to it'. And even now, if people listen properly to the album he has made 'they'll be gods'. Jesus had quoted Psalm 82:6 to his unbelieving Jewish audience, "Is it not written in your Law, 'I have said, "You are gods"'? If he called them 'gods', to whom the word of God came - and the scripture cannot be broken - what about the one whom the Father set apart as his very own and sent into the world? Why then do you accuse me of blasphemy because I said, 'I am God's Son'?" (John 10:34-36, NIV). Dylan reflects that his audience can be restored to their original god-like, unpolluted spiritual state by listening to his lyrics (which contained the good news of the gospel) and responding to them with a change of heart.

Another song, 'Let's Begin', (originally by Jimmy Webb) appears to be addressed to Christ. 'My new-found friend, let's begin... there's so much discover... we got to learn about each other, and in the end, we may find that we are lovers.' The Song of Songs, an Old Testament book of King Solomon's (King David's son), depicts the relationship between God and his people in the manner of a lover and his beloved. This was a concept that would feature prominently later on in Dylan's work. Dylan would borrow from different lyrical sources for his own purposes.

During this period Dylan covered the Dallas Holm number 'Rise Again', which depicts Jesus' resurrection from the dead in the first person. 'Go ahead, drive the nails through my hand, laugh at me where you stand. Go ahead, say it isn't me, but the day will come and you will see. 'Cause I'll rise again, ain't no power on earth can tie me down. Yes, I'll rise again; death can't keep me buried in the ground.' Dylan sings the chorus with a sense of overwhelming conviction of the truth of the words.

A further song from the period that didn't see the light of day was 'Thief On The Cross'. 'There's a thief on the cross, his chances are slim... I wanna talk to him.' Jesus was crucified between two thieves, each of which eventually had very different reactions to him. While one continued to curse him, the other confessed faith in him. [xiii]

[xiii] Luke 23:39-43: 'One of the criminals who hung there hurled insults at him: "Aren't you the Christ? Save yourself and us!" But the other criminal rebuked him. "Don't you fear God," he said, "since you are under the same sentence? We are punished justly, for we are getting what our deeds deserve. But this man has done nothing wrong." Then he said, "Jesus, remember me when you come into your kingdom." Jesus answered him, "I tell you the truth, today you will be with me in paradise."'

The track 'Blessed Is The Name' falls into the category of classic gospel music, with Dylan's black back-up singers in full voice. 'Blessed is the name of the Lord forever, wisdom and might are his... Well, to the just he will be faithful, let it rain fire and brimstone down. But he did not destroy Sodom and Gomorrah, till Lot was safely out of town.' The account of the patriarch Abraham's nephew, who was named Lot, leaving Sodom is found in Genesis chapter 19. Sodom was notorious for evil and God destroyed it with fire and brimstone; only Lot and his two daughters survived.

'Foot Of Pride' is another song from this period, later to make an appearance on 'The Bootleg Series Volume 1-3' album (1991) and 'The 30th Anniversary Concert Celebration' album (1993). The song takes its title from Psalm 36:11: 'Let not the foot of pride come against me, and let not the hand of the wicked remove me.' It is full of biblical imagery, starting with the devouring lion of 1 Peter 5:8. 'Be self-controlled and alert. Your enemy the devil prowls around like a roaring lion looking for someone to devour.' The next is the issue of cross-dressing; a woman passing herself off as a man. There was a strong prohibition against this in the Law of Moses. 'A woman must not wear men's clothing, nor a man wear women's clothing, for the Lord your God detests anyone who does this.' (Deuteronomy 22:5). God had gone to a lot of trouble to instill gender specific design into his creation and God's people Israel were taught the importance of respecting it.

The song then cuts to a funeral with a preacher talking about the betrayal of Christ by one of his followers, Judas Iscariot. 'Satan entered into Judas who was called Iscariot, belonging to the number of the twelve. And he went away and discussed with the chief priests and officers how he might betray him to them.' (Luke 22:3-4).

Dylan likens this act of betrayal ('It's like the earth just opened and swallowed him up') to that of one of the Israelite priests, Korah. He had opposed their leader Moses on grounds of jealousy masquerading as egalitarianism, despite Moses' clear role in leading the people out of Egypt. Moses and his brother Aaron put the matter to the test by having a simultaneous offering of incense with two hundred and fifty of

Korah's supporters. What happened next is described in Numbers 16:28-33. 'Moses said, "By this you shall know that the Lord has sent me to do all these deeds; for this is not my doing. If these men die the death of all men, or if they suffer the fate of all men, then the Lord has not sent me. But if the Lord brings about an entirely new thing and the ground opens its mouth and swallows them up with all that is theirs, and they descend alive into Sheol, then you will understand that these men have spurned the Lord." As he finished speaking all these words, the ground that was under them split open; and the earth opened its mouth and swallowed them up, and their households, and all the men who belonged to Korah with their possessions. So they and all that belonged to them went down alive to Sheol; and the earth closed over them, and they perished from the midst of the assembly.' It might be supposed that this would have settled matters. It did not; the next day the people began to complain that it was Moses (rather than Korah) who had caused the deaths!

Dylan identifies the real culprit with the next line of the song: 'He reached too high, was thrown back to the ground.' This is a reference to the fall of the devil from his position as an angel before the throne of God, described in Isaiah 14:12-15: 'How you have fallen from heaven, O star of the morning, son of the dawn! You have been cut down to the earth, you who have weakened the nations! But you said in your heart, "I will ascend to heaven; I will raise my throne above the stars of God, and I will sit on the mount of assembly, in the recesses of the north. I will ascend above the heights of the clouds; I will make myself like the Most High." Nevertheless you will be thrust down to Sheol, to the recesses of the pit.' Dylan then fires off a typically witty line about being nice to people going up who you might just meet on their way back down.

The song now switches direction to address Christ: 'Hear ya got a brother named James...' Mark 6:3 reads, 'Is not this the carpenter, the son of Mary, and brother of James and Joses and Judas and Simon?' The 'mixed' blood of the next line seems to be a reference to the fact that Christ was born of Mary while a virgin; his blood is that of hers and his father's - God. He could look 'straight into the sun' from the cross because at the point of crucifixion there was a lunar eclipse of the sun. Luke 23:44-46: 'It was now about the sixth hour, and darkness fell over the whole land until the ninth hour, because the sun was obscured; and the veil of the temple was torn in two. And Jesus, crying out with a loud voice said, "Father, into your hands I commit my spirit." Having said this, he breathed his last.'

The 'revenge' Dylan says that the character (evidently Christ) has is spoken of in the book of Jeremiah (46:10) - 'For that day *[the day of Christ's sacrifice]* belongs to the Lord God of hosts, a day of vengeance, so as to avenge himself on his foes *[those, particularly the devil, who oppose him]*.' Christ, as any human, ate and drank, and as Dylan says next, 'Drinks can be fixed'. This is very likely a reference to the account of the crucifixion. 'They brought him to the place Golgotha, which is translated, Place of a Skull. They tried to give him wine mixed with myrrh; but he did not take it.' (Mark 15:22-23). Myrrh was used as a sedative, and Jesus was determined to keep his faculties clear, even in the pain of crucifixion. The song's chorus reflects on stubbornness and pride. 'There ain't no going back when your foot of pride come down.' Pride is sometimes called a 'mortal' sin; Dylan would later distinguish it from 'venial' (thought to be less serious) sin in his 'Theme Time' radio show, showing a grasp of theology that puts most people to shame.

The next verse refers to a 'retired businessman named Red, cast down from heaven and he's out of his head.' This seems to be another reference to the devil, who was 'cast out of heaven' (Revelation 12:9). 'Then another sign appeared in heaven: and behold, a great red dragon having seven heads and ten horns, and on his heads were seven diadems.' (Revelation 12:3). Pride, his original sin, is the trap with which the devil seeks to bring men and women down to his level. The Apostle Paul's first letter to Timothy in the Bible speaks of how people should avoid being ensnared: 'Do not become conceited and fall into the condemnation incurred by the devil... have a good reputation with those outside the church, so... not to fall into reproach and the snare of the devil.' (1 Timothy 3:6-7).

The devil uses people to do his work, as Dylan sings; 'Miss Delilah is his, a Philistine is what she is.' Delilah causes the downfall of a Hebrew judge named Samson (Judges 16); the Philistines were the traditional enemies of God's people Israel. The song goes on to describe how the devil uses his influence to get people to carry a 'burden too heavy to be yours.' His influence also enables money to be made 'from sin'. The penultimate verse discusses how the devil can influence us through others. He uses 'beautiful people' who can make an impression on us, and so lull us into spiritual sleep like Delilah did. These people have ''Mystery' written all over their forehead'. This is a reference to the book of Revelation chapter 17, one of Dylan's most frequently referred to books of the Bible. Those under the devil's influence have some power of persuasion to subdue resistance to them; they try to control behaviour in just the same way that they accuse 'religion' or God of doing, but to a very negative end. The book of Revelation (17:3-7) refers to an adorned woman sitting on the demonic figure 'the Beast'; she has 'Mystery' written on her forehead. [xiv]

The last verse of the song reverts again to describing Christ: 'Yes, I guess I loved him too.' Dylan can still see him in his mind 'climbing that hill'; surely a reference to Christ climbing Calvary, the place of crucifixion. Having arrived at the top, Dylan then says that he was 'struck down by the strength of the will.' This line probably refers directly to the prophet Isaiah's accurate foretelling about Christ, some 750 years earlier. 'Surely our grief's he himself bore, and our sorrows he carried; yet we ourselves esteemed him stricken, smitten of God, and afflicted. But he was pierced through for our transgressions, he was

---

[xiv] Revelation 17:3-7: 'And he carried me away in the Spirit into a wilderness; and I saw a woman sitting on a scarlet beast, full of blasphemous names, having seven heads and ten horns. The woman was clothed in purple and scarlet, and adorned with gold and precious stones and pearls, having in her hand a gold cup full of abominations and of the unclean things of her immorality, and on her forehead a name was written, 'Mystery, Babylon the Great, the Mother of Harlots and of the Abominations of the Earth'. And I saw the woman drunk with the blood of the saints, and with the blood of the witnesses of Jesus. When I saw her, I wondered greatly. And the angel said to me, "Why do you wonder? I will tell you the mystery of the woman and of the beast that carries her, which has the seven heads and the ten horns."'

crushed for our iniquities; the chastening for our wellbeing fell upon him, and by his scourging we are healed.' (Isaiah 53:4-5).

Dylan concludes the song by quoting Christ: 'Another disciple said to him, "Lord, first let me go and bury my father." But Jesus told him, "Follow me, and let the dead bury their own dead."' (Matthew 8:21-22, ANIV). The disciple's father has not yet died; Jewish custom dictated that the son had to remain until his father had died, i.e. sometime in the future. Jesus' comment (which Dylan quotes) indicates that the spiritually dead will look after the burial; the spiritually alive can get on with following him.

Another unpublished song in this collection was 'City Of Gold'. The lyrics speak simply of heaven, the dwelling place of God. 'There is a city of gold, far from the rat race that eats at your soul, far from the confusion and the bars that hold, there is a city of gold.' The book of Revelation (21:18, 21) describes heaven in this way, 'The material of the wall was jasper: and the city was pure gold, like clear glass... And the twelve gates were twelve pearls; each one of the gates was a single pearl; and the street of the city was pure gold, like transparent glass.'

The second verse tells of a 'Country of light, raised up in glory and the streets are bright. Glory to God - not by deeds or by might, there is a city of light.' This resonates with Revelation 21:23-25: 'And the city had no need of the sun, neither of the moon, to shine in it: for the glory of God did lighten it, and the Lamb is the light thereof. And the nations of them which are saved shall walk in the light of it: and the kings of the earth do bring their glory and honour into it. And the gates of it shall not be shut at all by day: for there shall be no night there.'

Heaven's light is a pure light; the precious stones that the chapter mentions are all the type that refract polarized light, meaning that they shine with the colours of the rainbow. The absence of night is picked up in the next verse, which tells that in the place of heavenly light there are 'angels' in white, there is no illness and there is no night. The angels described in John's gospel (20:12) are 'in white', and heaven is a place devoid of sorrow, sickness and death. 'God shall wipe away all tears from their eyes; and there shall be no more death, neither sorrow, nor crying, neither shall there be any more pain: for the former things are passed away.' (Revelation 21:4).

The city is one of love; 'stuff dreams are made of' with no sunset or night-time fears, including fear of 'stars'. 1 John 4:16 states: "God is love', and Dylan defines the eternal city by this attribute. In heaven there is no night. 'There shall be no night there; and they need no candle, neither light of the sun; for the Lord God gives them light: and they shall reign forever and ever.' (Revelation 22:5, KJV). Fear of 'stars above' is probably a reference to the devil and his (fallen) angels. 'Then the fifth angel sounded, and I saw a star from heaven which had fallen to the earth; and the key of the bottomless pit was given to him.' (Revelation 9:1). The Hebrew prophet Daniel refers to angels as stars (Daniel 8:10).

The song continues with the message that this city is one of hope. Because there is no sickness, there is no need of doctors or medicines. The concept of 'hope' in scripture is much more than a fingers-crossed form of shallow optimism. It is closely linked to faith; a confident certainty that God is in control of circumstances on behalf of those who are following him. In heaven, God's children receive new bodies of the resurrection type that Jesus modelled, and they know no sickness. God will 'throw down a rope' to save anyone who calls upon him.

The final verse tells us that the city is one of gold, far from earth's 'rat race' and the prison 'bars that hold', a city that gives 'peace' for the human spirit and rest for our souls. Peace is one of the products (fruit) of the indwelling of the Holy Spirit. (See Galatians 5:22). Jesus had said: "Come to me, all you who are weary and burdened, and I will give you rest. Take my yoke upon you and learn from me, for I am gentle and humble in heart, and you will find rest for your souls. For my yoke is easy and my burden is light." (Matthew 11:28-30). The city is where Jesus, the Prince of Peace (Isaiah 9:6), is enthroned. (See Revelation 22:1).

'Ain't No Man Righteous' is another as yet unpublished song from this period. It demonstrates a mature understanding of the Christian faith, stating that it is serving the Lord that makes life worthwhile. One's own human status doesn't count and neither does lifestyle, in and of itself. Dylan has never seen human perfection, and he knows that there 'ain't no man righteous, no not one'. Dylan had an abundance of everything the world could offer; money, fame, status, women… and he had been left empty. In Jesus, he came to understand that true fulfillment lay in doing the will of his Father in heaven. Human beings may attain a level of self-righteousness (actually a form of pride), but never sufficient to qualify on God's terms; as they carry the taint of our sinful natures. As King David implored God, 'Do not enter into judgement with your servant, for in your sight no man living is righteous.' (Psalm 143:2).

The second verse warns of the devil who likes to oppose us by open hostility, or if that is not successful, will 'even work his ways through those whose intentions are good'. There are sun and moon worshippers, but there hasn't yet been found any man righteous - not even one. The proverb says that 'the road to hell is paved with good intentions.' There are many who intend to look for God one day, just not right now. The Bible warns that 'no one has authority over the day of his death' (Ecclesiastes 8:8), and no one knows the hour of Christ's return (Matthew 24:36), so Jesus advised that we had better be ready. Jeremiah (25:6) warned against the worship of other gods, no matter how many others seem to be following them.

Verse three speaks of the 'social hypocrites', people who impose their rules on others while not following them themselves. The 'raising and lowering of flags' points towards a sort of misguided patriotism; if we compare our own 'goodness' with God's we come off looking like a 'filthy rag'. Jesus had upbraided the Pharisees (religious lawyers) for their hypocrisy (Matthew 23:3-4) in saying 'Do not do what they *[the Pharisees]* do, for they do not practice what they preach. They tie up heavy loads and put them on men's shoulders, but they themselves are not willing to lift a finger to move them.' Nationalism and patriotism are not routes to God either. Dylan concludes the verse by quoting Isaiah 64:6; the filthy rags mentioned are in actual fact a woman's menstrual cloth, which the Jewish Law (Torah) regarded as being unclean until ritual washing had been performed.

The fourth verse describes the counterpart to the city of heaven that he has been singing about; a 'city of darkness' where there is no sun either - no light at all. A lot of 'evil things' have been done in love's name. In this last city there will be an inextinguishable and eternal flame, prepared for the devil. Matthew's gospel (25:41) finds Jesus saying to those who have ignored him and the needs of others, 'Depart from me, accursed ones, into the eternal fire which has been prepared for the devil and his angels'.

The fifth verse sardonically recommends keeping on futilely talking with the 'wool' firmly over the eyes 'until you run right out of alibis'. Dylan warns that one day there will be an accounting with God, an eternal reckoning when it will be seen that the only truly righteous person was the one who died as an acceptable offering for the sins of the whole world. While one may be able to deceive oneself ('pull the wool'), it is not possible to deceive God, before whom everybody will one day come for judgement. 'For we must all appear before the judgement seat of Christ, that each one may receive what is due him for the things done while in the body, whether good or bad.' (2 Corinthians 5:10, NIV). God judges 'the thoughts and intentions of the heart' by his word (Hebrews 4:12), and not just our actions, which though they may look good enough to us, do not meet the altogether purer standards of a holy God.

Verse six compares man's 'vanity' with God's 'power' which can set man free if man chooses to ask. 'Nothing new under the sun' is a quotation from the Old Testament book of Ecclesiastes (1:9, NIV). 'What has been will be again, what has been done will be done again; there is nothing new under the sun.' Vanity and pride are major obstacles to people choosing to follow Christ. God has the power to set anyone free but their freewill has to operate in cooperation with what God has already done through Christ's offering of himself on the cross, but 'Man gotta choose before God can set him free.'

The last verse states that we will have no need to 'wonder' where Dylan has gone after his death. All he asks is that we say that he 'trusted in God and that Christ was in him.' The Christ that defeated the devil was indeed God's chosen Son. Compared to him there 'ain't no man righteous, no not one.' With lyrics as simple yet profound as these, it is small wonder that Dylan says that he 'believes the songs', and that they are his 'lexicon'. [26] He says in two brilliant lines what theologians take great tomes to express.

There was also the song 'Cover Down Pray Through' (otherwise known as 'Cover Down Break Through', the title of which refers to the lack of response from God that the rebellious people of Israel are getting to their prayers. 'You have covered yourself with a cloud, so that no prayer can pass through.' (Lamentations 3:44). The song describes the Exodus of the people of Israel from slavery in Egypt. 'You heard about Pharaoh's army, trampling through the mud, you heard about the Hebrew children, redeemed by blood.' After Moses had led the people of Israel out of Egypt, they were pursued by Pharaoh to the Red Sea.

The account in Exodus records that God sent a wind and supernaturally drove back the water, so that the Israelites were able to pass through on the dry sea bed. But when Pharaoh's army tried to follow, the waters returned and they were drowned. Dylan sings that the same Spirit whose power drove back the Red Sea dwells in those who trust in Christ, and that the spirit that raised Christ from the dead can also quicken ('give life to') our mortal bodies. 'But if the Spirit of him that raised up Jesus from the dead dwell in you, he that raised up Christ from the dead shall also quicken your mortal bodies by his Spirit that dwells in you.' (Romans 8:11, KJV). But if we are not careful, we can let it 'run to our heads'; spiritual pride then hinders spiritual growth.

So we need 'protection', and God provides it in the 'armour of the Lord'; we have the sword of God's word, as described in the book of Hebrews (4:12). 'The word of God is living and active and sharper than any two-edged sword, and piercing as far as the division of soul and spirit, of both joints and marrow, and able to judge the thoughts and intentions of the heart.'

Dylan describes Jesus as 'the hammer of salvation', rather like Judas Maccabeus ('Judah the Hammer'). He was the Jewish priest who led the Maccabean revolt against the pagan Greeks of the Seleucid Empire (167-

160 BC). 'Genesis to Revelation, repent and confess', sings Dylan with great conviction. The song then describes what the Bible refers to as the 'conviction of sin'; the working of the conscience where you wake up restless because of an awareness of some wrongdoing which is eating away at you. The 'image' you have built of yourself 'will come a-tumblin' down', when God tests it. Death will not set you free until you have experienced the spiritual breakthrough that comes from turning to and trusting in Christ.

Dylan concluded the song on the live performance at the Massey Hall in Toronto, Canada (April 20, 1980) with the remark "Coverdown, breakthrough - I wish someone had told me that when I was coming up." The song seems to be saying that if you ask God to take away the cover and adopt a position of openness towards him, then you can experience a spiritual breakthrough similar to that of the people of Israel. They were spared the death of their first-born by painting the blood of a lamb on the lintels of their house doors, while slaves in the land of Egypt. This was symbolic of the blood that Christ would one day shed on behalf of all humanity. Judgement passed over the Israelites, and they were able to escape into the 'promised land' that stands for heaven; 'redeemed through blood' as Dylan put it.

'Yonder Comes Sin' illustrates what might have been released had it not been for the prevailing negativity and eye for the bottom-line of CBS. Dylan was finding out, like Johnny Cash before him, that the recording industry had the power to 'edit him out'. But the recording industry were reckoning without an adequate grasp of Dylan's intelligence and lyrical craft. He would simply find a way around their objections - using allegory.

Chapter 4

'Infidels'

"They were so rude, so nasty about Bob Dylan and said how they weren't gonna promote another gospel record... I was just astonished to hear these people, high-up people at CBS, talking about this man as if he were just someone... a 'f**k him' kind of attitude." [27]

In the light of this prevalent negativity, Dylan's 1983 album 'Infidels' was greeted with a sigh of relief by much of Dylan's public and especially the music industry. Finally, the religious thing was over.

Or was it?

There has perhaps never been a song as misunderstood as 'Jokerman'. Mainstream Jewish authors have ascribed the images therein to the Jewish Bob Dylan. This is not very flattering considering that almost all the illusions are evil. Dylan wrote the song while in the Caribbean, after learning about the evil spirits that the islanders call 'jumbis'; [28] hence the song's reference to idolatry (the iron headed idol's eyes are 'glowing').

'Casting bread' (in the first line) echoes the Bible's 'Cast your bread on the surface of the waters, for you will find it after many days.' (Ecclesiastes 11:1). Actions have consequences, something true even for spiritual beings like the Jokerman, who can stand on top of the water. The second line about idolatry resonates with St Paul's words to the Galatians. [xv] The 'glowing' of the idol's eyes indicate spiritual activity, but not for good. Scripture denotes idolatry as a sin which deceives people into worshipping what has been created instead of the Creator.

'Sailing into the mist' implies that the future is not clear; the next line, ('snake in your fists'), brings the first of two 'serpent' references in the song. This probably alludes to the book of Revelation. 'The great dragon

---

[xv] Galatians 5:19-20: 'The acts of the sinful nature are obvious: sexual immorality, impurity and debauchery; idolatry and witchcraft.'

was hurled down - that ancient serpent called the devil, or Satan, who leads the whole world astray.' (Revelation 12:9, ANIV). The 'hurricane' here is a reference to destruction, used similarly in the Bible in the book of Job. 'While Job was still speaking, yet another messenger came and said, "Your sons and daughters were feasting and drinking wine at the oldest brother's house, when suddenly a mighty wind swept in from the desert and struck the four corners of the house. It collapsed on them and they are dead, and I am the only one who has escaped to tell you!" (Job 1:18-19). This destruction, although allowed by God, is clearly the work of the devil, as the book of Job makes clear. [xvi] Snakes and hurricanes are both biblical images of considerable negative force.

The Jokerman does not have freedom - it is 'just around the corner'; his rebellious nature compels him to destructive acts. Worse still, he is someone for whom truth is very 'far off' indeed. Freedom is just around the corner from everyone, but often not attained. And in any case, it does not help much to have freedom without the guidance of truth to prevent the freedom leading to serious error. This spiritual principle is referred to in the gospel of John in reference to the freedom found in following Christ, who claimed (John 14:6) to be 'truth' personified. Spiritual truth sets us free. 'To the Jews who had believed him, Jesus said, "If you hold to my teaching, you are really my disciples. Then you will know the truth, and the truth will set you free."' (John 8:31-33). Having freedom while rejecting the truth is not a good combination at all.

The chorus tells us that the Jokerman is a dancer, but to the 'nightingale tune', i.e. at night; and by the 'light of the moon', the first two of the seventeen night-time references that the song makes. The nightingale is one of the few birds that sings at night, making it a bird of the darkness, when dark spiritual things often happen. For example, 'Then Jesus said

---

[xvi] Job 1:8-11: 'The Lord said to Satan, "Have you considered my servant Job? For there is no one like him on the earth, a blameless and upright man, fearing God and turning away from evil." Then Satan answered the Lord, "Does Job fear God for nothing? Have you not made a hedge about him and his house and all that he has, on every side? You have blessed the work of his hands, and his possessions have increased in the land. But put forth your hand now and touch all that he has; he will surely curse you to your face."'

to the chief priests, the officers of the temple guard, and the elders, who had come for him, "Am I leading a rebellion, that you have come with swords and clubs? Every day I was with you in the temple courts, and you did not lay a hand on me. But this is your hour - when darkness reigns.'" (Luke 22:52-53, ANIV).

The triple 'oh' of 'Oh, oh, oh Jokerman' indicates that the song, from a Jewish perspective, is a song of lament; an expression of great sadness for the poor spiritual state the 'Jokerman' is in. Laments were sung when someone died tragically, or when someone of stature was brought low. The Old Testament scripture of Isaiah 14:12 (KJV) contains an example in relation to the devil's fall from heaven. 'How art thou fallen from heaven, O Lucifer, son of the morning! How art thou cut down to the ground, which didst weaken the nations!' The devil had potential for spiritual greatness, but sadly threw it away through rebellious choices.

The second verse begins with another reference to the dark, because the Jokerman works alone and in secret, after the sun has set. 'Fools rush in where angels fear to tread' is a common proverb; the 'fools' here may be humankind whose fate, 'so full of dread' can be seen as consignment to hell and eternal punishment, something that is hidden until the end of life. In this context, Dylan's line 'where angels fear to tread' can refer to fallen angels or demons. The Jokerman is unable to reveal their future; only God can do this. In the original version (unreleased) of the song, Dylan added, 'No store bought shirt for you on your back, one of the women must sit in the shack and sew one.' The Jokerman is well dressed and has slaves to work for him.

Dylan then gives us a second 'snake' reference - shedding skin. The devil ('the great serpent') can manifest himself in many varied guises, as 'Man Of Peace' demonstrates. 'The persecutor within' is most likely the conscience, which the devil has completely hardened by his repeated sin. The devil works in what the Bible refers to as the 'high places', which have a close link to idolatry and false worship. For example, 'The high places were not taken away; the people still sacrificed and burned incense on the high places.' (2 Kings 14:4). Dylan uses an equivalent term 'mountains'. All angels can 'walk on the clouds'; they are spiritual beings without the restrictions of natural forces such as gravity, just as the Jokerman can stand 'on the water' (in line one). 'Manipulator of crowds' is very reminiscent of Christ's condemnation. [xvii] The devil cannot create or do anything truly good. He can only 'steal, kill and destroy' (John 10:10) by deception; he is truly a 'dream twister'. He was at home in Sodom and Gomorrah, towns that symbolised sin and depravity in the Old Testament and were destroyed by God after Lot had been persuaded to leave. (Genesis chapter 19). Dylan's sense of humour comes through in 'ain't nobody there would want to marry your sister' - no one would want the devil for a brother-in-law, and the Sodomites' sexual preferences make a heterosexual marriage to any 'sister' unlikely!

The 'friend' to the martyr and the woman of shame appears to be irony. The Jokerman is a friend who will not help them; instead he brings about their death by martyrdom with its eternal spiritual reward, and so unwittingly aids them. The 'fiery furnace' is a reference to the Old Testament prophet Daniel (chapter 3) and Babylonian King Nebuchadnezzar's threat. 'Whoever does not fall down and worship shall be cast into the midst of a burning fiery furnace'. This is reflected in Christ's warning about hell. 'They [God's angels] will throw them [evildoers] into the fiery furnace, where there will be weeping and gnashing of teeth.' (Matthew 13:42). The 'rich man' is a reference to the damned rich man in the parable Jesus taught about hell, traditionally referred to as 'Lazarus and Dives'. The rich man who cries out to Abraham for water from the flames of torment is not given any name. (Luke 16:19-31). Jesus used the parable to make the point that even someone returning from death (such as himself) would be insufficient to change very many people's (hardened) hearts towards God.

The reference to the 'Law' of Leviticus and Deuteronomy resonates with the message of the New Testament in the Bible; 'By works of the Law

---

[xvii] Mark 15:8-13: 'The crowd came up and asked Pilate to do for them what he usually did. "Do you want me to release to you the king of the Jews?" asked Pilate, knowing it was out of envy that the chief priests had handed Jesus over to him. But the chief priests stirred up the crowd to have Pilate release Barabbas instead. "What shall I do, then, with the one you call the king of the Jews?" Pilate asked them. "Crucify him!" they shouted.'

shall no one be justified.' (Galatians 2:16b). The devil uses the Law as a type of stick to beat over the heads of fallen mankind who cannot, in and of themselves, live up to its righteous demands. 'The Law is holy, and the commandment is holy and righteous and good.' (Romans 7:12). The problem is that mankind are unable to keep them. The Old Testament Law, which these two scriptural books relate is and was powerless to save. Salvation can only come through faith, just as Abraham was made right with God by his attitude of trust in God and his promise of a son.

'Jungle' and 'sea' both carry the connotation of danger and harm - the Jews were never historically a sea-faring nation - and the 'law of the jungle' is a simile for harm and danger. The next image, of 'smoke' and 'steed', can be a reference to the book of Revelation and the ashen horse that brought war and plagues. 'When the Lamb broke the fourth seal, I heard the voice of the fourth living creature saying, "Come". I looked, and behold, an ashen horse; and he who sat on it had the name Death; and Hades was following with him.' (Revelation 6:7-8). Once again, the image is one of night - it is 'twilight'.

The devil's beauty and resultant vanity is referred to with the reference to Michelangelo's willingness to 'carve out his features' (or as Dylan would later sing in 'Angelina' - 'a face that any painter would paint'); the devil's uncleanness also gets a mention. In Jewish society and scripture a dog is an unclean animal. The Bible records: 'Do not give dogs what is holy.' (Matthew 7:6). The devil is an unholy spiritual being, and the licking of his face by the dog is a powerful image of the transmission of uncleanness; dogs cleanse their rectums with their tongues.

The next imagery is of a conflict between the extermination carried out by the 'riflemen' of this world and the preacher who wants to see people saved. The original lyrics of the song went as follows: 'Well, the preacher-man talking about the deaf and the dumb, and a world to come, that's already been pre-determined.' It is pre-determined in the sense that God knows the outcomes of our lives already because he is outside of time, and so can see our the past, present and future choices and their consequences simultaneously.

Then comes a reference to many kinds of violence. The original lyrics read: 'Molotov cocktails can't drown out his *[the preacher-man's]* sermon.' 'Night comes steppin' in' appears to be an allusion to the final culmination of Satan's power over the world. Jesus said: 'As long as it is day, we must do the work of him who sent me. Night is coming, when no one can work.' (John 9:4, ANIV). Dylan then adds two other references to darkness ('shadowy' and 'grey skies'). Jesus refers to the devil as the 'prince of this world.' (John 12:31).

'Priest in his pocket' may stand for false religion on an organised level. More death and destruction is implied by the image of the blade being heated, preparatory to sharpening. One of the works of the Jokerman is to take orphans and raise them to be prostitutes, another reference to the 'Babylon' of scripture, so named the 'The Great, the Mother of Prostitutes'. (Revelation 17:5). The original lyrics for the song read: 'Take a woman who could have been Joan-of-Arc and turn her into a harlot'; in other words, take a noble minded woman and degrade her into prostitution.

Jokerman knows what 'he' (i.e. God) wants (right living in accordance with God's word), but does not 'show any response'; he is just not interested in doing God's will. It really is stretching credulity to suggest that this classic song could be about anyone other than the devil. Every line (with the possible exception of 'friend') points to it.

'Infidels' second track, 'Sweetheart Like You' addresses all those trapped on a dead-end street. The track starts off featuring a woman's 'boss' who has allowed vanity to get the better of him. Pride was the downfall of the devil, which the Old Testament prophet Isaiah describes. 'How you have fallen from heaven, O star of the morning, son of the dawn! You have been cut down to the earth, you who have weakened the nations! But you said in your heart, 'I will ascend to heaven; I will raise my throne above the stars of God, and I will sit on the mount of assembly in the recesses of the north. I will ascend above the heights of the clouds; I will make myself like the Most High. Nevertheless you will be thrust down to Sheol, to the recesses of the pit.' (Isaiah 14:12-15). The published version has the amusing 'he sure left here in style.' In an earlier version Dylan has the boss going up north 'to start a graveyard up there'! [29]

Dylan takes a liking to the woman, who has a smile that is 'hard to resist', and asks the song's question: "What's a sweetheart like you doing in a dump like this?" Men and women are supposed to have, in God's perfect plan, a fulfilling relationship with him. Instead, some have traded that in for spiritual servitude with the devil for a master, and like the prodigal son in Christ's parable (Luke 15:11), have to feed pigs in the sty of the devil's making. The question may have been inspired by the 1942 Vincent Sherman film 'All Through The Night', in which Humphrey Bogart asks, "What would a sweetheart like that Miss Hamilton dame be doing in a dump like this?"

The 'game' that the woman is embroiled in entails deception (a playing card disappearing with the flick of a wrist). Dylan thinks that rather than doing what she is doing, she belongs 'at home', with someone who won't 'do her wrong'. Dylan poses the question, just how much more abuse is she able to take, having been deceived by 'that first kiss'? She, like us all, has a choice: she can either stay crawling 'across cut glass to make a deal', or she can exit toward someone with rather healthier plans for her both spiritually and physically.

When Dylan sings that in her father's house are 'many mansions', he is quoting from John 14:2 (KJV), where Jesus says, 'In my Father's house are many mansions: if it were not so, I would have told you. I go to prepare a place for you.' 'Fireproof floors' implies safety from hell's influences. To be where the woman is at the moment she has had to have done 'some evil deed', and is certainly suffering with her current lifestyle. She is made to perform on the harmonica ('harp') until her 'lips bleed' from over-use.

Dylan closes the song with a quotation ('Patriotism is the last refuge of a scoundrel') from 'The Life Of Johnson' by James Boswell. [30] This life does not always deliver justice (e.g. thieves prosper), but the next one certainly will. The woman can enter the Kingdom of Heaven ('The land of permanent bliss'), if she will take a 'step down', i.e. if she takes a step of humility in approaching God and seeking his forgiveness.

'Infidels' third track was 'Neighbourhood Bully', where Dylan's concern for his spiritual heritage among God's chosen people is what is being expressed. Israel, the world's favourite whipping boy, gets singled out for any blame that's going within the region. Since Dylan told Kurt Loder [31] that 'Neighbourhood Bully' was not a political song; that leaves it as a statement of spiritual truth, or as Dylan acquiesced, 'a heartfelt statement of belief', rather than a party-political statement. For Dylan, politics is 'what kills'; it is 'corrupt'. The song is about the survival of the only democracy in the whole Middle East region.

Turning to the lyrics, Israel is merely 'one man' (one nation), but has many enemies who think that 'he's on their land'. In the biblical narrative, the Palestinians had been occupying some of the land promised by God to Abraham and his descendants. 'The Lord said to Abram, after Lot had separated from him, "Now lift up your eyes and look from the place where you are, northward and southward and eastward and westward; for all the land which you see, I will give it to you and to your descendants forever. I will make your descendants as the dust of the earth, so that if anyone can number the dust of the earth, then your descendants can also be numbered. Arise, walk about the land through its length and breadth; for I will give it to you."' (Genesis 13:14-17).

Muslim nations had previously occupied the territory taken back by Israel in the 'Six Days War' (June 5-10 1967), and the Islamic mind sees the land as permanently belonging to Islam. Israel, Dylan sings, is massively outnumbered by the surrounding Arab nations, but is still labeled as the 'neighbourhood bully' because Israel often gets the blame for the trouble arising as a result of their neighbours desire to 'wipe them from the map'. In the words of one of those neighbours' leaders: "There is no doubt that the new wave *[of attacks]* in Palestine will wipe off this stigma *[Israel]* from the face of the Islamic world... Israel must be wiped off the map." (Mahmoud Ahmadinejad, the - then new - President of Iran, speaking in 2005.) [32]

Israel, widely 'criticized and condemned', 'just lives to survive'. Pacifism is the best recourse for Israel, according to their critics - don't 'fight back', just 'lay down and die'. Israel has 'been driven out of every land'; sometimes in cattle trains from supposedly civilized 'Christian' Western countries, being deported to Auschwitz and other places of extermination. The Jews have been persecuted the world over. Why? Because they have an enemy in common with God? Israel, Dylan explains, is in 'exile', dispersed by the Romans from their homeland, but restored there, as the Bible foretold would happen, in 1948, following Hitler's acts of genocide.

Israel is always on trial. Why? For 'being born'. (The Bible describes Israel as having been birthed by God.) [xviii] Anytime an attack on Israel is repulsed, Israel, the only democracy in the Middle East, is blamed. Both the Muslim Arab states and the left-wing Western European journalists writing from the safety of their western offices, say that Israel should 'apologise'. Dylan, as a Jew, recognizes that Israel is not going to lie down quietly and die. Israel will not play by other's rules when 'a gun' is being held to him and 'a noose' prepared for him. Israel stands alone and outnumbered massively in the region, but is still labeled as a 'bully' despite neighbours calling for its destruction. Israel is 'surrounded by pacifists who all want peace', but it is a 'peace' the price of which is Israel's destruction. The idea is an extension of the prophet Jeremiah's who warned of those who said to Israel, '"Peace, peace"; when there is no peace.' (Jeremiah 8:11, KJV).

[xviii] Ezekiel 16:1-7: 'Then the word of the Lord came to me, saying, "Son of man, make known to Jerusalem her abominations and say, "Thus says the Lord God to Jerusalem, 'Your origin and your birth are from the land of the Canaanite, your father was an Amorite and your mother a Hittite. As for your birth, on the day you were born your navel cord was not cut, nor were you washed with water for cleansing; you were not rubbed with salt or even wrapped in cloths. No eye looked with pity on you to do any of these things for you, to have compassion on you. Rather you were thrown out into the open field, for you were abhorred on the day you were born. When I passed by you and saw you squirming in your blood, I said to you while you were in your blood, 'Live!' Yes, I said to you while you were in your blood, 'Live!' I made you numerous like plants of the field.'"

Israel's Muslim neighbours follow the Islamic practice of 'Taqiyya'. The term 'al-Taqiyya' literally means, 'Concealing or disguising one's beliefs, convictions, ideas, feelings, opinions, or strategies at a time of eminent danger, whether now or later in time, to save oneself from physical or mental injury.' As the Muslim cleric Muhammad Taqi Usmani recently said, 'Muslims should live peacefully in countries such as Britain, where they have the freedom to practice Islam, only until they gain enough power to engage in battle'. [33] A one-word translation of 'taqiyya' would be 'dissimulation'. Mohammed (Quran 3:28) taught and practiced dissimulation in order to gain an advantage over non-Muslims.

The fact that Israel has a habit of out-living its enemies is a sign that God is with her; 'Every empire that's enslaved him is gone, Egypt and Rome, even the great Babylon.' Dylan sings that Israel's 'holiest books have been trampled upon' - much of the ancient Jewish Bible has been re-written very differently in the Koran, and the scriptures as a whole have been ridiculed by the liberal West. The song ends with a reference to the life of Joshua, the man who took over from Moses in leading Israel into the Promised Land. Dylan sings, 'Running out the clock, time standing still.' Joshua 10:12-14 reads: 'Then Joshua spoke to the Lord in the day when the Lord delivered up the Amorites before the sons of Israel, and he said in the sight of Israel, "O sun, stand still at Gibeon, and O moon in the valley of Aijalon." So the sun stood still, and the moon stopped, until the nation avenged themselves of their enemies. Is it not written in the book of Jashar? And the sun stopped in the middle of the sky and did not hasten to go down for about a whole day. There was no day like that before it or after it, when the Lord listened to the voice of a man; for the Lord fought for Israel.' These last five words seem to sum up the song's integral message - the Lord fights for Israel.

The fourth track, 'License To Kill', laments the problems that the misuse of technology can so easily cause as a result of man pretending to be God while denying his existence and ignoring moral restraints. The song recounts man's steps away from being a steward of the world to being its exploiter, 'hell-bent for destruction'. Man is living out of synchrony with his maker; the result is that man is 'afraid and confused' (and consequentially depressed). His brain bears the marks of having been mismanaged with great skill, probably by the 'Man Of Peace' that Dylan sings about on 'Infidels', and certainly also by his political and social will-masters. Man believes what his eyes tell him, but 'his eyes, they just tell him lies', because everything he sees has been distorted by a false reality. You may be 'a noisemaker, spirit maker, heartbreaker, backbreaker... an actor in a plot' strikes a similar note to 'Gotta Serve Somebody' ('You might be an ambassador to England or France...') on 'Slow Train Coming'.

Dylan clearly felt that the resources going into the space programme would have been better spent on human needs closer to home, and that the technological advances achieved would hasten man's 'doom'. When the January 1986 space shuttle 'Challenger' broke up 73 seconds after launch, killing all seven crew members, Dylan gave the following introduction to the song on his Australian tour. "Here's a song I wrote a way back; it's all about the space programme. I suppose you heard about this recent tragedy, right? I don't need to tell you it really was a tragedy. You see, these people had no business going up there. Like, there's not enough problems on earth to solve? So I want to dedicate this song to all those poor people, who were fooled into going up there." [34]

Man worshipping at the 'altar of a stagnant pool' sums up man's spiritual reality; dead and odorous, only seeing his own reflection, which in his vanity is his sole source of fulfillment in his worship of himself.

According to many reviewers at the time, the album 'Infidels' marked a sea change away from Christianity. Commentators such as the Discographer wrote, "'Infidels' was Bob Dylan's 1983 album release and it brought a sigh of relief from legions of his fans. He had returned to the secular world and left his Christian fundamentalist teachings behind.' [35] This book will show that time has proved them wrong.

The next track exposed the error of that viewpoint at the time of release. It beggars belief that the song 'Man Of Peace' could be thought of as being 'post-Christian'. Satan is portrayed as a man on the street, with his arm outstretched. Who is he? 'The Fuhrer?' 'The local priest?' The devil has many faces, including that of 'a man of peace.' Tradition has it that,

59

as one of the most beautiful of angels, Satan was responsible for leading the worship in heaven; Dylan sings of his 'harmonious tongue', and his knowledge of love songs. 'Good intentions can be evil', Dylan tells us, which is often the case if they are not guided by truth, something 'so far off' from the Jokerman. Dylan told Kurt Loder ('Rolling Stone' Magazine) that he did not believe that there would be world peace, just a 'pause to reload the rifles'. To Dylan, 'None of this matters, if you believe in another world. If you believe in this world you're stuck, you really don't have a chance. You'll go mad, 'cause you won't see the end of it. You may want to stick around, but you won't be able to. On another level though, you will be able to see this world; you'll look back and say, "Ah, that's what it was all about all the time. Wow, why didn't I get that?"' [36]

The song portrays the devil as a person constantly on the move, all over the place, with a word here and a word there, working the crowd, with eyes 'looking like they're on a rabbit hunt'; constantly shifting visual direction. The devil will try and catch you out 'when you're hoping for a glimpse of the sun', such as being open to God but are looking in the wrong direction, or when 'your troubles feel like they weigh a ton.' The devil loves depression and will do everything he can to bring it on. The devil can ride you 'down Niagara Falls in the barrels of your skull'; he will manipulate you if you entertain him in your mind. His end will be to 'get a burning himself'. 'Then he (God) will also say to those on his left, 'Depart from me, accursed ones, into the eternal fire which has been prepared for the devil and his angels.' (Matthew 25:41). Contrary to popular belief, hell is a place of torment for the devil, not a place where he and his minions participate in the torture of others.

The devil can pose as a 'humanitarian' or as 'a great philanthropist'; whatever he needs to be at any given moment. 'He knows just where to touch you' because he has information based upon his and others' observations. If you let him put his arms around you then 'you can feel the tender touch of the beast.' [xix] Dylan likens the devil to a 'howling

---

[xix] Revelation 13:1-2: 'Then I saw a beast coming up out of the sea, having ten horns and seven heads, and on his horns were ten diadems, and on his heads

wolf', just as Jesus did. 'I am the good shepherd; the good shepherd lays down his life for the sheep. He who is a hired hand, and not a shepherd, who is not the owner of the sheep, sees the wolf coming, and leaves the sheep and flees, and the wolf snatches them and scatters them.' (John 10:11-12).

The song ends with an image of a 'blue-eyed boy' and tokens of a lost childhood ('little white shoes and a broken toy'). The boy is 'following a star, the same one them three men followed from the East'. This is a reference to Matthew 2:1-2. 'Now after Jesus was born in Bethlehem of Judea in the days of Herod the king, Magi from the east arrived in Jerusalem, saying, "Where is he who has been born king of the Jews? For we saw his star in the east and have come to worship him."' The wise men are traditionally numbered as being three, after the number of gifts that they brought to the infant Christ; this 'little boy' grew up to be a man who defeated Satan through his own death on a cross, with his subsequent resurrection disarming the power of death.

Next on the album came 'Union Sundown'. 'Sundown on the union, and what's made in the USA', expresses Dylan's concern for the nation's economy based on the amount of consumer goods imported from Singapore, Taiwan, Malaysia, the Amazon and other places where people will work for a pittance. Greed has got in the way, Dylan sings, and profit has come before maintaining jobs at home. The line 'capitalism is above the law' could have come from Dylan's earliest protest materials, and 'until greed got in the way' sums up the root problem at the heart of the issues addressed in the song.

The lyrics evoke the memory of Jesus' words in Luke 12:15. 'Jesus said to them, "Beware, and be on your guard against every form of greed; for not even when one has an abundance does his life consist of his possessions." Dylan sings: 'They used to grow food in Kansas, now they want to grow it on the moon...' This witty use of hyperbole reinforces

---

were blasphemous names. And the beast which I saw was like a leopard, and his feet were like those of a bear, and his mouth like the mouth of a lion. And the dragon gave him his power and his throne and great authority.'

the point that greed sets no limits to its demands. As the Old Testament Jewish proverb says, 'The leech has two daughters, 'Give', and 'Give'. There are three things that will not be satisfied, four that will not say, 'Enough': Sheol, and the barren womb, earth that is never satisfied with water, and fire that never says, "Enough."' (Proverbs 30:15-16).

As Dylan said to Kurt Loder, "What's thirty cents a day? He *[the worker in Argentina]* don't need thirty cents a day. I mean, people survived for 6000 years without having to work for a slave wage." [37] At his insightful best, Dylan points out that 'Democracy don't rule the world' *[i.e. greed does]*. 'The world' is a term used in the scripture to define that spiritual territory that Satan has usurped control over. As Jesus said, "I have given them your word; and the world has hated them, because they are not of the world, even as I am not of the world. I do not ask you to take them out of the world, but to keep them from the evil one. They are not of the world, even as I am not of the world." (John 17:14-16). Dylan concludes his description of the terrible power of greed with "a man's gonna do what he has to do..." *[i.e. the 'man' standing for the person motivating the greed and motivated by greed]*, "... when he's got a hungry mouth to feed" *[his own]*.

Next up was the masterpiece 'I and I'. Said by Dylan to have been written in the West Indies; he told Leonard Cohen that he wrote it in fifteen minutes. [38] The track is an allegorical masterpiece, one of the first among Dylan's new art of conveying spiritual truth, as Christ himself did, within the allegorical language of a 'parable' - a story with spiritual meaning for those able to discern it. For this purpose, while not actually sporting dreadlocks and reverting to marijuana use, Dylan adopts the language of the Rastafarians, who use the term 'I and I' to refer to themselves and God. In so doing they indicate the presence and divinity of the Almighty (from the Hebrew 'Yahweh' - 'I Am') within themselves, whilst also stating that they belong to the world and are not somehow removed from it. Rastafarian scholar E. E. Cashmore says, "'I and I' is an expression to totalize the concept of oneness, the oneness of two persons." This is similar to the Christian idea of being 'in Christ'. Jesus had said in John 15:19: "You are not of the world, but I chose you out of the world." Dylan told Kurt Loder, "I know a lot of Rastas. I know they're Bible-believing people, and it's very easy for me to relate to any Bible-believing person." [39]

The song begins with Dylan observing a 'strange woman' in his bed. Who is she? We are not told. What we are told is a series of thoughts and reactions Dylan has to her, for example, marriage to a 'righteous king who wrote psalms beside moonlit streams'. This is a reference to King David who penned many of the Jewish prayer-songs that make up the book of Psalms. Perhaps the woman stands for Israel, with whose spiritual heritage Dylan is now re-connecting in his faith-journey, in a way now informed by his relationship with the Jewish Messiah. Israel is described in the Old Testament scriptures as having been 'wed' to God. 'As the bridegroom rejoices over the bride, so your God will rejoice over you.' (Isaiah 62:5). And, 'Turn, O backsliding children,' says the Lord; 'for I am married unto you.' (Jeremiah 3:14, KJV).

The chorus is a fine example of Dylan's craft of allegory and the skilful interweaving of scriptural concepts. 'I *[the human me]* and I, *[the 'I am' - Yahweh, the God of Israel]*, in creation where one's nature neither honours nor forgives.' The human nature fallen away from God and his grace can do neither of these basic spiritual things. 'I and I, one says to the other, no man sees my face and lives.' (As God had said to Moses in Exodus 33:20: "You cannot see my face, for no man can see me and live.")

In the song Dylan decides to go for a walk, because if she awakens she will 'want me to talk.' It is possible that he didn't want to talk about his faith in an open way anymore, given the flak he had received for it. Dylan has 'nothing to say, especially about whatever was'. His attempts to be straightforward and open about his faith had often led to him being abused and rejected, as Christ himself had been. The song describes an 'untrodden path' which he once took, (surely meaning the path of discipleship), 'where the swift don't win the race', echoing the Jewish scripture of the Old Testament. 'I again saw under the sun that *the race is not to the swift* and the battle is not to the warriors, and neither is bread to the wise nor wealth to the discerning nor favour to men of ability; for time and chance overtake them all.' (Ecclesiastes 9:11, *italics mine.*) This 'race' of life is also described in the book of Hebrews (12:1, KJV): 'Let us run with patience the race that is set before us.' In God's economy, it is not always the fastest who wins, but rather the faithful, and also 'the worthy, who can divide the word of truth' *[the scripture]*. This echoes Paul's words to Timothy: 'Study to show yourself approved unto God, a workman that need not be ashamed, rightly dividing the word of truth.' (2 Timothy 2:15, KJV).

The 'stranger' who taught Dylan to 'look into justice's beautiful face' is a biblical term for a Gentile (a non-Jew), probably one of the pastors in the Californian Vineyard Church, or his African-American girlfriend at that time, Mary Alice Artes, who contacted her Vineyard Church pastors on Dylan's behalf. They apparently also taught Dylan 'to see an eye for an eye and a tooth for a tooth', standing for the Jewish Law (the Torah), and in particular the distinctions that Christ drew between it and his own message of faith and trust. "You have heard it said, 'An eye for an eye, and a tooth for a tooth': but I say unto you, that you resist not evil: but whosoever shall smite you on your right cheek, turn to him the other also." (Matthew 5:38-39). Dylan has been taught how to discern the difference between Law and grace; the old covenant and the new one that Christ offers.

The final verse gives another good insight into Dylan's spiritual experience. 'Noontime *[the brightest time of day]*, and I'm still pushin' myself along the road, the darkest part.' *['Dark' presumably because, despite it being 'noon', it has become the dark night of the soul's testing.]* 'Into the narrow lanes, I can't stumble or stay put', echoes the Bible. Proverbs 4:12: 'When you walk, your steps will not be impeded; and if you run, you will not stumble', and, 'Your word is a lamp to my feet, and a light to my path.' (Psalm 119:105). Dylan is in partnership with God who guides his feet and leads him forward, in both conscious and subconscious ways. 'Someone else is speaking with my mouth' *[others in the recording industry may be speaking in his name]*, '…but I'm listening only to my heart' *[where Christ dwells by faith]*. 'You are a letter of Christ, cared for by us, written not with ink but with the Spirit of the living God, not on tablets of stone but on tablets of human hearts.' (2 Corinthians 3:3). 'I've made shoes for everyone, even you, while I still go barefoot.' Dylan, surely one of the world's richest and most successful recording artists of all time, still lives a comparatively very simple lifestyle, touring much of the time and living in trailers and fairly inexpensive hotels. He has made a lot of money for others and worked hard for them and for his public, but doesn't indulge himself with much in the way of materialism.

'Infidels' concludes with 'Don't Fall Apart On Me Tonight', in which Dylan reasons with an unnamed 'girl' about her plight. He 'needs' her but she seems not certain what she wants or needs - possibly describing Dylan's relationship with his fan base, which have expressed rejection of his newfound faith and a desire to return to the old ways. Dylan obliges by communicating the new through the old type of language. 'Just a minute before you leave, girl' *[before you walk away from my music and its message]*. 'What is it that you're trying to achieve?' *[i.e. what are you really seeking?]*

Dylan warns her of 'vipers'; those who speak of him and his music with forked tongues and so can't be trusted. These people or beings have 'lost all ray of hope'; even ready to enter hell, the place of abandoned hope. Dangers abound; even in 'the palace of the Pope'. Pope John Paul II, had recently (May 13, 1981) been shot and badly wounded by a Turkish gunman named Mehmet Agca, as he entered St Peter's Square at the Vatican. [40]

While Dylan 'needs' her, he is realistic about where the relationship is going - nowhere. There are too many fundamental differences between them. He can't see the two of them 'going anywhere'; presumably because they are too far apart spiritually. He can't take her to the 'only place open'; she has to get to that place herself, he can't do it for her. He muses that he wished that he could have been a doctor - maybe he could have saved people that would otherwise have been lost. As he said to Dave Herman in 1981, "There's other things I would enjoy doing, besides playing - like become a doctor, who can save somebody's life on the highway. I mean, that's a man I'm going to look up to." [41] Dylan seems to be communicating spiritually through his words and music, and has burned 'every bridge I crossed'; he knows there is no turning back. As he sang in 'Solid Rock', 'Won't let go and I can't let go.'

He sings, 'I ain't too good at conversation.' Presumably his efforts to communicate his faith have not always been successful. What he wants to do most of all is bring her 'to the mountaintop', the place where she could meet God for herself, as the people of Israel had at Mount Sinai. 'Now Mount Sinai was all in smoke because, the Lord descended upon it in fire; and its smoke ascended like the smoke of a furnace, and the whole mountain quaked violently.' (Exodus 19:18). Dylan feels 'stuck', like a character in a painting; observed by many but unable to make a response in and of himself that will satisfy their true needs. Some people then appear, walking towards them - are they people she knows or 'will there be a fight'? They are humourless and devoid of any moral compass, unable to distinguish right from wrong. Could they represent some of the anti-Christian executives at Dylan's record company? Dylan wants reality (which includes spiritual reality); he wants to 'get beneath the surface waste', to a place without criticism or threats, or 'decadence and charm', which flatters to deceive. Misplaced affection and harming herself with 'mudcake creatures' in her arms are not what are good for her. They can reminisce about the past times of Clark Gable, but in the end 'yesterday's gone', and 'tomorrow is just one step beyond'. That is what we should all be living for.

The quantity of scriptural references on 'Infidels', and the album's title itself, should have provided a clue at the time that his 'Christian phase' was more than just a phase. His comments in 1985 to Bill Flanagan make his position clear. "I'll tell you one thing, if you're talking just on a scriptural type of thing, there's no way I could write anything that would be scripturally incorrect. I mean, I'm not going to put forth ideas that aren't scripturally true. I might reverse them, or make them come out a different way, but I'm not going to say anything that's just totally 'wrong'; that there's not a law for." [42] There are many ways of conveying spiritual truth. The years to come would demonstrate the use of allegory; of 'reversing them', or 'making them come out a different way', while remaining true in meaning to the textual source.

Chapter 5

'Empire Burlesque'

"I just have to hope there's some kind of way this music that I've always played is a healing kind of music. I mean if it isn't I don't wanna do it. Because there's enough stuff, so-called music, out there, which is sick music. It's just sick. It's made by sick people and it's played to sick people to further a whole world of sickness. Now, that's not only true of music, this is true in film industry, it's true in the magazine industry. You know it caters to people's sickness. There's a lot of that. And if I can do something that is telling people or... hoping anyway that... whatever their sickness is, and we're all sick, whatever it is, you can be healed and well and set straight." [43]

1985 brought the release of 'Empire Burlesque'; 'burlesque' meaning 'a satirical literary or dramatic work that presents a solemn subject in an undignified way or an inconsequential subject in a dignified way'. The opening track, 'Tight Connection To My Heart' (which Dylan had written previously under the title 'Someone's Got A Hold Of My Heart'), is an example of burlesque of the first type. Dylan employs the language of allegory to describe what is closest to him - his 'love', even his 'baby' (i.e. of Bethlehem) that has the tightest of all tight connections to his 'heart'. The Bible denotes the heart as 'the seat of the affections, the perceptions, the thoughts, the understanding, the reasoning powers, the imagination, conscience, intentions, purpose and the will'. [44]

With the added hindsight of 'Christmas In The Heart', the clarity of the spiritual message that Dylan was communicating comes across more strongly, for example, the reference to that most un-Jewish of practices, the Christian celebration of the Eucharist (communion), where Christ's blood is sometimes represented by wine.

'Tight Connection To My Heart' appears to move backwards and forwards between Dylan's relations with his commercial taskmasters, his public and God. The chorus is a direct quotation from the Old Testament poetic book 'Song of Solomon.' Dylan starts by borrowing a line from the Humphrey Bogart film 'Sirocco'; 'I've got to move fast; I can't with you around my neck.' Who is 'you'? It may be the recording industry, whose goals and priorities rarely coincide with those who want to serve a higher purpose. Dylan admits to nerves ('hands sweating'), but says that he will 'go along with the charade' (from this perspective, the need to keep recording their way). That is, at least until he can come up with a 'way out'; a quote from the 1949 Humphrey Bogart film 'Tokyo Joe', in which Bogart says, 'I'll go along with the charade until I can think my way out.' Yes, he has contractual obligations to the music industry, but to him it is possibly 'all a big joke', not to be taken too seriously.

The song goes on to relate that Dylan can 'feel the breath of a storm', and so has to 'get his coat'; because there's something he has 'to do tonight'. What is it? Well, for a start, it involves being outside at night in a storm. Much later, in 'Ain't Talkin'' (from the album 'Modern Times'), Dylan sings about walking 'out tonight in the mystic garden', where he encounters someone - presumably God. The concept of going out at night for a spiritual meeting is a common theme of Dylan's, e.g. 'Working Man's Blues #2': 'In the dark I hear the night birds call, I can feel *[not 'hear' as on the official lyrics' website]* a lover's breath'. So who is the lover? Presumably it is the same person who goes out at night in the Jewish love song recounted in the Old Testament in the Song of Solomon, from which the song's chorus is derived. This ancient love poem, said to be prophetically describing the love relationship between Christ and the church, provided a rich source of allegory for the allegedly 'post-Christian' Dylan to continue his spiritual writing in a somewhat undercover kind of way.

'Has anybody seen my love?' sings Dylan, perfectly mirroring the beloved's words 'Have you seen him whom my soul loves?' in the Song of Solomon. 'On my bed night after night I sought him whom my soul loves; I sought him but did not find him. I must arise now and go about the city; in the streets and in the squares. I must seek him whom my soul loves. I sought him but did not find him. The watchmen who make the rounds in the city found me, and I said, "Have you seen him whom my soul loves?"' (Song of Solomon 3:1-3).

The beloved, a dark skinned Shulammite [45] woman, is seeking and being sought by her lover, King Solomon. From a New Testament perspective this passage is seen as describing the relationship between Christ and his Church. As the Apostle Paul wrote to the Ephesians (5:31-32): 'For this cause shall a man leave his father and mother, and shall be joined unto his wife, and the two shall be one flesh. This is a great mystery, but I speak concerning Christ and the church.'

Dylan then appears to address his public in words reminiscent of Humphrey Bogart ('You want to talk to me, go ahead and talk' - 'The Maltese Falcon.') Nothing that can be said will 'shock' Dylan (he has been around the block too many times for that), and he realizes, tongue in cheek, that he 'must be guilty of something'. He alludes to Madame Butterfly, an opera in which a Japanese wife is betrayed by her American naval husband; surely a fitting analogy to Dylan and the recording industry's response to his declarations of faith. Madame Butterfly has 'lulled' him to sleep, in a 'town without pity' (the recording industry knows no pity, only the value of the bottom line: "What are you f**king moaning about? You want 20 million bucks from us? Well, you gotta do what we tell you. And what we're telling you is ... No Torah! No Bible! No Koran! No Jesus! No God!") [46]

Dylan then sings, 'You're the one I've been looking for', a sentiment duplicated in a later song on the album, 'Emotionally Yours' ('You're the one I'm living for'). Given the preceding references to the Song of Solomon, this verse would seem to be addressed to Christ. 'You're the one that's got the key' (to my heart). Dylan tries to 'figure out' which of them is too good for the other, using another line borrowed from Humphrey Bogart in Sirocco: 'I don't know whether I'm too good for you or if you're too good for me.' The truth is that God is too good for any of us, but he accepts us anyway, out of the undying love he has for each of us.

The penultimate verse describes a character that is 'shot for resisting arrest'. Dylan can 'still hear his voice crying in the wilderness', just like Jesus' cousin, the prophet known as John the Baptist, had done so many years earlier. [xx] Dylan closes with a very clear expression of his faith, 'Never could learn to drink that blood and call it wine.' This is based on the gospel's accounts of Jesus' last Passover Seder meal. 'While they were eating, Jesus took some bread, and after a blessing, he broke it and gave it to the disciples, and said, "Take, eat; this is my body." And when he had taken a cup and given thanks, he gave it to them, saying, "Drink from it, all of you; for this is my blood of the covenant, which is poured out for many for forgiveness of sins. But I say to you, I will not drink of this fruit of the vine from now on until that day when I drink it new with you in my Father's kingdom." (Matthew 26:26-29). Dylan was learning to 'hold you' (Christ), and all his love, and call Christ his own.

'Seeing The Real You At Last', track number two, seems to address the issue that all encounter as they grow in faith, and so gain the 'conviction of things not seen' with natural eyes. (Hebrews 1:1). As before, if 'you' is seen as being used spiritually, then we have the scriptural idea that faith ignites an ability to understand and so 'see' and take hold of things that are otherwise invisible to the natural eye. As Jesus said, "Abraham rejoiced to see my day: and he saw it, and was glad." (John 8:56, KJV).

By the time 'Empire Burlesque' was recorded, Dylan had covered some miles in his relationship with God, and had seen some false images of what Christ is like stripped away to reveal the true man from Nazareth.

The opening line ('the rain not having cooled things down') may be a paraphrase of an Edward G Robinson line from the 1948 Humphrey Bogart film 'Key Largo'; 'Think this rain would cool things off, but it didn't.' (Alternatively it may be a rendering of a line from the 1954 Alfred Hitchcock film 'Rear Window': 'I thought the rain would cool things down but all it did was make the heat wet.') The later line 'Didn't

---

[xx] Luke 3:1-4: 'Now in the fifteenth year of the reign of Tiberius Caesar, Pontius Pilate being governor of Judaea… the word of God came unto John the son of Zacharias [John the Baptist] in the wilderness. And he came into all the country about Jordan, preaching the baptism of repentance for the remission of sins; As it is written in the book of the words of Isaiah the prophet, saying, "The voice of one crying in the wilderness, 'Prepare the way of the Lord, make his paths straight.'" (KJV).

I take chances?' is certainly found in 'Key Largo'. 'What's the matter, you guys? Didn't I take chances? I make the run from Cuba, risk my neck, my boat and the shipment…'

The song's first verse has Dylan intoning that he'd like to be able to 'get you to change your mind, but it looks like you won't.' As the prophet Samuel said: "He who is the Glory of Israel does not lie or change his mind; for he is not a man, that he should change his mind." (1 Samuel 15:29). Dylan concludes, therefore, that he will now be busy (presumably doing what he thinks God wants of him), while at the same time avoiding 'going nowhere fast', in other words, staying on-track. Dylan is 'glad it's over'; whatever he needed to have learned seems to have been learned. Now he is 'seeing the real you at last'; for example the real Jesus who allows people to be themselves, and even be free to make mistakes as part of the learning curve of developing their own faith.

Dylan goes on, again reminiscent of 'Key Largo', 'Didn't I risk my neck for you?' He had certainly stuck his neck out in his proclamation of the gospel. This mirrors a later song from the album 'Modern Times', 'Thunder On The Mountain': 'I did all I could, I did it right there and then.' He had certainly risked his artistic reputation and career for the sake of the message of the gospel and the spiritual 'good news' it embodies. Dylan says he rose above it all (all of the criticism and flak?) for 'you' (i.e. God). He admits to having had some 'rotten nights' (another Bogart line, from 'The Maltese Falcon'), where he may have felt self-torment and been robbed of sleep. These it seems have now passed, and he is seeing the 'real you' (presumably the authentic Messiah) 'at last'.

Despite his faith, Dylan is still very much a human being, subject to human weakness and all the associated issues, such as hunger and irritability. He is 'tired of this bag of tricks' (and all the old ways of doing things), and appears to be getting tested on a level of grace somewhat less than he has experienced to date. The Bible speaks of God's grace (unearned favour) flowing like water, and therefore, like all waves, having peaks and troughs. 'Deep calls to deep at the noise of your waterfalls; all your waves and billows have gone over me.' (Psalm 2:7, NKJV). Ups and downs are a normal part of any spirituality.

Dylan appears to borrow from another Bogart movie, 'The Big Sleep', in the line about the time when 'there was nothing wrong with me, that you could not fix'. This happens when God (rather than Dylan himself or his past experiences of God's grace) was what was being relied upon. Dylan has come through 'the storm' of testing, he intimates, even though he had needed to be 'strapped to the mast' (like Ulysses of classical Greek mythology, rather than be drawn onto the rocks by the singing of the Sirens). There is now a great expression of hope; it is 'time' for his spiritual vision to clear, so he can see 'the real you at last'.

The Orthodox Church have a long tradition of representing Christ in their icons as a baby (albeit a grown-up one), and Dylan seems to have hit on that as another way to allegorise his faith; this time by using the term 'baby' as a way of addressing Christ (the baby of Bethlehem). This 'baby', he says 'didn't show no visible scars' at their first meeting. When someone first meets Christ by faith and revelation, the joy often experienced means that the scars Christ still bears from his crucifixion aren't seen. 'Then said he to Thomas, "Reach hither thy finger, and behold my hands; and reach hither thy hand, and thrust it into my side: and be not faithless, but believing." (John 20:27, KJV). It is possible that the marks of suffering, and their implications in what St Peter described as 'sharing in Christ's sufferings' ('to the degree that you share the sufferings of Christ, keep on rejoicing' - 1 Peter 4:13) were not obvious to Dylan in the enthusiasm of the early part of his conversion. If not, it wasn't to be long before they became apparent in a variety of ways.

Dylan then compares this figure ('you') to Annie Oakley and Belle Starr, deliberately reversing their gifts (shooting and riding respectively), in a line borrowed from the 1980 Clint Eastwood film 'Bronco Billy'. Dylan is then back to 'The Maltese Falcon', with another line of Humphrey Bogart's ('I don't mind a reasonable amount of trouble'), perhaps applying that to his faith journey. His next line, 'Trouble always comes to pass', certainly echoes the words of Jesus in John 16:33 (ANIV). "I have told you these things, so that in me you may have peace. In this

world you will have trouble. But take heart! I have overcome the world."
'I got troubles, I think maybe you got troubles' is a line by Piper Laurie
from the 1961 film 'The Hustler'. 'I got troubles, I think maybe you got
troubles; I think maybe we better just leave each other alone.'

The main reality for Dylan now is that he is 'seeing the real you at last';
presumably the real Jesus, and no invention of the mind. Dylan will now
end 'this baby talk'; he has his troubles and he knows that 'you' (i.e. the
Messiah) has troubles too, in terms of those he cares for. A substantial
portion of humanity is still separated from relationship with him. God
knows about every single problem we have, and bears them with us.
'Whatever you gonna do, please do it fast,' echoes Jesus' words to Judas
at the Last Supper. '"What you are about to do, do quickly." (John
13:27, ANIV).

The message being communicated is that while we can know God in a
personal and experiential way through Christ's sacrifice, God continues
to reveal himself thereafter through a process of bringing us closer to
himself. This process is what the Bible calls 'sanctification', meaning we
get to have a closer and closer relationship with God. Whilst making
himself knowable in this life, God can never be fully known until the
next. Then we will have a new body and a new mind, without any
barriers to the spiritual realm, and be able to know as we are known.

The album's next track, 'I'll Remember You', is a wonderful love song;
but who is 'you'? This person is 'true', 'the best' and 'quick to cut to the
core'. For a Jew, and indeed a Jewish believer in (and follower of)
Y'shua, these descriptions all apply to the word of God, as wielded by
the Spirit of God. The book of Hebrews reads (4:12, KJV): 'For the
word of God is quick, and powerful, and sharper than any two-edged
sword, piercing even to the dividing asunder of soul and spirit, and of
the joints and marrow, and is a discerner of the thoughts and intents of
the heart.' The Jewish wisdom literature and proverbs personify God's
word and its wisdom (Proverbs 8:12 and 18, KJV: 'I wisdom dwell with
prudence... riches and honour are with me'; and Proverbs 7:4, KJV: 'Say
unto wisdom, you are my sister').

Dylan tells us that he will be thinking about this person when he is 'all alone', and 'at the end of the trail'; i.e. when his life here on earth comes to an end. When he first found God in this way, Dylan said that 'Jesus put his hand on me. It was a physical thing. I felt it. I felt it all over me. I felt my whole body tremble. The glory of the Lord knocked me down and picked me up.' [47]

The line 'there's some people you don't forget, even though you've only seen them one time or two' is a paraphrase from another Bogart movie, 'The Big Sleep', but it could easily be applied to Christ. For Dylan, this person (presumably Jesus, whom the Bible calls 'The wisdom of God' - 1 Corinthians 1:24) 'came right through'. Even the painful memories of his personal failures, described in his saying that he couldn't claim to have done things the way 'you' would have liked or wanted, can't take away his knowing that he was 'understood' by the one that he loves so much and who promised to be there for him at life's end.

The next track 'Clean Cut Kid' is something of a journey down memory lane to the days of the Vietnam anti-war protests, such as the 1963 number 'Masters Of War'. Dylan recounts what happens inside the head (and with disastrous consequences) of young people when they are taken out of their society and taught to kill. Only the 'kid' in question is not just anybody, he 'goes to church on Sunday' (no synagogue-goer this; he even sings in the church choir), and turns 'his pockets inside out' for friends in need. Only after the Vietnam (or any other war you want to mention) experience, he is so messed up psychologically that he commits suicide by jumping off San Francisco's Golden Gate Bridge into China Bay, an area notorious for its treacherous sea currents.

The song lays bare some of corrupting influences of American society, such as the American dream of material success that only serves to put the 'kid' into debt. If the main message of the song is to warn of the corruption of power through war and other things that destroy the soul of man, it succeeds brilliantly. As Dylan told Bill Flanagan, "We're all sinners. People seem to think that because their sins are different from other people's sins, they're not sinners. People don't like to think of themselves as sinners. It makes them feel uncomfortable. "What do you mean 'sinner'?" It puts them at a disadvantage in their mind. Most people walking around have this strange conception that they're born good, that they're really good people - but the 'world' has just made a mess of their lives. I had another point of view. But it's not hard for me to identify with anybody who's on the wrong side. We're all on the wrong side, really." [48]

Next was 'Never Gonna Be The Same Again', a non-subtle faith 'conversion' title if ever there was one. In this track Dylan once more seems to adopt the device of addressing Christ, once a baby of the Bethlehem manger, as a lover after the pattern of the scripture in the Song of Solomon. Dylan's 'baby' is right there with him, just as Jesus had promised he would be in Matthew 28:20. "I am with you always, even to the end of the age." As the book of Hebrews (13:5, ANIV) teaches, 'Keep your lives free from the love of money and be content with what you have, because God has said, "Never will I leave you; never will I forsake you."' This 'baby' can be so close that his presence in Dylan's waking and sleeping makes Dylan 'want to scream'. This person Dylan is singing to has 'touched' him, as Dylan himself related about his experience of meeting Jesus for the first time.

But relationships (even spiritual ones) have their ups and downs, and Dylan has had his fair share of those, even some that have 'hurt' this one he loves so much. But this person means more to Dylan 'than everything', and the encounter has meant that Dylan is irrevocably changed, never to be the same again. This exactly patterns the new birth start-all-over-again chance that Christ offers to all who will place their trust in him and the sacrifice at Calvary that he made on their behalf. Dylan, he says, now has 'something to think about'. The ego hasn't quite gone (does it ever in this life?). So Dylan would like any 'leaving' to have been his idea, not his 'baby's', who has taught him how to love him, in a line borrowed from Alan Ladd in the 1953 Western 'Shane'. 'I don't mind leaving; I'd just like it to be my idea.'

Dylan has been 'taught how to love', but is probably well aware of incidents of disobedience to Christ's (the baby's) commands, (e.g. 'Whatever you want men to do to you, do also to them.' Matthew 7:12).

75

Fortunately for us, love is something we don't have to manufacture ourselves, but it is love that God gives us. As the apostle Paul (Romans 5:5) said, 'The love of God has been poured out within our hearts through the Holy Spirit who was given to us.'

Dylan tells us that he unable to 'go back' to the past; and he doesn't seem to want to. Jesus had taught, "No one, after putting his hand to the plough and looking back, is fit for the kingdom of God." (Luke 9:62). Dylan's poetic genius shines through in a line concerning the impossibility of 'unringing' a bell; he can't go back to 'what was'; as St Paul had said (2 Corinthians 5:17, KJV). 'If any man be in Christ, he is a new creature: old things are passed away; behold all things are become new.' In Christ, the 'new' never becomes old, because his 'mercies are new every morning.' (Lamentations 3:23). He has changed, and the old, including the sometimes bitter 'reality' of Dylan's past, has gone, cast off as Hebrews 10:16-17 indicates. "This is the covenant that I will make with them after those days", says the Lord, "I will put my laws into their hearts, and in their minds will I write them; and their sins and iniquities will I remember no more." Dylan's (old) 'reality' has been 'cast to the wind', and he 'will never be the same again.'

One of the messages of the next song, 'Trust Yourself', is that while we live amongst 'wolves and thieves', we have (a God-given) innate and instinctive ability to discern the difference between truth and lies. Jesus said (John 8:32, KJV) that his disciples would 'know the truth, and the truth shall make you free.' Dylan has always been realistic in his summaries of human nature with its pride and fickleness. Because we are all responsible for ourselves, Dylan's advice is that we should back ourselves, with God's help, to 'know the way', rather than trusting in him (Dylan) or anyone else to show us truth and (genuinely spiritual) beauty. Dylan knows that what seems like love may in fact only be 'lust', so we should not put our trust in others who are basically 'ungodly', otherwise you will end up being disappointed. Rather, personalise your faith, so that it is truly yours and not just what 'someone else believes'.

'Emotionally Yours' is another outstanding example of both Bob Dylan's music and also his ability to allegorise. The lyrics, published some 10 years after his separation from his first wife and eight years after their divorce, point to something deeper than the undoubted depth of emotion shown towards a woman that he loves. If the song is applied allegorically to Christ, the baby of Bethlehem, then it becomes easily comprehensible from a spiritual perspective. The song opens with Dylan requesting his 'baby' to remind him of the place their relationship began.

This again appears to be the language of the book of Revelation (the subject of Dylan's keen interest and the topic of many an on-stage reflection in 1979 and 1980). Revelation 2:2-4 finds Christ upbraiding the church at Ephesus. 'I know your deeds and your toil and perseverance… But I have this against you, that you have left your first love.' Dylan sings of getting back to that place of his first love; 'of where I once begun', and his 'Tell me you're the one', has a ring of John the Baptist's words about it. 'When John, while imprisoned, heard of the works of Christ, he sent word by his disciples and said to him, "Are you the expected one, or shall we look for someone else?" (Luke 7:19).

Dylan keeps on 'believing', and can sing with heartfelt passion that 'You're the one I'm living for', which makes perfect sense if seen as being directed toward God. It makes less sense if it is seen as directed towards a woman, given that Dylan was between marriages at the time of writing. A new birth ('from above') as Jesus taught in John 3:3, seems to be behind the statements 'It's like my whole life never happened', and 'When I see you, it's as if I never had a thought'. The spiritual inference is that the whole of his past life has been washed clean and God has given him a new start. As the Apostle Paul said in 2 Corinthians 5:17, (ANIV), 'Therefore, if anyone is in Christ, he is a new creation; the old has gone, the new has come!'

This 'dream' might seem 'crazy' to those who thought Dylan had 'lost his marbles' in proclaiming Christ, but to Dylan it is all-consuming; 'It's the only one I've got.' In fact it is the only one worth having. The idea that if Dylan gets 'taken' by this 'baby', he will be 'satisfied' seems to point towards another nod to the book of Revelation. Therein is a view commonly known as the 'rapture' of the Church and its removal from the earth before the Great Tribulation of Revelation chapter 11 and onwards. It would seem that to Dylan, like another Jew, the Apostle Paul wrote centuries earlier, 'For to me, to live is Christ and to die is gain.' (Philippians 1:21).

The next song, 'When The Night Comes Falling From The Sky', seems to address Dylan's relationship with his fan-base, some of whom may have taken umbrage with his newfound faith relationship with Christ. The title evokes images of the world's end. 'See me returning over fields' is evocative of the second coming of Christ (John 4:35: 'fields white for harvest'), when 'the host of heaven shall be dissolved, and the heavens shall be rolled together as a scroll: and all their host shall fall down, as the leaf falls off from the vine, and as a falling fig from the fig tree.' (Isaiah 34:4, KJV). Dylan's songs are the 'letters' that he wrote; letters that he send his 'feelings' and which tell the truth that Dylan knows will fit the recipients 'like a glove.'

Dylan says that he has seen 'thousands who could have overcome the darkness', thousands of souls with the potential to respond to the good news of Christ's sacrifice, yet who have been condemned to die because of love of a 'lousy buck'. This may be a reference to the commercial interests of the recording industry that would not permit him to continue recording more overtly Christian material. There is a hint of Humphrey Bogart in the line 'Stick around, baby. We're not through'. The 1945 Howard Hawk's film 'To Have And Have Not' finds Bogart saying to Lauren Bacall "Stick around, we're not through yet."

The song introduces another of the allegorical devices that Dylan would usefully employ in his declaring spiritual beliefs in a way that was below the critic's radar - the slave trade and escape from slavery. This is alluded to in the line about crossing over a line drawn at the 'northern border of Texas', out of the southern state's slavery into freedom. Like 'Caribbean Wind' before it, the concept of deliverance from the power of sin is likened to being set free from slavery. As the Apostle Paul put it, 'our old self was crucified with him, in order that our body of sin might be done away with, so that we would no longer be slaves to sin;

for he who has died is freed from sin.' (Romans 6:6-7). The song concludes with Dylan asking for 'freedom', a freedom of a (spiritual) world that some of his audience denies the existence of; a spiritual world accessed by faith that brings certainty to that which is unseen (Hebrews 11:1). This 'freedom' will become apparent to everyone when 'the night falls from the sky', and the final Day of Judgement comes. 'A world which you deny' is also a clever re-phrasing of Jesus command that his disciples 'deny themselves' the attractions of the 'world' (the spiritual territory in rebellion to him), and follow him. (Matthew 16:24).

This type of spiritual concern shown by Dylan towards his fan-base is typically Dylanesque. The author personally witnessed it at the end of his 2009 European tour in Dublin; when after his final encore in a show which had featured not one single word spoken to the audience, not even to introduce his band, Dylan stood in silence for a full minute with his hand raised, palm facing the crowd, in an apparent act of benediction.

This concern is shown in the penultimate track, 'Something's Burning, Baby'. There is a blatant spiritual message to those with ears to hear it - get out of that burning building before it collapses on top of you. 'Something is burning, baby, are you aware?' asks Dylan, to which the answer is self-evidently, 'No.' People are a mortal body around an eternal spiritual being, as Dylan has said. "We're all spirit. That's all we are, we're just walking dressed up in a suit of skin, and we're going to leave that behind." [49] In the light of this the most important question that a person can ask is: 'Where will the real me be spending eternity?'

The song is about the oblivious or indifferent attitude that many have towards their own spirituality and eternal destiny. They are unable to discern the danger they are in or to smell the smoke of it. Something bad is happening to them, possibly an attitude of indifference to God, of whom they do not appear to be aware or even care about. Their 'love' has gone blind; though they are a substantial portion of Dylan's fan-base, their love for him has become 'blind' too. They are unable to appreciate the nature of the spiritual change he has gone through. The light in their eyes has almost gone out.

Dylan asks if he is 'no longer a part' of their 'plans or dreams?' Do they no longer consider what he says to be true or relevant now that they do not find it immediately comfortable? Their relationship of mutual trust has changed - they have begun to act 'strange' towards him. What is it that has caused them to act like this toward him? Dylan says that he can 'see the shadow of a man' - a shadowy figure - making her 'blue'. 'Who is he?' Dylan asks. Presumably it is Satan, the 'Man Of Peace', who would like to be a whole lot more than he is entitled to be right now. All we have to do is nothing and he will be.

Dylan describes an alternative, a 'pasture' where 'charity *[love]* is supposed to cover up a multitude of sins', a direct quotation from 1 Peter 4:8. 'Above all, keep fervent in your love for one another, because love covers a multitude of sins.' God's love and free forgiveness overlooks all our wrongdoing if we come to him trusting in the sacrifice that he offered on our behalf rather than in our own efforts or our own goodness. The song is addressed to someone in a precarious condition that Dylan can 'feel in the night' when he is 'thinking' of them. ('Thinking' about something or someone is Christian shorthand for prayer, as expressed in the song 'Thunder On The Mountain' from 'Modern Times' - 'I was thinking about Alicia Keys, I couldn't keep from crying', written at the time of Alicia Keys' disappearance.) [50]

His audience needs something from God because they 'can't live by bread alone', and expect to be truly satisfied. As Jesus told the devil after his 40-day temptation: 'It is written, that man shall not live by bread alone, but by every word of God.' (Luke 4:4, KJV). Only God and his word to us, including his son, the 'Word made flesh', can truly satisfy. Dylan says that there is a stone that needs to be rolled away, but 'their hands are tied'. This appears to be a direct reference to the gospel's accounts of the resurrection, when 'there was a great earthquake: for the angel of the Lord descended from heaven, and came and rolled back the stone from the door, and sat upon it. His countenance was like lightning, and his raiment white as snow.' (Matthew 28:2-3, KJV). Dylan's public will only understand what he means when they too have experienced the power that raised Jesus from the dead, as evidenced by the empty tomb.

Dylan can feel a 'wind' that is 'upside down', possibly standing for the Holy Spirit, whose coming enabled beaten fisherman, whose Saviour was crucified and buried, to go out and change the world, turning it 'upside down'. As Jesus said, 'Do not be amazed that I said to you, "You must be born again." The wind blows where it wishes and you hear the sound of it, but do not know where it comes from and where it is going; so is everyone who is born of the Spirit.' (John 3:7-8).

The message that is communicated is one of an upside-down kingdom, as Acts 17:6-7 describes: 'They *[some antagonistic Jews]* drew Jason and certain brethren unto the rulers of the city, crying, "These that have turned the world upside down are come hither also."' (Acts 17:6-7, KJV). Bleeding, flames and burning abound, but the message of hope that Dylan leaves us with is that, like Christ, he can wait for people to respond, because he believes 'in the impossible' along with Jesus who said, "With men this is impossible; but with God all things are possible." (Matthew 19:26, KJV).

The last track, 'Dark Eyes' is another heartfelt expression of Dylan's concern for the needs of others. Dylan relates in 'Chronicles Volume 1' that the sight of a call girl who told him that she badly needed a drink inspired this song. There is a brilliant inter-play between the darkness of the eye makeup she was wearing and the spiritual darkness in which she, along with countless others, was living. The song opens with a description of an evening scene of relaxation and socialising, which Dylan is observing from 'another world' which he inhabits, one where living and dying have been 'memorized'. This appears to represent the spiritual world, in which God, who dwells outside of time, can see in one moment everything that ever was, is and ever will be.

In this world, which runs parallel with (yet is quite different to) the natural world we all inhabit, the 'earth is strung with lovers' pearls'; a fabulous image of all the wonder that God, the lover of his creation, has placed in it by virtue of the amazing beauty of what he has made. And yet, despite being cognisant of this, all Dylan can see are the 'dark eyes' of those that do not yet know their creator - the lover of their souls, and so are not yet spiritually illuminated from within. Next, from 'far away' a cock crowing, evocative of the bird that crowed when Peter denied Christ for the third time in the courtyard of the High Priest following Jesus' arrest. [xxi]

To further back up the biblical imagery, the next line tells of a soldier who is 'deep in prayer', probably a reference to the effect Christ's crucifixion had on the Roman centurion in charge of the execution squad. 'When the centurion, and they that were with him, watching Jesus, saw the earthquake, and those things that were done, they feared greatly, saying, "Truly this was the Son of God."' (Matthew 27:54, KJV). And again, in the next line, there is the reference to a mother's child who has got himself lost so that she cannot find him despite much searching. The account of Jesus being lost in Jerusalem aged twelve completes the biblical references. [xxii]

Any lingering doubt about the spiritual intent of the song is surely dispelled by the next line which speaks of the resurrection of the dead ('another drum beating for the dead that rise'), and 'nature's beast' who

---

[xxi] Matthew 26:73-75: 'A little later the bystanders came up and said to Peter, "Surely you too are one of them; for even the way you talk gives you away." Then he began to curse and swear, "I do not know the man! And immediately a rooster crowed. And Peter remembered the word which Jesus had said, "Before a rooster crows, you will deny me three times." And he went out and wept bitterly.'

[xxii] Luke 2:41-49: 'Now his parents went to Jerusalem every year at the Feast of the Passover. And when he became twelve, they went up there according to the custom of the Feast; and as they were returning, after spending the full number of days, the boy Jesus stayed behind in Jerusalem. But his parents were unaware, of it, but supposed him to be in the caravan, and went a day's journey; and they began looking for him among their relatives and acquaintances. When they did not find him, they returned to Jerusalem looking for him. Then, after three days they found him in the temple, sitting in the midst of the teachers, both listening to them and asking them questions. And all who heard him were amazed at his understanding and his answers. When they saw him, they were astonished; and his mother said to him, "Son, why have you treated us this way? Behold, your father and I have been anxiously looking for you." And he said to them, "Why is it that you were looking for me? Did you not know that I had to be in my Father's house."'

meets their rising with fear, presumably because the judgement that is coming is especially for those spiritual (demonic) enemies of God.

Yet despite this knowledge, all Dylan can see is the darkness in the eyes of those around him. This seems to reflect a spiritual concern based on Christ's words: "The eye is the lamp of the body; so then if your eye is clear, your whole body will be full of light. But if your eye is bad, your whole body will be full of darkness. If then the light that is in you is darkness, how great is the darkness!" (Matthew 6:22-23).

In the next verse we learn that Dylan has apparently been told to be 'discreet for all intended purposes', presumably including his faith, and that while revenge may seem to be 'sweet' from the perspective of those who have so advised him, they surely do not share God's perspective on eternal realities. The Bible teaches that 'judgement will be merciless to one who has shown no mercy; mercy triumphs over judgement.' (James 2:13). Dylan is a man of mercy, hence has compassion for those cut off from their Creator by their own willfulness and pride. He tells us that he feels 'nothing for their game where beauty goes unrecognized.' Some cannot discern spiritual truth and beauty even when it is right under their noses (from their perspective 'revenge is sweet'). What Dylan is aware of in that context is only 'heat and flame', suggestive of a coming judgement; 'a terrifying expectation of judgement and the fury of a fire which will consume the adversaries.' (Hebrews 10:27).

Then comes a rather enigmatic line about a 'French girl' who is in 'paradise', with 'a drunken man at the wheel'. This has an eerily prophetic ring about it, having come 12 years before the death of Princess Diana in Paris, in a limousine driven by a man with a blood-alcohol level three times that legally permitted when driving in France.

Whatever the connotation, Dylan warns against the 'Falling gods of speed and steel', because the 'time is short' and emotions ('passions') can easily get 'out of control' when they are driven by sin. Dylan would repeat this thought in 'Ninety Miles An Hour Down A Dead End Street', on 'Down In The Groove.' There is a spiritual blindness in people's eyes, and he sees so much of it in front of his concert stages. He had said his message as best he could, and received hostility. When asked about his faith, he told Robert Hilburn: "I feel like pretty soon I am going to write about that", he said. "I feel like I got something to say but more than you can say in a few paragraphs in a newspaper." [51]

Say it he would. But for a while he would often use other people's words, as his next album. 'Knocked Out Loaded' would prove.

Chapter 6

'Knocked Out Loaded'

"Well, for me, there is no right and there is no left. There's truth and there's untruth, ya'know? There's honesty and there's hypocrisy. Look in the Bible, and you don't see nothing about right or left. Other people might have other ideas about things, but I don't, because I'm not that smart. I hate to keep beating people over the head with the Bible, but that's the only instrument I know, the only thing that stays true." [52]

How would Dylan use the Bible ('the only instrument he knows'), without 'beating people over the head' with it? Using other people's songs was certainly one method. 'Knocked Out Loaded', released in 1986, during a tour with Tom Petty and the Heartbreakers, had a generally unenthusiastic media response, perhaps in part because it included covers of other artist's songs. The album title itself came from an Irving Berlin song 'Junco Partner'. 'Down the road, came a junco partner, he was loaded as could be, he was knocked-out, knocked-out loaded...' (i.e. drunk).

The first track, 'You Wanna Ramble', was a version of the 1955 Herman 'Little Junior' Parker 'I Wanna Ramble', performed in a lively fashion to open the album. Parker had had a background in gospel music, and the song, most of which Dylan re-wrote, decries the state of the world we all live in - 'For only fifteen hundred dollars, you can have anybody killed.' The line, 'What happens tomorrow is on your head not mine' is a quote from the 1958 film 'The Big Country', starring Gregory Peck.

The second track, 'They Killed Him', written by Kris Kristofferson (an American army captain turned musician) is a memorial to Mahatma Gandhi, Martin Luther King and Jesus Christ. Gandhi led the struggle in India for independence from British rule in the first half of the twentieth century, promoting a policy of 'total non-violence'. A Hindu assassin shot him on 30 January 1948, after Gandhi left a Hindu prayer meeting which his killer had attended. Rev Martin Luther King was an Afro-American Baptist Christian Minister and US Civil Rights Movement leader who also promoted non-violent protest in the bid for racial equality. He was shot while standing on a Memphis motel balcony on April 4, 1968; conspiracy theories abound. King's last speech included these words, 'I would like to live a long life. Longevity has its place. But I'm not concerned about that now. I just want to do God's will. And he's allowed me to go up to the mountain. And I've looked over. And I've seen the Promised Land. I may not get there with you.' [53] Then the song addresses Jesus: 'The only Son of God Almighty, the holy one called Jesus Christ. He healed the sick and fed the hungry, and for his love they took his life away… the holy Son of Man.' Enough said.

The third track was the first all-Dylan composition of the album. 'Driftin' Too Far From Shore' shares a title with a Charles Moody hymn (1923) that was covered by the Stanley Brothers (bluegrass gospel singers), which is presumably how it came to Dylan's notice. The lyrics appear to address Dylan's concern about the spiritual distance between him and someone with whom he used to be in a relationship. The song starts with the subject 'leaving' (possibly reflecting some of Dylan's experience of being rejected). The line 'I figure we're even, or maybe I'm one up on you' is from the 1951 film 'Bend Of The River' starring James Stewart. Dylan has tried to communicate his newfound message of spiritual freedom, but the subject of the song seems to be 'driftin' too far from shore' to be able to hear or respond. Dylan, on the other hand, seems to have found an anchor that prevents drift. 'This hope we have as an anchor of the soul, a hope both sure and steadfast.' (Hebrews 6:19).

There is a strong 'current' running, such as the prevalent undercurrent of unbelief in the music business, which Dylan says he is not going to get 'lost' in. At this point in his career, Dylan frequently used movie allusions; this song contains an adaptation from a Humphrey Bogart film 'Sabrina' (1954). 'Father, remember your basal metabolism. Making love to a servant in your mother's house! She is not a servant; she's a servant's daughter.' Or as Dylan puts it: 'No gentleman likes making love to a servant, especially when he's in his father's house.' The song warns the listener that at any moment they could 'go under', and that there are 'haunted' places that are best avoided if they want to avoid not just getting on the wrong side, but being 'the wrong side' itself. 'We weren't on the wrong side, sweetness, we were the wrong side.'

Next up on this supposedly 'post-Christian' album was a traditional gospel song, 'Precious Memories', providing further evidence of Dylan's grasp of spiritual realities. Written by J.B.F. Wright (born in Tennessee, February 21, 1877), the original also contains this first verse: 'I remember mother praying, father too, on bended knee, sun is sinking, shadows falling, but their prayers still follow me.' Dylan sang the rest of the song, about 'precious memories' flooding his soul; reminders of God's faithfulness to him, the God who says 'never will I leave you or forsake you.' (Hebrews 13:5).

With 'Maybe Someday', it was back to original Dylan lyrics and a song re-worked from the 'Empire Burlesque' sessions. Dylan surmises that sometimes it takes losing everything to bring people to their senses and to the point where they 'have nothing left to hide' and so come before God with no pretences. 'When you've lost everything you'll have nothing left to hide.' Dylan sings that the love he had for them was never his own, maybe it was from 'on high'; he seems to hope that they won't reject it, for their sakes.

T.S. Eliot had written a poem (in 1927), the 'Journey Of The Magi' (based on the account of the 'Wise Men's' visit to the nativity in Bethlehem in Matthew chapter 2), which reads 'the cities hostile and the towns unfriendly'. For Dylan, Eliot's words become 'through hostile cities and unfriendly towns', immediately followed by a reference to the betrayal of Christ, and the price (thirty pieces of silver) of the blood money paid to Judas Iscariot. [xxiii] The listener may want 'something for nothing', but that is actually an empty delusion that is a waste of time pursuing. The song invites them to cast their mind back to the time they saw 'blood on the moon'; presumably standing for a lunar eclipse,

---

[xxiii] Matthew 26:14-16: 'Then one of the twelve, named Judas Iscariot, went to the chief priests and said, "What are you willing to give me to betray him to you?" And they weighed out thirty pieces of silver to him. From then on he began looking for a good opportunity to betray Jesus.'

occurring when the sun, earth, and moon are aligned so that the moon passes behind the earth, such that the earth prevents the sun from illuminating the moon. The moon's surface appears blood red because the sunlight is refracted through the Earth's atmosphere on the edges of the earth. 'Blood on the moon' in scripture stands for God's intervention, and is predicted to occur at Christ's return, when 'The sun will be turned into darkness, and the moon into blood, before the great and awesome day of the Lord comes.' (Joel 2:31).

According to Dylan, they are 'going though some sort of a test'. In scripture, temptation to do wrong represents a kind of spiritual test, one that is intended to strengthen rather than to harm. Dylan is hoping for the day when they will 'hear a voice from on high', which will ask "For whose sake did you live, for whose sake did you die?" The Bible teaches that God will speak to us all at the end and that the sooner we listen and respond the better. The line about 'breaking down bedroom doors to get to you' is from Burt Lancaster in the 1958 film 'Separate Tables', starring Rita Hayworth. Dylan goes on to sing that he always 'a sucker for the right cross'; a play on the title of the 1950 John Sturges film 'Right Cross'; or perhaps the Roman execution stake between the two crucified thieves at Calvary. The song closes with a quote from the 1947 Robert Mitchum film 'Out Of The Past'. 'Do you know San Francisco? I was there for a party once', which Dylan renders as 'I always liked San Francisco; I was there for a party once.'

Then came the album's classic, 'Brownsville Girl'. Co-written with Sam Shepard and recorded during the 1984 Cherokee sessions, it was originally known as 'New Danville Girl', after the Woody Guthrie song 'Danville Girl'. Guthrie sings words made more familiar by Dylan, 'Got stuck on a Danville girl, bet your life she was a pearl, she wore that Danville curl.' From whence came 'Brownsville' (a town in the Rio Grande valley, Cameron County, near the Texas-Mexico border)? Presumably Dylan opted for Brownsville through his friend songwriter Kris Kristofferson, who was born there, and because the song is set in Texas, being based on the 1950's Gregory Peck movie 'The Gunfighter'. The album's cover art, by Charles Sappington, features another Gregory Peck western, 'Duel In The Sun'. The song dominates the album, not just in length (11 minutes and 5 seconds), but like many of Dylan's longer pieces (for example 'Desolation Row' - 11 minutes 21 seconds, 'Idiot Wind' - 7 minutes 48 seconds, or more recently, 'Highlands' - 16 minutes 31 seconds), the long poetry (almost prose, given Dylan's outstanding ability to make almost anything scan) gives the listener a glimpse inside Dylan's head, where his often-enigmatic craft is manufactured.

The meaning? As Dylan said, to Bill Flanagan in 2004, "I'm not good at defining things. Even if I could tell you what the song was about I wouldn't. It's up to the listener to figure out what it means to him." The song was inspired by Lou Reed's 'Doin' The Things That We Want To' and its reference to Sam Shepard's play 'Fool For Love'. The first verse of Reed's song is 'The other night we went to see Sam's play, doin' the things that we want to. It was very physical; it held you to the stage, doin' the things that he wants to.'

Dylan said that Reed's song had inspired Dylan and Shepard to write 'a sort of response', which emerged in 1986 as 'Brownsville Girl.' Dylan said that just as Reed's song opened with the narrator at the play, the Shepard/Dylan song would open with the narrator at the movie.

The song moves between the movie (a Western) and two unnamed women, the first of which comes to him 'on the painted desert' (a desert area in Arizona in the south-western USA, east of the Little Colorado River), in a 'busted down Ford' and 'platform heels'. She leaves him after a night near the Alamo, a Christian mission and fort named 'Misión San Antonio de Valero', or, as Dylan sings, 'San Anton'. The Alamo played a central role in the Texas Revolution (gaining independence from Mexico) when, in December 1835, local volunteers defeated Mexican troops to take the fort. They were (with men such as Davey Crockett and James Bowie of Bowie-knife fame) later annihilated following a Mexican army siege in March 1836, in an event that became defined in US history as part of the developing nation's psyche. 'Remember the Alamo!' (the rallying call of the victorious avenging American army in their routing of the Mexicans), became their inspirational cry of many a future battle.

The somewhat whimsical nature of the poetry reflects, among other things, Dylan's love for the Southern states and their part in US history. Dylan recounts the movie's gun fight and then relates, 'I keep seeing this stuff and it just comes a-rolling in.' Presumably he takes part of the film away in his mind where it keeps replaying, bringing with it associated thoughts and their messages from the sub-conscious part of the mind that generates what we call memories.

After the first woman leaves ('to find a doctor'), the song continues with another woman who has a 'dark rhythm in her soul'. They continue driving to Amarillo (in Northern Texas), to a mysterious friend's house (named Henry Porter - 'The only thing we knew for sure about Henry Porter is that his name wasn't Henry Porter'), where his wife (Ruby) meets them. She has fallen on hard times (but won't ask him for help), and is 'broken-hearted'. Dylan supplies a classic line in 'Even the swap meets around here are getting pretty corrupt.' When told how far the second woman and Dylan plan to drive, Ruby just smiled and said, "Ah, you know some babies never learn", as if to say, '"You keep repeating the same mistakes."

All the time the movie is playing on inside Dylan's poetic mind, and a lot of the cast seem to be looking at him ('lookin' my way'). Then another character appears, a man with an Elvis Presley style 'pompadour' quaffed hairstyle. Shots ring out, and we are told the gunman has been 'cornered in the churchyard'. Dylan seems to take the man's place in a kind of substitutionary self-sacrifice, reminiscent of what Christ did on the cross, an image backed up by the next line, 'You saw my picture in the Corpus Christi Tribune.' ('Corpus Christi' means the body of Christ, and is a festival in honour of the Eucharist.) The 'Corpus Christi Caller-Times' is a Texan newspaper from the town of that name on the Gulf of Mexico. Dylan's picture is captioned 'a man with no alibi', but he is freed after the second woman 'goes out on a limb to testify' that she was with Dylan at the time of the shooting, in a dramatic testimony that borders on perjury. We are then treated to another classically Dylanesque line: 'If there's an original thought out there, I could use it right now', before it is back to the movies again, with Dylan queuing in line to watch another Gregory Peck production. It is a different film, 'a new one', but Dylan doesn't 'even know what it's about'. It may have been 'The Scarlet And The Black', from 1983, about a priest (Hugh O'Flaherty) who lived in Rome in during World War 2, and who smuggled Jews and other refugees to safety from the Nazis.

Dylan reflects that 'People who suffer together have stronger connections than people who are most content', because hardship can produce a human bonding stronger than that created during times of comfort and ease. He doesn't 'have any regrets'; he knows his life will reflect what he believes in. The woman seems to share his perspective, as she opines that 'People don't do what they believe in, they just do what's most convenient, then they repent.' ('Repent' means to change their way of thinking and to turn away from their own self-centred path and move towards God.) The song concludes with typical good humour - 'Let's hope that the roof stays on!'

After 'Brownsville Girl' came 'Got My Mind Made Up', co-authored with Tom Petty, with whose 'Heartbreakers' band Dylan was touring at the time. It's a track that appears to affirm Dylan's commitment to his faith and to his personal integrity; someone who has been around the block enough times to know which way 'is up' in relation to spiritual truths. 'Don't ever try to change me', Dylan leads with. He has been 'in this thing too long' to be dissuaded; nothing can be said or done to make him alter his view, presumably about something he believes in deeply enough and has sufficient personal experience of to be absolutely sure about. Well, his faith does spring to mind, although that is a little easier to say in 2011, after 'Christmas In The Heart', than it was in the mid-1980's. The song describes a planned visit to Libya; an odd destination given the tense political situation at the time, [xxiv] and reassures the subject of the song that they 'Will be alright' because 'Someone's watching over you.' The song closes with the emphatic and much

---

[xxiv] In April 1986 the USA were bombing Libya following the bombing of a Berlin discotheque frequented by US soldiers, using aircraft based on British soil (the British WPC Yvonne Fletcher having been shot dead from within the Libyan Embassy during a protest outside the building in April 1984).

repeated line, 'I got my mind made up, presumably a re-iteration of a faith perspective.

The album's final song, 'Under Your Spell', was co-written with Carol Bayer Sager. Sager said, 'We arranged for a time to write at his barn in Malibu. And it was really weird. I'd say something and he'd say he liked, it but he was all the way over on the other side of the room and he was covering his paper as if I was going to look and cheat. It was the most private collaboration.... I mean it's hard to call it collaboration because we were never exactly doing anything together at the same time. And at the end of the day he really didn't use a whole lot of my lyric, maybe a third, but he gave me a credit.' [54]

The song contains the line from which the album's title is derived. 'I was knocked out and loaded in the naked night' (a term for inebriation taken from the song 'Junco Partner'), itself based on an old (1940) blues composition by Willie Hall (entitled 'Junker's Blues'). Dylan sings that he is 'caught between heaven and hell', but is confident that he 'will survive.' He is hearing his baby's 'words', which are ringing in his head 'like a bell'. Dylan has 'trusted you, baby'; he had certainly trusted in Christ, now seems to be saying that Christ can have confidence in him. In future he might 'let the dead bury the dead' as Jesus said: "Follow me, and allow the dead to bury their own dead." (Matthew 8:22). He asks that his audience prays that he not 'die of thirst two feet from the well' on a 'cursed mountain', knowing that there is a source of (presumably spiritual) water close to us all. We just have to recognize it.

Dylan was entering a phase of recording a greater proportion of numbers published by other artists. Whereas five of the eight tracks on 'Knocked Out Loaded' were written or co-written by him, he would have a hand in writing only four of the ten songs on his next album 'Down In The Groove'. As on 'Knocked Out Loaded', both the choice of song and his handling of them would prove instructive, reflecting his own spiritual message, but using other people's material to do so.

Chapter 7

'Down In The Groove'

Sam Shepard: 'Do you ever think about angels?'
Bob Dylan: 'Angels. Yeah, now, angels - the Pope says this about angels - he says they exist.'
Sam Shepard: 'Yeah? The Pope?'
Bob Dylan: 'Yeah. And they're spiritual beings. That's what he says.'
Sam Shepard: 'Do you believe it?'
Bob Dylan: 'Yeah.'
Sam Shepard: 'Have you had any direct experience with angels?'
Bob Dylan: 'Yeah. Yeah, I have.' (Sam Shepard, 'Esquire', July 1987).

'Down In The Groove', released in 1988 and later described by 'Rolling Stone' magazine as Dylan's worst album, was another mixture of Dylan originals and cover songs. He was beginning what would become known as 'The Never Ending Tour', and inspiration was apparently becoming harder to come by. Despite the negative reviews, the album presents an unusual choice of material for an artist supposedly in a 'post-Christian' phase. Five of the ten songs - 'When Did You Leave Heaven?', 'Death Is Not The End', 'Silvio', 'Ninety Miles An Hour (Down A Dead End Street)', and 'Rank Strangers To Me' all have a strongly spiritual or directly Christian element, and one of the others ('Sally Sue Brown') was sung with a subtle lyrical addition to substantially alter the meaning in a very positive moral way.

The remaining three songs, 'Let's Stick Together', 'Had A Dream About You, Baby' and 'Ugliest Girl In The World' (co-written with Robert Hunter of 'The Grateful Dead'), all present sentiment that could easily be classified as broadly Christian. That just left the traditional mid-Western folk song 'Shenandoah'. If the critics hadn't been so busy panning 'Down In The Groove' musically, they might have seen it for what it really was; a spiritual album mistakenly labelled 'post-Christian'.

First up was 'Let's Stick Together', the Roxy Music dance favourite and a song affirming the solemnity of marital vows. A 'marriage vow, you know, it's very sacred' (i.e. holy before God). The song strongly makes the case for putting the needs of your children first before a precipitate divorce; a sentiment deeply rooted in Christian morality.

'When Did You Leave Heaven?' is a traditional gospel piece addressing one of the spiritual beings known in scripture as angels, who act as God's messengers. The song asks, "How's everything in heaven?" and "Why did you give up your place there for all these earthly things?" According to the book of Hebrews (1:7, NKJV), 'Of the angels he says, "Who makes his angels spirits, and his ministers a flame of fire."

'Sally Sue Brown' (originally written by Arthur Alexander, Earl Montgomery and Tom Stafford) is a love-crazed ditty about a promiscuous young woman of tight skirts and 'cheating misery'. In covering it, Dylan made an important but generally unrecognized change (and one to date not even recorded by the official lyrics site). 'Like a fool you're gonna hear me say, "Lay at your bed, Sally Sue Brown, please let me love you"', becomes, when sung by Dylan, 'You're not gonna hear me say, "Lay at your bed..."; an important change from a moral perspective! Also the original 'Like she broke that poor heart of mine' has been altered to 'I'd like to see her ruin this a-heart of mine', the inference being; she won't!

'Death Is Not The End' (an outtake from the 'Infidels' recordings) is a clear expression of faith in the one whose 'bright light of salvation' is still shining for those with eyes to see it. It is a message of hope that this life is not all that there is. It is followed by something where wrongs will be righted and hurts mended. Religion is not, in itself, the answer; what is 'held sacred, falls down and does not mend' encapsulates the futility of human effort alone to find God. In Christ, God comes to find us, if we receive him on his terms rather than trying to impose our own. The 'crossroads' of life cannot always be understood; dreams sometimes 'vanish' into an uncertain future, but knowing that there is more on an eternal level gives a reason and a hope for pressing on regardless. 'Storm clouds gather' over us all from time to time, but when things look bleak and you feel alone, remember this life is preparation for something much better, assuming you have eyes that have been opened spiritually to see.

Dylan sings of a 'tree of life growing', surely a reference to Revelation (22:1-3). [xxv] Its location (heaven) is confirmed by the next line 'where the spirit never dies', and where 'the bright light of salvation shines'.

The Bible makes it clear that this 'city has no need of the sun or of the moon to shine on it, for the glory of God has illumined it, and its lamp is the Lamb.' (Revelation 21:23). There is even a reference to hell in 'cities... on fire with the burning flesh of men.' Truly, death is not our final ending. But we have choices to make that carry eternal consequences. Dylan's reference to a 'search in vain to find just one law abiding citizen' is a reference to the Hebrew patriarch Abraham's nephew Lot in Sodom, where none could be found to be righteous outside of Lot's immediate family, and Sodom was destroyed along with the neighbouring Gomorrah. The lyric also reflects Solomon's words, 'Indeed; there is not a righteous man on earth who continually does good and who never sins.' (Ecclesiastes 7:20). In that regard the song re-visits Dylan's song 'Ain't No Man Righteous' on 'Yonder Comes Sin'.

Viewed from a spiritual perspective, death is definitely not the end of life, because our spirits are not mortal - they live on forever. The vital question of 'where?' is up to us to decide.

Next is another Dylan composition, 'Had A Dream About You Baby'. In scripture dreams can be portents of what is to come (at least for old men! - Joel 2:28). Dylan here appears to be trying to urgently communicate some spiritual realities - a very similar message to 'Something's Burning Baby' from 'Empire Burlesque'. His alarm comes through in the line that his 'heart is breakin'' for her and not in passion; when she kisses him 'it just makes me mad, I tell you to stop'. She and he are not on the same wavelength; she misunderstands the urgency of the message he has to bring. In Dylan's dream, she has 'a rag wrapped around her head', as in the scriptural manner of the burial cloth. Attendant death and danger

---

[xxv] Revelation 22:1-3: 'Then he showed me a river of the water of life, clear as crystal, coming from the throne of God and of the Lamb, in the middle of its street. On either side of the river was the tree of life, bearing twelve kinds of fruit, yielding its fruit every, month; and the leaves of the tree were for the healing of the nations'.

are highlighted in the next line about the 'fire engine red' dress she is wearing. Dylan is giving warning, but who will listen?

'Ugliest Girl In The World' (co-written with Robert Hunter of 'The Grateful Dead') seems to demonstrate Dylan's newfound attitude to life in the way he relates to women. As the Bible says, 'Your adornment must not be merely external; braiding the hair, and wearing gold jewelry, or putting on dresses; but let it be the hidden person of the heart, with the imperishable quality of a gentle and quiet spirit, which is precious in the sight of God.' (1 Peter 3:3-4). And as the Lord said to Samuel, "Do not look at his appearance or at the height of his stature, because I have rejected him; for God sees not as man sees, for man looks at the outward appearance, but the Lord looks at the heart."' (1 Samuel 16:7).

After detailing some of her less attractive features (surely not the Semitic hook nose?), we learn that if he loses her he 'will go insane'. Who is this woman? Perhaps she stands allegorically for the Nation of Israel; the 'weird sense of humour that's all her own', the 'prize-fighter nose' and similar ears all point to the scars of battle to which Israel is no stranger. Dylan doesn't know why he loves her, but just like the many supporters of Israel, he 'just can't stop'. Blood is thicker than water, and as God promised to Dylan's forefather Abraham, 'I will bless those who bless you, and the one who curses you I will curse, and in you all the families of the earth will be blessed.' (Genesis 12:3).

In 'Silvio' (the second track co-written with Robert Hunter of 'The Grateful Dead', and later chosen for release as a single), the idea is communicated that Dylan's new priorities extend past beauty to money too. His career may have dipped in the mid-eighties, but he surely knows that there is much more to life than material success. He can 'stake his future on a hell of a past', but he seems determined to move forward from there without 'complaining'. What is important to him has been adjusted; as someone who is now a very wealthy man he knows from first-hand experience that 'silver and gold won't buy back the beat of a heart grown cold'. Rather, what he seems interested in now is finding out what 'only dead men know', i.e. where the real meaning of life is to be found - in the next life when after death it has been discovered that death is 'not the end'. He describes himself as an 'old boll weevil'; a beetle found on cotton buds and flowers, and also (for a future supporter of US President Barack Obama), a term used for conservative Democrats in the southern states. He sings that he is 'looking for a home', and we can take him as we find him or leave him well alone.

'I can... require the rain' is to do as the Old Testament prophet Elijah did. 'Elijah went up to the top of Carmel; and he crouched down on the earth and put his face between his knees. He said to his servant, "Go up now, look toward the sea... in a little while the sky grew black with clouds and wind, and there was a heavy shower."' (1 Kings 18:42-45).

Dylan goes on to sing, 'You know I love you', and that when it is time for us to go we have 'an open door', perhaps having in mind the Apostle John who 'looked, and behold, a door standing open in heaven, and the first voice which I had heard, like the sound of a trumpet speaking with me, said, "Come up here, and I will show you what must take place after these things."' (Revelation 4:1). 'You give something up for everything you gain' is very reminiscent of Jesus' words "Truly I say to you, there is no one who has left house or brothers or sisters or mother or father or children or farms, for my sake and for the gospel's sake, but that he will receive a hundred times as much now in the present age, houses and brothers and sisters and mothers and children and farms, along with persecutions; and in the age to come, eternal life."' (Mark 10:29-30). With the benefit of hindsight, it is clear that Dylan was right to predict that he would be 'sing it loud and sing it strong'.

Blair and Robertson's country piece 'Ninety Miles An Hour (Down A Dead End Street)' is another song with a strong moral to it. After dealing with physical beauty and money, Dylan turns his attention to sex in a song which describes the dangers of playing around with what the Bible clearly defines as wrong-doing and sin. 'Kissing in fun - no harm was done', but the next thing you know is that the 'brakes have gone' and you can't stop. Both of them 'belong to someone else' and the (adulterous) relationship is described as being like a 'bad motorcycle with the devil in the seat'.

The behaviour, like all sin, quickly becomes something that the participants lose their ability to choose their way out of. It is now 'too late to listen' to the voice of conscience warning of the impending disaster one normally associates with driving at 'ninety miles an hour down a dead end street'. The clear moral of the song is not to ignore God's warnings and pretend that you can control the emotions that are stirred up by sinful and wrong behaviour. You can light the fuse; putting out the firework is another matter all together.

The penultimate track is 'Shenandoah', a traditional American folk song about the Shenandoah River (a tributary of the Potomac River) in the states of Virginia and West Virginia. Like all traditional songs, the song has been added to and altered over the years since its first printing in the July 1882 edition of Harper's New Monthly Magazine. The version chosen by Dylan concerns a white man who loves an Indian maiden and longs to take her 'away across the wide Missouri'. It is a beautiful song and one Dylan handles with tenderness worthy of its subject matter.

The album closes with 'Rank Strangers To Me', a gospel song written by Albert E. Brumley, a gospel singer and composer born in Spiro, Oklahoma (October 29, 1905 - November 15, 1977) and author of the more famous 'I'll Fly Away' ('Some glad morning when this life is o'er, I'll fly away. To a home on God's celestial shore, I'll fly away...') 'Rank Strangers' expresses the loneliness often felt at first by those who change spiritual kingdom and find a sense of distance between those whom they love, but who have not yet made the switch themselves. Such appears to have been the case with Dylan too.

The song opens with a description of the writer returning home replete with memories of a happy youth only to find that everyone he meets is a 'rank stranger', whom he cannot recognise despite having known them previously. It seems that their state of being has changed; 'they all moved away'. And so he looks forward to arriving one day in heaven where no-one will be 'a rank stranger', because though 'now we see in a mirror dimly, but then face to face; now I know in part, but then I will know fully just as I also have been fully known.' (1 Corinthians 13:12).

Aside from two (contractually necessary) albums of folk-music material, 'Down In The Groove' would be Dylan's last album with a substantial amount of non-Dylan written material until 'Christmas In The Heart' (2009). With 'Oh Mercy', he would be back to telling his own story, his way.

Chapter 8

'Oh Mercy'

1989 saw the release of an album made up entirely of songs of Dylan's own composition. 'Oh Mercy' was produced, apparently at Bono's suggestion, [55] by Canadian Daniel Lanois after Lanois had produced U2's 'The Joshua Tree' in 1987. The recording of the all-new Dylan material reflected a resurgence of creativity.

The album opens with 'Political World', which sees societal norms being held up to the light of the truth that scripture reveals. In the political world in which we live, 'love don't have any place'. There is only avarice and worldly power, or as Dylan would put it in 'Working Man's Blues #2', 'Power and greed, and corruptible seed, seems to be all that there is.' 'Crimes' are committed with impunity, and 'crime don't have a face'; in other words, there is no personal responsibility. In this world 'icicles' are on the ceiling, i.e. we are in a cave with stalactites hanging down, and the law of the caveman prevails. The song was accompanied by the release of a video depicting politicians feasting and committing every manner of vile behaviour while the house band, led by Dylan, played the song.

In the song's 'political' world, wisdom has been imprisoned; so that it cannot affect man's folly. It is thought to be 'misguided as hell' by its opponents who see to it that no-one can easily follow it. In this world 'mercy walks the plank' in a pirate-style execution; life is deceptive and death itself is seen disappearing inside 'the nearest bank', presumably to cash in its profits. Courage is now resigned to history ('a thing of the past'), and no one will stand up to anyone or anything. 'Houses are haunted' (evil spirits abound), with children being 'unwanted' (their lives often now conveniently terminated in the womb). No one knows whether tomorrow will bring one's death.

All man is interested in is what he is able to 'see and feel' - a temporal world that will eventually pass away. Legitimate authority has gone (there is 'no one to check') and the odds are heavily against you (a 'stacked deck'). Our cities are noted for their 'lonesome fear', i.e. an artificially created sense of isolation with an attendant distrust of neighbours, in which people become changed into something less than themselves and what God intends for them. 'You're never why you're here' seems to suggest that we will never get to achieve the full potential that God intends us to achieve, unless we actively include him in our lives.

In this 'Political World' we are constantly being scrutinized by others (the 'microscope'). Travel is easy but so too is suicide ('hang yourself'); the 'rope' needed is not in short supply, neither is there any shortage of things in modern life to drag you down. In this world we 'thrash about' as though in death throes and we are conditioned towards finding the 'easy way out', by trying to take a shortcut to fulfilment. Peace is not really wanted, especially by those who wish to profit from war, as Dylan has pointed out. [56] In this world, possession is everything, and many are willing to 'shout God's name' when it suits them, even if they don't know 'what it is'. 'God' has become a confused concept rather than a living Person who can be known, loved and loved by.

The second song, 'Where Teardrops Fall', finds Dylan singing of a place where one can go 'far away' from all of life's stresses and strains. It is a place 'where teardrops fall' and is surely a place of reflection, meditation and prayer, which in scripture is often marked by weeping. On his later album, 'Modern Times', Dylan would pen 'I was thinking about Alicia Keys, couldn't keep from crying...' 'Thinking about' is Messianic/Christian shorthand for reflecting on something prayerfully; in this instance Keys' disappearance. The Bible says of Christ 'In the days of his flesh, when he had offered up prayers and supplications with strong crying and tears.' (Hebrews 5:7, KJV). This place is a private place 'over the wall'. Jesus had said 'When you pray, go into your inner room, close your door and pray to your Father who is in secret, and your Father who sees what is done in secret will reward you.' (Matthew 6:6).

In this secret place Dylan says, 'You are there'. But who is 'you'? Presumably it is the one whom Dylan is spiritually communing with. Dylan has been beating a drum 'slowly' and playing a 'fife lowly'. The fife is a small, high-pitched, flute used by armies to accompany the drums while on the march as well as for military signalling. Dylan appears to be sounding, in a 'lowly' (humble) way a call to arms on behalf of the one who knows 'the song in my heart' because he has placed it there.

In this secret place he is shown 'a new place to start'. He can begin over, or, as Jesus put it, 'be born again - from above.' (John 3:7). Dylan has rent his clothing, a Hebrew phrase for sorrowing for sin. For example King David, to his commander Joab and the people, after the death of Saul's cousin (1 Samuel 14:50) and army commander Abner. 'Tear your clothes and put on sackcloth and lament for Abner.' (2 Samuel 3:31).

Dylan has 'drained the cup', like Jesus' disciples James and John were invited to do, in participating to some extent in his sufferings. [xxvi] Night-time seems to be a favourite time of Dylan's to reflect and meditate, for example, 'Ain't Talking' from 'Modern Times' ('As I walked out tonight in the mystic garden'). His autobiography 'Chronicles' indicates that night-time is certainly a favourite time to record. We see Dylan 'strippin' away', all the vestiges of his old life, and still meditating ('thinking of you') when dawn arrives.

Dylan is motivated by 'love and with kindness'. He will celebrate with the song's subject the 'cutting of fences', such as ones that divide people spiritually. The Apostle Paul wrote, 'For he himself [Christ] is our peace, who made both groups into one and broke down the barrier of the dividing wall, by abolishing in his flesh the enmity.' (Ephesians 2:14-15). This 'cutting' 'sharpens senses' (presumably spiritually); he can better hear from God and see what he is doing, lingering in 'fireball heat'. In early North American revival prayer meetings the Holy Spirit was seen to move like 'great balls of fire' (as in the Jerry Lee Lewis

---

[xxvi] Mark 10:38-39: 'Jesus said to them, "You do not know what you are asking. Are you able to drink the cup that I drink, or to be baptized with the baptism with which I am baptized?" They said to him, "We are able." And Jesus said to them, "The cup that I drink you shall drink; and you shall be baptized with the baptism with which I am baptized."

song of that title). When things slow down, Dylan has a particular place he can go to and 'see you'. As he would later record, 'I know a place where there's still something going on' - a place of meeting where spiritual things happen ('Summer Days', 'Modern Times').

The next song, 'Everything Is Broken' addresses a universal spiritual problem; without the one who 'holds everything together' in people's lives, everything gets broken. The song seems to reflect the biblical view that everything humans do is tainted by an attitude of indifference or rebellion to God (which is what the Bible calls 'sin'). Consequently, in God's eyes, 'everything is broken'. Among the litany of things that are 'broken' come idols, i.e. things that take the place of God in people's lives. 'Broken hearts' abound, as do 'broken promises'. Who is it that 'every time they leave' 'things fall to pieces', in Dylan's experience? Could it be the same person he is singing to in 'Where Teardrops Fall?'

'Ring Them Bells' is yet another song that refutes the popular idea that Dylan was somehow 'post-Christian' in this phase of his distinguished career. Bell ringing serves many purposes: to sing God's praises, to summon the faithful to worship and to call an alarm. It is not something that figures large in the Jewish faith. In this song Dylan seems to call on the bell ringers (who, oddly enough, are mainly Christian saints) to be active in making their many proclamations.

The song begins by noting that even 'heathens' and unbelievers can make a lot of noise with bells. Indeed, much that passes as 'religion' is run by those with apparently little personal encounter with the life-changing power of God. The image of the world we live in being 'on its side' is reminiscent of the allegations brought against the Apostle Paul in the Greek city of Thessalonica, where the rioting crowd cry out that "These that have turned the world upside down are come hither also; whom Jason hath received, and these all do contrary to the decrees of Caesar, saying that there is another king, one Jesus." (Acts 17:6-7, KJV). Dylan also recounts that 'time is running backwards' as in the time of the prophet Isaiah. 'This shall be the sign to you from the Lord, that the Lord will do this thing that he has spoken: "Behold, I will cause the shadow on the stairway, which has gone down with the sun on the stairway of Ahaz, to go back ten steps." So the sun's shadow went back ten steps on the stairway on which it had gone down.' (Isaiah 38:7-8). Not content with putting time into reverse gear, Dylan has 'the bride' doing the same thing too. The people of God are referred to in scripture as the 'Bride of Christ'. [xxvii] The image of the church (especially in the West) being like a car in reverse gear is an insightful one indeed, given the modern church's ineffectiveness relative to that of the early church.

The second verse calls upon St Peter to ring his bells 'Where the four winds blow', surely a reference to Revelation 7:1. "After this I saw four angels standing at the four corners of the earth, holding back the four winds of the earth so no wind could blow on the earth, on the sea, or on any tree'. Many people ('rush hour') on 'the wheel' is an image also found in scripture. 'A wise king winnows the wicked, and drives the threshing wheel over them' (Proverbs 20:26); providing a link to 'the plough' in the song. Threshing wheat involved beating the head of grain from the stalk, done in ancient times by flail arms attached to the wheels of a cart. The sun sinking tells us that the 'rush hour' in question is the evening homeward one rather than the morning one, indicating that time is drawing to a close. This signals an end for the 'sacred cow' of materialism; alluding to the original 'sacred cow' of false worship made while Moses was absent from the Israelites when receiving the Law on Mount Sinai. 'All the people tore off the gold rings which were in their ears and brought them to Aaron. He took this from their hand, and fashioned it with a graving tool and made it into a molten calf; and they said, "This is your god, O Israel, who brought you up from the land of Egypt."' (Exodus 32:3-4).

'Ring Them Bells' third verse features 'Sweet Martha'; probably a reference to the Negro spiritual song, 'Mary and Martha' (friends of Christ found in John 11:5). This begins: 'Mary and Martha who have gone 'long, to ring them charming bells' *[in heaven]*. The bells call out

---

[xxvii] Revelation 21:2-3: 'I saw the holy city, new Jerusalem, coming down out of heaven from God, made ready as a bride adorned for her husband. And I heard a loud voice from the throne, saying, "Behold, the tabernacle of God is among men, and he will dwell among them, and they shall be his people, and God himself will be among them."'

that 'God is one', because there is only one, and not all 'gods' are the same, despite some religions claims to the contrary. In the live version released on the 'Tell Tale Signs' album, Dylan sings 'that the Lord is one', a subtle but significant clarification of the song's strongly Messianic/Christian content. The bells are to waken 'the shepherd' who is asleep. Consequently God's flock is not being properly cared for; this was certainly the case in the time of the Hebrew prophet Ezekiel. [xxviii]

As a result the area is full of 'lost sheep', surely a reference to Jesus' teaching. 'So he told them this parable, saying, "What man among you, if he has a hundred sheep and has lost one of them, does not leave the ninety-nine, in the open pasture and go after the one which is lost until he finds it? When he has found it, he lays it on his shoulders, rejoicing. And when he comes home, he calls together his friends and his neighbours, saying to them, "Rejoice with me, for I have found my sheep which was lost!" I tell you that in the same way, there will be more joy in heaven over one sinner who repents than over ninety-nine, righteous persons who need no repentance.' (Luke 15:3-7). Isaiah (53:6) wrote, 'All we like sheep have gone astray', and Jesus had defined his own mission statement as 'The Son of Man has come to seek and to save that which was lost.' (Luke 19:10).

The fourth verse has the bells being rung on behalf of the 'blind and the deaf'. On the face of it, of what use is bell-ringing to the deaf? Dylan, who clearly has a wide-ranging understanding and knowledge of both the Jewish and Christian scriptures, is surely aware that 'On that day *[of the Lord's coming]* the deaf will hear words of a book, And out of their gloom and darkness the eyes of the blind will see.' (Isaiah 29:18). Jesus fulfilled this by healing the deaf and blind. The bells are also ringing on

---

[xxviii] Ezekiel 34:7-10: 'Therefore, you shepherds, hear the word of the Lord: "As I live," declares the Lord God, "surely, because my flock has become a prey, my flock has even become food for all the beasts of the field for lack of a shepherd, and my shepherds did not search for my flock, but rather the shepherds fed themselves and did not feed my flock"; therefore, you shepherds, hear the word of the Lord: Thus says the Lord God, "Behold, I am against the shepherds, and I will demand my sheep from them and make them cease from feeding sheep."'

account of the 'chosen few', yet another reference to Jesus' teaching, this time about a king who prepared a wedding feast for his son but has trouble with people not responding to his invitation. 'When the king came in to look over the dinner guests, he saw a man there who was not dressed in wedding clothes, and he said to him, "Friend, how did you come in here without, wedding clothes?" And the man was speechless. Then the king said to the servants, "Bind him hand and foot, and throw him into the outer darkness; in that place there will be weeping and gnashing of teeth. For many are called, but few are chosen."' (Matthew 22:11-14). The 'chosen few' 'will judge the many when the game is through', as the Apostle Paul had written: 'Do you not know that we will judge angels? How much more matters of this life?' (1 Corinthians 6:3).

The fifth and final verse has the bells ringing under the hand of St Catherine (of Alexandria, a 4th century Roman Christian martyr). They ring because the 'fighting is strong'; as it was when the Apostle Paul wrote to his friend Timothy that he should 'Fight the good fight of faith; take hold of the eternal life to which you were called, and you made the good confession in the presence of many witnesses.' (1 Timothy 6:12). One of the reasons for the fight is on behalf of the 'child that cries' when its 'innocence dies' (e.g. from abuse). 'They' (presumably immoral people) are 'breaking down the distance between right and wrong' (thus reversing the request of King Solomon in 1 Kings 3 verse 9 to 'distinguish the difference between right and wrong'). They thereby obscure the moral distinctions that God has established to rightly order human life, and so leave the vulnerable (e.g. children) at risk of harm.

This is followed by another distinctively spiritual (and scripture-based) song, 'Man In The Long Black Coat', a slow paced sombre song (with accompanying cricket insect-noises), and somewhat enigmatic. The man himself has many signs of being up to no good spiritually; he wears black, and has dust on him, which is associated in scripture with death (Ecclesiastes 3:20) and also sorrow (Revelation 18:19). He has an expressionless (mask-like) face, and is able to quote from the Bible, something even the devil can do (e.g. Luke 4:29). The preacher's sermon topic (that man's conscience is vile and depraved) represents a common and unbiblical error (it 'sticks in the throat'). The conscience is a key means of God communicating with our spirits. It can become insensitive - 'seared' (1 Timothy 4:2), or 'defiled' (Titus 1:15) in extreme cases, but it mainly speaks to the mind about the innate difference between right and wrong. [xxix] People make 'choices', for better or for worse, but other people just 'float', drifting from one poor choice to another. We are not told who is blamed for the woman's choice - her or her former husband - but the song ends with several notes of destruction (e.g. trees uprooted in the night), leading the hearer to understand that it was not a good choice that was made. Dylan expert Clinton Heylin [57] opines that the song is Dylan's rendering of the old English ballad 'The Daemon Lover', in which the devil entices a woman away from her husband and to her eventual doom. Heylin is almost certainly correct.

The next track, 'Most Of The Time', sees Dylan bearing his own soul. By 1989 his marriage of 1986 to Carolyn Dennis may have been starting to get rocky (she filed for divorce on August 7 1990). What was then still unknown is revealed in this song. 'Most of the time', sings Dylan, he can see clearly and is fairly stable in terms of running his own affairs. He can 'follow the path', maybe even find the right way. Jesus had said, "I am the way, and the truth, and the life; no one comes to the Father but through me." (John 14:6). Dylan can also interpret 'the signs'. Jesus had said, "When it is evening, you say, "It will be fair weather, for the sky is red." And in the morning, "There will be a storm today, for the sky is red and threatening." Do you know how to discern the appearance of the sky, but cannot discern the signs of the times?" (Matthew 16:2-3).

We can all handle things in our own strength, up to a point, 'most of the time', because we feel we can work things out for ourselves. Mostly Dylan is 'strong enough not to hate' those who oppose him, and he doesn't deceive himself with 'illusion', neither is he too worried about 'confusion'. His spiritual compass is apparently still working.

[xxix] Romans 2:14-16: 'For when Gentiles who do not have the Law do instinctively the things of the Law, these, not having the Law, are a law to themselves, in that they show the work of the Law written in their hearts, their conscience bearing witness and their thoughts alternately accusing or else defending them, on the day when, according to my gospel, God will judge the secrets of men through Christ Jesus.'

The next song 'What Good Am I?' was, according to 'Chronicles Volume 1', written after Dylan witnessed an arrest of a homeless person whom he had passed on the street. Dylan illustrates the point made in James 4:17 about those who know the good they should do but don't do it: 'to one who knows the right thing to do and does not do it, to him it is sin'. What benefit is that? To themselves or those they don't bother helping, none at all. It is easy to ignore the homeless, when we see how they 'are dressed'. Reminiscent of James (2:1-4), Jesus' half-brother, he challenges the tendency we all have to judge by appearances. [xxx]

'What good am I if I'm like all the rest, if I just turn away, when I see how you're dressed?' sings Dylan. 'What good am I?' is another way of stating James' 'What use is it?' 'What use is it, my brethren, if someone says he has faith but he has no works? Can that faith save him? If a brother or sister is without clothing and in need of daily food, and one of you says to them, "Go in peace, be warmed and be filled," and yet you do not give them what is necessary for their body, what use is that? Even so faith, if it has no works, is dead, being by itself.' (James 2:14-17). Actions are what counts, not simply good intentions.

The question, 'What good are we if we know what is right and don't do anything about it?' is a perfect paraphrase of James 4:17. Seeing without responding is mealy-mouthed ineptitude; looking through people while ignoring their spiritual and physical needs is not what God wants. Dylan speaks of turning 'a deaf ear to the thunderin' sky', in other words, being deaf to the God who speaks from there. [xxxi] What good are we if we can

---

[xxx] James 2:1-4: 'My brethren, do not hold your faith in our glorious Lord Jesus Christ with an attitude of personal favouritism. For if a man comes into your assembly with a gold ring and dressed in fine clothes, and there also comes in a poor man in dirty clothes, and you pay special attention to the one who is wearing the fine clothes, and say, "You sit here in a good place," and you say to the poor man, "You stand over there, or sit down by my footstool," have you not made distinctions among yourselves, and become judges with evil motives?'

[xxxi] John 12:27-32: 'Jesus said: "Now my soul has become troubled; and what shall I say, "Father, save me from this hour?" But for this purpose I came to

hear weeping and even know the hidden concerns of others (what they say in their sleep), and then 'freeze' in the way 'the rest who don't try' do? What good are we even to ourselves (spiritually) if, despite having every opportunity, we still can't see that our 'hands are tied'? Dylan insists on asking the most pertinent of questions - who tied our hands? And why? And where must we have been for this to have happened to us? These rhetorical questions point to the state described in Ephesians 4:26-27 (ANIV). 'Do not let the sun go down while you are still angry, and do not give the devil a foothold.' A little foothold is all the devil needs to divert us away from behaving in the way God intends us to towards one another.

What good are we if we say 'foolish things' and then compound it by laughing 'in the face of what sorrow brings' instead of 'weeping with those who weep'? (as the Apostle Paul had taught in Romans 12:15). What good are we if we keep our backs turned while others 'silently die', and so remain separated from God, instead of communicating with them and helping them in their spiritual condition? What good are we indeed?

Composed in the first part of 1988, 'Disease Of Conceit' provides further evidence that Dylan's 'Christian phase' was something more than just a phase. The Apostle Paul could say that he was 'confident of this very thing, that he who has begun a good work in you will perform it until the day of Jesus Christ' (Philippians 1:6, KJV); certainly there was no letting up in Dylan's case. Pride, the ultimate original sin and the downfall of the devil, is what is dealt with in this highly insightful composition about the root of all spiritual ills. Dylan opens the song: 'There's a whole lot of people suffering tonight from the disease of conceit.' Pride is a universal sin, easily affecting us and causing us to

---

this hour. Father, glorify your name." Then a voice came out of heaven: "I have both glorified it, and will glorify it again." So the crowd of people who stood by and heard it were saying that it had thundered; others were saying, "An angel has spoken to him." Jesus answered and said, "This voice has not come for my sake, but for your sakes. Now judgement is upon this world; now the ruler of this world will be cast out. And I, if I am lifted up from the earth, will draw all men to myself."'

'struggle' with it, and we may not even recognize it or even see pride as being a good thing. It comes straight at us at high speed, according to Dylan, who (with all of his accomplishments) is well positioned to know about it. Pride is a master of disguise and can take many forms. It 'rips' into us, dulling us towards God by taking the credit for what he has done or for what we have done with what he has given us. It affects us 'body and mind', and can break our hearts without our even being aware that it is there. It comes into us without asking our permission, 'eating' away at 'our souls', taking over our 'senses' and leaving us with 'no control'. Pride tends to flaunt itself; it is not known for discretion.

People are not just suffering from it, they are 'dying' from it, Dylan tells us. The sin of pride kills them spiritually, causing misery and 'crying tonight'. Pride can come 'out of nowhere', when we are least able to resist it, even if we are able to discern it (which often we are not). Pride is relentless in its work, rendering us spiritually unresponsive to God, like a 'piece of meat'. Physicians have no remedy for it - they can recognize it, but are uncertain as to its true nature - is it a good or a bad thing? Pride causes 'trouble', even giving us double vision by disturbing our perception of reality. Dylan likens its ultimate effect to the grandiose ideas associated with end-stage syphilis, but these 'delusions of grandeur' are even harder to treat than that caused by the syphilis spirochete. Their 'evil eye' makes us believe, erroneously, that we are 'too good to die'; that somehow mortal ills no longer apply to us. We end up being buried alive, yet spiritually dead, being cut off from God by pride. A deadly disease indeed. The song does not point us to the remedy, but we need a new birth, 'from above', that God's Spirit brings when we turn to him trusting in the remedy of Jesus' own sacrificial death. But as Dylan said, 'Being born again is a hard thing' (page 19).

The penultimate track, 'What Was It You Wanted?' seems to address the many demands that the music industry and the artist's fan base can place on a performer. They cannot always be met, and anyway, there are so many. What are the important ones? Are they simply the agenda of the 'one who is looking'? And who is he anyway? The song is a series of questions that Dylan is asking, presumably of a fan or one of the myriad of others who want a piece, just a little piece, of his time. What is it that they want? What is going on inside them - in their heart and mind - in the 'show' that is their life? What is their motive in 'kissing' Dylan? Is there an ulterior motive concealed beneath their expressions of affection? Dylan thinks he may have seen someone else watching, somebody 'in the shadows', observing their lives. Who is it? They are not there for good if their shadowy location is any guide. They were watching the 'kiss' being given, reminiscent of another kiss, one of betrayal. 'A crowd came, and the one called Judas, one of the twelve, was preceding them; and he approached Jesus to kiss him. But Jesus said to him, "Judas, are you betraying the Son of Man with a kiss?"' (Luke 22:47-48).

The demands of others are always there, and can be a distraction; they tend to 'slip out' of his mind, because they are really not on his list of priorities anyway, because they are not to God's glory. The repetitive and presumably empty requests are likened to a vinyl gramophone record with a defect that causes the playing needle to jump and replay itself ('did the needle just skip?'). A 'slip of the lip' gives away the request's pointlessness - meaninglessness reinforced by Dylan's inability to keep track of the number of such requests or even of the identity of the person making them. So few have God's heart perspective; their desires seem to Dylan unimportant from an eternal point of view.

'Something that comes natural' is a good contrast to something that has spiritual meaning, but who is it who is making the request, and what is their motive? It is easy to become spiritually disorientated, to 'get it wrong' because our surroundings appear to alter and our perspectives can be easily reversed ('the whole thing going backwards. Many people want something for nothing, yet following God comes with a price. 'Whoever does not carry his own cross and come after me cannot be my disciple.' (Luke 14:27). Dylan appears to be having trouble focusing on the enquirer and their persistent requests, possibly because he doesn't think that what they are asking for is (spiritually) important and so he is having trouble listening to them.

The album closes with 'Shooting Star', a beautiful series of enigmatic reflections on, it would seem, the one Dylan described on introducing his song 'In The Garden' in 1987, as his 'hero' - Jesus of Nazareth. On witnessing the shooting star, Dylan's mind turns to someone who he says was 'trying to break into another world'. Jesus came from the world of heaven to break into our world of sin with a rescue plan for us, but we still have to break into the world of heaven, access to which his death on the Cross made possible. As Jesus said: 'From the days of John the Baptist until now the kingdom of heaven has suffered violence, and the violent take it by force.' (Matthew 11:12). Dylan refers to a place he 'never knew' - surely a spiritual world that was at work long before he discovered its reality in a personal way.

He wonders whether the subject of the song 'made it through' - perhaps how Christ's rescue mission affected him. Dylan's attention then turns to himself - was he 'still the same'? Had he become what the subject of the song intended him to become? God works in us to restore the image that the divine artist originally intended before the beauty of the painting became besmirched by negativity and sin. Is the image of God being re-created in us or are we 'still the same'? As the Apostle Paul wrote to the Colossians, 'You have put on the new self who is being renewed to a true knowledge according to the image of the one who created him.' (Colossians 3:10).

In the Greek of the New Testament 'sin' is translated from 'hamartia'; the Greek archery term for 'missing the mark'. And so we find Dylan asking whether he had 'missed the mark' or 'over-stepped the line' of what is acceptable; a line that only the subject of the song could see, in other words, a spiritual line. The song then moves back to Dylan, who can hear the 'engine' and 'bell' of 'the last fire truck from hell' passing him, at a time when 'all good people are praying'. He is referring to what the Bible calls the 'end times', before Christ's return as judge. So he sings of the 'last temptation', the ultimate 'account' (of God's final reckoning) and 'the last time you might hear the Sermon on the Mount' (the teaching of Christ found in Matthew's gospel chapters 5- 7). The end of the world imagery is completed by the reference to a 'tomorrow' when it will be 'too late' to say anything further that needed to be said. 'Time' will have been called - 'slipped away', something that Dylan seems acutely aware of and wished, in 1989, to still communicate.

Chapter 9

'Under The Red Sky'

'Under the Red Sky' was released by Columbia Records in September 1990. Produced by Don and David Was (of 'Was, not Was' fame; born Weiss and Fagenson respectively); it confounded critics by exploring yet another musical genre, this time the imaginative world of children's nursery rhymes. The album was dedicated to one 'Gabby Goo Goo'. Desiree Gabrielle Dennis-Dylan, his then four-year-old daughter, had been born on January 31, 1986 to his second wife Carolyn Dennis. Carolyn Dennis had been one of his back-up singers and was the daughter of Madelyn Quebec, herself also a member of Dylan's touring vocal quartet. The marriage, birth and subsequent divorce were kept a secret for many years; reviewers at the time were unaware of the significance of the dedication or indeed of Gabby Goo Goo's existence.

The album opened with the (deliberately?) infuriating 'Wiggle Wiggle', a song that, if nothing else, shows that Dylan can pen nursery rhymes with the best of them. Despite the song's line 'You can raise the dead', there seems to be nothing to suggest that the song is anything other than what is says on the label - a nursery rhyme for the amusement of a little girl. And as such it succeeds beautifully.

The second number was the album's title track. 'Under The Red Sky' was, again, apparently written for children, and contained a few grains of spiritual truth mixed in with a number of different nursery rhyme themes. According to Don Was, Dylan 'Wrote it like a little biblical song. It was actually a very moving night when he put the vocal in. It was about six in the morning, we'd been working all day and he went out there... There was something really special to that thing. I could tell from the minute we started playing that this was just coalescing fast, and it had a lot of heart, a lot of feeling. I misunderstood it. I thought it's about ecology... and he looked at me like I'm a total asshole and he said, 'Well, it's not about ecology', and he walked out of the room. So I followed him out and I explained why I thought that. And he just shook his head. He said, 'I can't believe people read this much into it.' That's the only time I really ever asked him about a lyric and he told me… It's about people who got trapped in their home town.' [58]

Whatever the case, the line 'Someday little girl, everything for you is gonna be new' must surely be directed towards his young daughter, Desiree. It also echoes words from the book of Revelation: 'And he that sat upon the throne said, "Behold, I make all things new." And he said unto me, "Write, for these words are true and faithful."' (Revelation 21:5). The 'diamond as big as your shoe' that follows this promise might easily stand for the eternal reward that awaits God's children in heaven.

The chorus goes on to speak of 'the key to the kingdom', which Christ promised to the Apostle Peter. 'I will give you the keys of the kingdom of heaven; and whatever you bind on earth shall have been bound in heaven, and whatever, you loose on earth shall have been loosed in heaven.' (Matthew 16:19). The line about a 'blind horse that leads you around' may be a reference to the prophecy of Zechariah (12:4) about the judgement that will befall those who assail Jerusalem. 'I will watch over the house of Judah, while I strike every horse of the peoples with blindness.'

The song, along with other nursery rhyme inspired numbers, resonates with the words of Jesus in Luke 18:16-17. 'Jesus called for them, saying, "Permit the children to come to me, and do not hinder them, for the kingdom of God belongs to such as these. Truly I say to you, whoever, does not receive the kingdom of God like a child will not enter it."'Jesus took time to share with little children, and, as 'Man Gave Names To All The Animals' had shown in 1979, so does Dylan.

The third track, 'Unbelievable', seems to outline the plight of those who say they do not believe in God, and instead end up believing in everything and hence in nothing of any eternal value. 'Strange but true' indeed is human behaviour that puts us on the level of 'bait in a fish's mouth' - helpless and out of control - that might well be explained by our 'livin' in the shadow of an evil star.' 'Stars' in scripture stand for angels, some of whom chose evil and rebellion against God rather than good. 'Then the fifth angel sounded, and I saw a star from heaven which had fallen to the earth; and the key of the bottomless pit was given to him. He opened the bottomless pit, and smoke went up... like the smoke of a great furnace... the sun and the air were darkened ... Then out of the smoke came locusts upon the earth, and power was given them, as the scorpions of the earth have power.' (Revelation 9:1-3).

Dylan finds it 'unbelievable' that 'it' (surely man's plight) would ever 'get this far', but spiritual foolishness comes more naturally than wisdom does to most of us. Being led by our noses into wrong thinking can 'drive you to drink' (to alcoholism and depression). The Israelites were promised a 'land of milk and honey'; now this has been reduced to being described as 'the land of money', i.e. greed and materialism. (Exodus 3:8, ANIV: 'I have come down to rescue them from the hand of the Egyptians and to bring them up out of that land into a good and spacious land, a land flowing with milk and honey.') Our heads and minds have become 'so dignified' (numbed intellectually by pride), that 'every moon is sanctified'. Rather than worship nothing, man now worships everything, left having to 'feed that swine', like the prodigal son [xxxii] who turned his back on his father only to discover that what the world had to offer was not all it was made out to be. Our malady may be that we have 'no eyes' (and so are blind to spiritual truth), and we are 'told lies' (and so are deceived), our hearts bleeding beneath a thin

---

[xxxii] Luke 15:15-24: 'So he went and hired himself out to one of the citizens of that country, and he sent him into his fields to feed swine. And he would have gladly filled his stomach with the pods that the swine were eating, and no one was giving anything to him. But when he came to his senses, he said, "How many of my father's hired men have more than enough bread, but I am dying here with hunger! I will get up and go to my father, and will say to him, "Father, I have sinned against heaven, and in your sight; I am no longer worthy to be called your son; make me as one of your hired men."" So he got up and came to his father. But while he was still a long way off, his father saw him and felt compassion for him, and ran and embraced, him and kissed him. And the son said to him, "Father, I have sinned against heaven and in your sight; I am no longer worthy to be called your son." But the father said to his slaves, "Quickly bring out the best robe and put it on him, and put a ring on his hand and sandals on his feet; and bring the fattened calf, kill it, and let us eat and celebrate; for this son of mine was dead and has come to life again; he was lost and has been found." And they began to celebrate.'

veneer of the appearance of being 'civilized'. We are so much 'in need', yet so little cognizant of it, that it really is 'unbelievable'.

'Born In Time' is surely a deeply personal song that seems to speak of Dylan's reluctance to go back to the past and that which has been of great cost to him emotionally. It seems to address his feelings towards his second wife, Carolyn Dennis, one of his Christian back-up singers. She had filed for divorce on August 7, 1990, the year the song was published. The song emphasizes that what happens in this life (in the realm of 'time') can, but does not have to, affect eternity.

Something is coming through to Dylan in a state of loneliness, typically in the night-time, in the 'black and white' of old memories, the substance of 'dreams' which stand in harsh contrast to the more painful reality of the present moment. If the 'you' of this poignant song is indeed his ex-wife (unknown at the time), then Dylan does not seem to be able to muster the emotional energy to return. 'No more of this' has a scary finality to it, as does 'You came, you saw', directed to someone who, like Julius Caesar (after his brief war with the Kingdom of Pontus), has 'come, seen and conquered'. The relationship is taking 'too much skill' and 'will' - it seems too demanding to carry on with. Dylan compares this to 'the law', most probably the Law of Moses, which was intended to show us of our need of help when all our own self-improvement programmes had failed. 'The Law has become our tutor to lead us to Christ, so that we may be justified by faith.' (Galatians 3:24).

There is an intensely personal note to the line about 'marrying young, just like your Ma' (presumably a reference to Carolyn Dennis' mother, Madelyn Quebec, also one of his back-up singers). It seems from the lyric that despite Carolyn 'trying', Dylan 'slid' and 'reeled' on a trajectory that whilst being upward, 'tests every nerve'. One of the problems is that it is based on the 'ways of nature' (the version sung on 'Tell Tale Signs' speaks of 'scheming'). 'Nature's ways' are not always a good guide to how to behave; the 'natural' is a scriptural term meaning that which is inherent to the (fallen) human state of being; a state of separation from God. It is frequently contrasted in scripture with that which represents God's pure intentions (and so denoted as the 'spiritual'). [xxxiii] In the light of Dylan's lyrics, it seems that the Apostle Paul, in his description of the struggle between the 'natural' and the 'spiritual' would have understood where Dylan was coming from. (Romans 17:14-20).

Dylan goes on to say that the person addressed 'won't get anything they don't deserve', knowing that God sees everything and will reward us according to what we deserve. 'Behold, the Lord God will come with might, with his arm ruling for him. Behold, his reward is with him, and his recompense before him.' (Isaiah 40:10).

The song's descriptions of their relationship shows Dylan being very open and transparent. The fire (presumably of his feelings towards Carolyn) continues to smoke, and she is described in flowing poetry as being 'snow', 'rain', 'striped' and 'plain'. The poignancy and pain comes across powerfully when Dylan concludes his emotional rhyming by singing 'truer words have not been spoken or broken', surely a description of his marriage promises made with the best of intentions but then sadly broken.

The song ends with a description of a place of 'mystery', because none of us always understand why some things happen. Instead we perceive a 'foggy web of destiny', where God sees all and knows all. Sometimes we just have to trust in his ability to work things out, despite our own ability to mess things up.

There is a much lighter, but still spiritually meaningful tone to the next piece, 'TV Talkin' Song'. Many people can only see the good things that television can do. But from a psychological, and certainly from a

---

[xxxiii] Romans 7:14-20: 'For we know that the Law is spiritual, but I am of flesh, sold into bondage to sin. For what I am doing, I do not understand; for I am not practicing what I would like to do, but I am doing the very thing I hate... For I know that nothing good dwells in me, that is, in my flesh; for the willing is present in me, but the doing of the good is not. For the good that I want, I do not do, but I practice the very evil that I do not want. But if I am doing the very thing I do not want, I am no longer the one doing it, but sin which dwells in me.'

spiritual perspective, there is another side; a much darker side. A historical case study bears this out. In 1989 when the Buddhist nation of Bhutan finally succumbed to the introduction of television, a crime-wave born of material dissatisfaction soon followed. The minister for health and education, Sangay Ngedup said: "Until recently, we shied away from killing insects, and yet now we Bhutanese are asked to watch people on TV blowing heads off with shotguns. Will we now be blowing each other's heads off?" [59] Or, as Dylan said to Charles Kaiser in December 1985, "TV is so super-powerful. When I was growing up, and even in the Sixties, that was never the case. You had to go out and experience things to form opinions. Now you don't have to move. You get knowledge brought into you, without the experience of it. I think there's something really dangerous in that."

The song recounts a visit to Hyde Park in London and a place called Speaker's Corner (at the northeast corner of the park), which has for years been a place of public oration and debate. There is a man discoursing 'about all kinds of different gods', and another man talking 'about the TV god' and all 'the pain that it invokes', presumably from the false images it projects. There is a concern expressed for 'children when they're young'; who often grow up with the TV babysitting for them, and so losing innocence to materialism and unreality. TV pollutes the 'temple' that is our 'minds', Dylan sings, echoing the words of the Apostle Paul. 'Do you not know that you are a temple of God and that the Spirit of God dwells in you?' (1 Corinthians 3:16), and warns against letting 'an egg get laid' inside, which will hatch into something you might not want.

The orator calls on his audience to 'pray for peace', and to resist being led to 'the land of forbidden fruits', rather like the one in the Garden of Eden. 'The Lord God commanded the man, saying, "From any tree of the garden you may eat freely; but from the tree of the knowledge of good and evil you shall not eat, for in the day that you eat from it you will surely die."' (Genesis 2:16-17). Rather than let TV 'drag your brain about', you might have, like Elvis, to 'shoot the damn thing out.' (Elvis Presley once famously shot out his TV when the actor Robert Goulet

118

came on the screen.) The song ends with a violent disturbance, one that Dylan is able, with fitting irony, to watch on TV later that evening.

Another nursery rhyme inspired track was '10,000 Men', presumably based on the 'Grand Old Duke Of York, who 'had 10,000 men. He marched them up to the top of the hill and he marched them down again.' Maybe it was good for their discipline. In Dylan's version, the song seems to be more about release from 'spiritual slavery', and where real treasure is to be found. Dylan's men are 'dressed in Oxford blue', the uniform of the Unionist army in the American Civil War (1860-1865) against slavery. (US Army dress uniform is still dark blue in colour.)

They are 'coming for you', and Dylan employs a triple negative (nothing is done by halves) to say that their behaviour is not what your mother would want. Then we find them 'digging for silver and gold'. The US Civil War gave place to the opening up of frontier areas such as Arizona in the pursuit of mineral wealth, which in scripture stands for the search for spiritual truth 'of greater worth than gold', because its benefit will last forever. As Psalm 119:72 says, 'The law of your mouth is better to me than thousands of gold and silver pieces.'

Dylan asks, 'Who could your lover be?' (Do you know his true identity? Is he really good for you?). He offers to get behind his disguise by eating 'off his head so you can really see!' Next come 'ten thousand women all dressed in white', presumably dressed ready for a wedding, as the book of Revelation depicts the New Jerusalem: 'I saw the holy city, new Jerusalem, coming down out of heaven from God, made ready as a bride adorned for her husband.' (Revelation 21:2).

Whereas 'Wiggle Wiggle' may have thrown people off the scent, the spiritual is soon back in evidence with '2 x 2', a song that looks at the purpose of life and its intended outcome - entering the kingdom of heaven. Dylan expert Clinton Heylin has uncovered a verse from an early studio recording that didn't make the final cut but nevertheless indicates where Dylan was coming from. 'One by one, thy will be done; two by two. I'm telling it true; three by three, why can't you see? Four by four, you've seen it before.' The reference is to the Lord's Prayer - 'Thy will be done, thy kingdom come, on earth as it is in heaven.' (Matthew 6:10). This is followed up by Dylan's own declaration of veracity ('telling it true'), reminiscent of St John's (21:24). 'This is the disciple who is testifying to these things and wrote these things, and we know that his testimony is true.' Dylan had told it time and time again, but many of his audience didn't 'get it' then and many still don't, despite having 'seen it before'.

The official lyric runs: 'How many paths did they try and fail?', presumably in their search for fulfillment, and how many 'lingered in jail?', like Christian and Hopeful in the 'Doubting Castle' of John Bunyan's 'Pilgrim's Progress'. They too were 'headed for heaven', and having made it passed 'the gate', they were able to 'drink the wine', in the biggest and best party ever. As the angel said to St John: "Write, 'Blessed are those who are invited to the marriage supper of the Lamb.'" (Revelation 19:9). This is the other 'rendezvous' (surely heaven) that they 'follow the sun' towards.

The album follows up this clearly biblically based song with 'God Knows'. This song deals with the fact that God is all knowing and is especially concerned about the attitude of indifference or rebellion to him that is destroying us from within - which scripture calls sin. For someone who supposedly had lost interest in his faith, this track contains a remarkably large number of references (twenty-five) to God. The second verse gets to the point; there is 'a struggle' going on. As the Apostle Paul put it to the church at Ephesus (modern day Turkey), 'Our struggle is not against flesh and blood, but against the rulers, against the powers, against the world forces of this darkness, against the spiritual forces of wickedness in the heavenly places. Therefore, take up the full armour of God, so that you will be able to resist in the evil day, and having done everything, to stand firm.' (Ephesians 6:12-13).

The 'crime' of the next line is whatever breaks God's word and his laws, the outcome of which will be eventual judgement, not by 'water' though, as happened on the last occasion with Noah's flood (Genesis chapter 6), but rather, 'fire next time'. Which is just how the Bible tells it will be. 'If we deliberately keep on sinning after we have received the knowledge of the truth, no sacrifice for sins is left, but only a fearful expectation of judgement and of raging fire that will consume the enemies of God.' (Hebrews 10:26-27, ANIV).

The next verse addresses sin; that attitude of indifference to or rebellion against God that began with our first ancestors in the Garden of Eden. God knew it was going to happen, and he made provision for it. This sin thing is not deliberate 'treason' or purposeful wrong-doing, but is an in-bred attitude and disposition that leads to behaviour that is harmful and not as the maker intended. As Dylan sings, 'It was supposed to last a season'; the trouble being that it is a rather long season. 'It's been so strong for so long', but the reign of sin and death will, one day, come to an end. God knows all too well, having become a man himself for a time, how 'fragile' our lives are. As Psalm 103:14 says, 'He himself knows our frame; he is mindful that we are but dust.' 'God knows everything', the song tells us. God even knows the number of hairs on our heads. (Luke 12:7).

Because God exists outside of the realm of human time, he 'sees it all unfold' but is surprised by none of it; he has seen it all already. Although he does not direct our choices, his existence outside of time means that he is aware of what our actions will be before we are. We really should 'be crying', out of sorrow for the trouble that our sins have caused; the problem is with our hearts and our inner attitudes - we have been 'so bold and so cold'; bold in continuing in sin but cold towards God. We should all, according to Dylan, be ready to 'weep' tears of remorse as you turn towards him, having seen our wretched state spiritually separated from him. 'God knows the secrets of your heart', sings Dylan. God's thoughts to us may come to us during sleep, in dreams sometimes, as well as in our conscience. Dylan's 'you ain't gonna be taking nothing with you when you go' (after this life ends) resonates with Jesus' words. 'Do not store up for yourselves treasures on earth, where moth and rust destroy, and where thieves break in and steal. But store up for yourselves treasures in heaven, where neither moth nor rust destroys, and where thieves do not break in or steal; for where your treasure is, there your heart will be also.' (Matthew 6:19-21).

God does indeed have 'a purpose' in everything. As the Apostle Paul had said, 'And we know that God causes all things to work together for good to those who love God, to those who are called according to his purpose.' (Romans 8:28). Everyone has 'a chance'; everyone has an opportunity to turn to him, though whether they take it is up to them. God has given us all the ability to 'rise above the darkest hour of any circumstance', with his help. As Dylan says, there 'is a heaven' where God dwells, 'out of sight' to the natural human eye, and he has made a way 'from here to there'; a way that sometimes might not be easy ('a million miles by candlelight'). But with his help we can make it.

Sometimes the Christian life ('walk') is not easy but 'we do not lose heart, though our outer man is decaying; yet our inner man is being renewed day by day. For this momentary light affliction is producing for us an eternal weight of glory far beyond all comparison, while we look not at the things which are seen, but at the things which are not seen; for the things which are seen are temporal, but the things which are not seen are eternal.' (2 Corinthians 4:16-18).

The nursery rhymes of 'Under The Red Sky' would be the last original Dylan album for seven years, the longest gap in his recording history. The reason, in the opinion of this medically qualified author, was (post-divorce) severe reactive depression, following his second (and at the time a closely guarded secret) marriage. No one gets married to get divorced, certainly not two people of strong Christian faith. The consequential psychological trauma of self-reproach, recriminatory guilt feelings (and probable spiritual attack) inevitably resulted in a dearth of creativity, eventually resulting in a set of hitherto unnoted depressive symptoms being clearly expressed in his next album, 'Time Out Of Mind'.

The album's title ought to have given a clue to his depressed state of 'Time Out Of [my] Mind' at the point of its release. It would not be until 2001 and 'Love And Theft' that the mood and music tempo would lift. Ten years is a painfully long time for anyone to be living with post-divorce (and loss of child) 'blues wrapped around my head'. ('Standing In The Doorway', from 'Time Out Of Mind').

Chapter 10

1991-1996 and 'The Bootleg Series Volumes 1-3'

After releasing 'Under The Red Sky' in 1990, Dylan fans would have to wait until 1997 before further new and original material would be released in 'Time Out Of Mind'. The seven year period was filled with 'The Bootleg Series Volumes 1-3' (released in 1991 to celebrate Dylan's fiftieth birthday), 'The 30th Anniversary Concert Celebration' (1993), a 'Greatest Hits' album (1994), a live album: 'MTV Unplugged' (1995), and in 1992 and 1993, two albums of folk song 'covers'. These comprised of traditional material that Dylan took and rendered in his own unique style; some of which he brought into his live shows.

The folk albums were 'Good As I Been To You' (1992) and 'World Gone Wrong' (1993). The first was recorded initially in Chicago with David Bromberg as producer, and completed at Dylan's home studio largely under his own production. The original session had included 'Rise Again' (found on the bootleg 'Yonder Comes Sin'); in the end Dylan chose to release purely covers of folk numbers, stating that "I needed a short time to record these songs; these songs are really important to me, *[they]* followed me during all these years so I treated them as if they were my songs, not like covers. It took a short time, you know, these are folk songs and do not need too many ornaments." [60]

The second album of folk material, 'World Gone Wrong', was released as Dylan's final offering under his 1981 contract with Columbia Records, before his move to Sony. For many, the most enjoyable expression of Dylan's timeless originality was the wit and wisdom of the album's liner notes, which, presumably in response to the controversy around song-rights that 'Good As I Been To You' had generated, were written personally and in-depth. The 'lords of the illogical in smoking jackets' (for 'Ragged And Dirty') is pure poetic Dylan. Despite the pieces being not of his own composing, spirituality still figured prominently. For example, his description of 'Lone Pilgrim' (by 'Doc' Watson, himself a committed Christian): 'The lunacy of trying to fool the self is set aside at some given point... Salvation and the needs of mankind are prominent, and hegemony *[the dominating influence or leadership of one social group or nation over others]* takes a breathing spell.' 'My soul flew to mansions on high' - 'what's essentially true is virtual reality.' The song 'Delia' has 'rectitude' *[moral uprightness]*, 'the singer's not talking from a head full of booze.'

Prior to these albums, Dylan fans had been treated to some high-quality recordings of tracks previously only available in inferior quality on bootlegs. 'The Bootleg Series Volumes 1-3' saw absolute classics such as 'Blind Willie McTell' see the official light of day for the first time, a brainwave on the part of Dylan's management, who deserve thanks and credit for the decision. This chapter, in keeping with the overall theme of the book, will not cover all the earlier material, but only that from (or after) Dylan's 'Christian period', with one or two notable exceptions.

'Nobody 'Cept You' (disc 2), was written in 1973 and recorded (though not released) as part of the material for the 1974 'Planet Waves' album. In the song, Dylan demonstrates beyond any shadow of doubt his willingness to use spiritual and biblical language prior to his personal encounter with Christ. 'There's nothing 'round here I believe in, 'cept you' is surely addressed to a human object of his affection - or is it, given his use of the word 'sacred'? 'There's nothing to me that's sacred, 'cept you' is an uncommon choice of phrase. Whichever it is, the song's subject 'reaches' Dylan, he 'admires' them, and when they meet he experiences 'fire' in his 'soul'. This person is one that he is now to 'live or die for'.

The song goes on to liken his feelings to those encountered previously in a church setting where hymn singing would bring about an experience of peace he describes as 'sublime'. Dylan recalls his childhood when to play and generally enjoy games in the local cemetery was quite natural, as for most children. Now however, this expression of a natural joie de vivre is lost to him and he is reduced to passing by 'mournfully'; he has become a 'stranger' only visible to this person who remains the object of his desire.

'Quit Your Low Down Ways' was an outtake from 'The Freewheelin' Bob Dylan' sessions in 1962, and also carried a scriptural message. It is no good relying on outward signs of piety (such as Bible reading and prayer) if you are going to carry on in your old and rotten ways of behaving. 'If you can't quit your sinnin', at least 'quit your low down ways'. Fair enough.

From the post 1978 period, disc 3 contained 'Ye Shall Be Changed' (1982), based on a verse in a letter of St Paul's to the church at Corinth in which Paul speaks of the second coming of Christ. Dylan sings of the all too human state of resentment) and other types of negative emotions that do not come from God) and compares it with the natural desire for 'contentment', and the God-shaped space that is in every person's life, that only God can fill. Once 'hatred' has exhausted itself, Dylan predicts that 'Ye shall be changed', directly quoting 1 Corinthians 15:50-57. [xxxiv]

Dylan knows that most of what men and women achieve is by their own 'sweat, blood and muscle'; because man's original choice of rebellion toward God meant that we have to work much harder than was originally intended. As God had said to Adam, "Cursed is the ground because of you; in toil you will eat of it all the days of your life." (Genesis 3:17-19). Life's stresses are summed up with 'All you ever do is hustle' (and generally get hassled), while our 'loved ones' leave us due to a lack of interpersonal commitment in our lives. We may not even be too sure of those closest to us (the 'wife and kids'), but we 'shall be changed', if we

---

[xxxiv] 1 Corinthians 15:50-57: 'Now I say this, brethren, that flesh and blood cannot, inherit the kingdom of God; nor does the perishable inherit the imperishable. Behold, I tell you a mystery; we will not all sleep, but we will all be changed, in a moment, in the twinkling of an eye, at the last trumpet; for the trumpet will sound, and the dead will be raised imperishable, and we will be changed. For this perishable must put on the imperishable, and this mortal must put on immortality. But when this perishable will have put on the imperishable, and this mortal will have put on immortality, then will come about the saying that is written, "Death is swallowed up in victory. O death, where is your victory? O Death, where is your sting?" The sting of death is sin, and the power of sin is the Law; but thanks be to God, who gives us the victory through our Lord Jesus Christ.'

have faith in Christ. What has passed does not need to 'control' you, and our uncertain future can have 'a whole new beginning'. As Jesus had said, "Truly, truly, I say to you, unless, one is born of water and the Spirit he cannot enter into the kingdom of God. That which is born of the flesh is flesh, and that which is born of the Spirit is spirit. Do not be amazed that I said to you, 'You must be born again.'" (John 3:5-7). We don't even have to 'go' anywhere, such as 'Russia or Iran'. Just 'surrender to God and he'll move you right here where you stand.' 'When the last trumpet blows, the dead will arise'; just as Paul said.

The song goes on to speak of the 'bitter water', a reference to the book of Exodus (15:23-25). [xxxv] Dylan also sings of the 'bread of sorrow', another reference to the Exodus and the 'bread of affliction' eaten in Egypt by the children of Israel. Don't live as if trapped by your past ('it don't control you'). When you've had 'enough' of enduring a path that's 'been rough', (and if you decide to follow Dylan in his faith in Messiah), then Paul's words will be as true for you as they were for Dylan, and 'ye shall be changed', into something much better.

'Angelina' was an outtake from the 'Shot Of Love' recordings in 1981, and it stands as yet another of Dylan's poetic masterpieces, raising the question of which track on that album got included in preference to it! An artist that can write lyrics in such fashion and then not publish them has to be a genius, and most likely one of extremely high standards or who thinks his work might be misunderstood. The track, sung in the manner of a Jewish lament, appears to describe Dylan's heart for those who are spiritually lost, and especially those who are in flat opposition to God by virtue of a contrary spirituality. As such it stands as in the same category of spiritual perspective as 'Jokerman' on 'Infidels', only addressed to a female. ('Angelina', as in the feminine form of angel, of which Satan represents the 'fallen' type.) Dylan opens the song by saying that he has always been someone willing to take risks, but in a

---

[xxxv] Exodus 15:23-25: 'When they came to Marah, they could not drink the waters of Marah, for they were bitter; therefore, it was named Marah. So the people grumbled at Moses, saying, "What shall we drink?" Then he cried out to the Lord, and the Lord showed him a tree; and he threw it into the waters, and the waters became sweet.'

calculated way (one hand 'advances' while the other is being drawn back), and this includes atypical situations where the forces that humans experience (the 'current') are powerful and unusual (dancing monkeys).

Why is there 'blood drying' in Dylan's hair? Is it an allusion to Christ with his crown of thorns? And why is the hair 'yellow'? (Renaissance art frequently depicts Jesus, although a Hebrew, as having blond hair.) Something is 'drawing' him to Angelina's door (a love born out of spiritual concern?), and it brings to her a sense of recognition. She is not completely impervious (yet) to what is motivating him. The refrain 'Oh, Angelina, oh, Angelina' is sung as a lament; the Hebrew custom of expressing sorrow for one's own or another's poor condition. Dylan used this in his epic song 'Jokerman' ('Oh Jokerman, oh oh oh o-h Jokerman.') A sense of deep concern for a spiritually lost state - in this case the devil's - is what is being conveyed. This notion of spiritual lament is confirmed by the next line, which describes a figure that has eyes like 'slits' that 'any snake' would be proud of.

This is surely, as in 'Jokerman', a reference to what the scripture calls 'the ancient serpent' described by the Apostle John in the book of Revelation (a favourite book of Dylan's) as 'the great dragon' who was cast out of heaven. [xxxvi] This snake-like figure ('Jokerman' contained several serpent images) has a 'face that any painter would [love to] paint', just like the 'Jokerman' ('Michelangelo indeed could've carved out your features'). Lamenting the downfall of those who had the potential to be great is a common Jewish scriptural theme. For example, the devil was created by God originally as a being of great beauty, and is lamented over by the Jewish prophet Ezekiel. 'The word of the Lord came to me saying, "Son of man, take up a lamentation over the king of Tyre [symbolic of the devil] and say to him, 'Thus says the Lord God,

---

[xxxvi] Revelation 12:9-11. 'That old serpent, called the devil, and Satan, which deceives the whole world: he was cast out into the earth, and his angels were cast out with him. And I heard a loud voice saying in heaven, "Now is come salvation, and strength, and the kingdom of our God, and the power of his Christ: for the accuser of our brethren is cast down, which accused them before our God day and night. And they overcame him by the blood of the Lamb, and by the word of their testimony; and they loved not their lives unto the death."'

"You had the seal of perfection, full of wisdom and perfect in beauty. You were in Eden, the garden of God; every precious stone was your covering."' (Ezekiel 28:11-13).

The picture is completed with a description of an ancient idol whose features are mixed between that of a voluptuous woman and a 'hyena'. Dylan asks whether he has to ask their 'permission to turn the other cheek', as Christ taught his followers to do in the Sermon on the Mount. 'You have heard that it has been said, 'An eye for an eye, and a tooth for a tooth'. But I say unto you, that you resist not evil: but whosoever shall smite you on your right cheek, turn to him the other also.' (Matthew 5:38-39, KJV). Jesus is turning the requirement of the Law of Moses on its head (in limiting the retaliation that an injured person could legally require), and so demonstrating an ultimate reliance on God as Father to protect his children. [61] Dylan demonstrates a brilliant (and typically Jewish) grasp of logic in asking, 'If you can read my mind, why must I speak?' He is speaking to someone with a claim to particular form of spiritual discernment; but from what source? Is Angelina's from God, or not?

The next verse makes reference to a valley of 'giants' (probably a reference to the book of Genesis (6:4, KJV) and its account of spiritually demonic interference with humankind. 'There were giants in the earth in those days; and also after that, when the sons of God *[in this case demonic angels]* came in unto the daughters of men, and they bore children to them, the same became mighty men which were of old, men of renown.' The consequences are rather dire - Dylan pictorialises the American flag exploding. The biblical imagery continues with a description of the land of 'milk and honey' - the Promised Land described by God to Moses in the book of Exodus. [xxxvii] Dylan tells Angelina that he is just a messenger, one sent under instructions from 'the judge' with her subpoena. The judge is ordering a meeting with her.

[xxxvii] Exodus 3:8: 'So I have come down to deliver them from the power of the Egyptians, and to bring them up from that land to a good and spacious land, to a land flowing with milk and honey, to the place of the Canaanite and the Hittite and the Amorite and the Perizzite and the Hivite and the Jebusite.'

Will she respond and listen, or will the consequence of her ignoring the judge's order mean that she will 'cease to exist'? If she does, she had better not blame Dylan, who is acting out of a love's pure motives, but who cannot stay around indefinitely waiting for a response. Truly, for Angelina, her 'best friend' is Dylan's 'worst enemy' - surely the devil.

This perspective is supported by the darkness of the next verse, which describes a 'black Mercedes' being driven through a war scene. Angelina's servants (and/or the devil's servants) are in a state of living death, right 'down to the bone', and Dylan can foresee their impending destruction, asking that they pick the place of his coming downfall - 'Jerusalem or Argentina?' Angelina has a history; one of being stolen 'when she was three days old'. Apparently her mother has since sought 'vengeance' and, to some extent, found it, but to what end? The person concerned is then described as being 'surrounded by God's angels', but Angelina's mother cannot see them - she is 'blindfolded', as, alas, is Angelina. Both are blind to the ultimate spiritual realities being depicted.

Dylan can see what can only be a spiritual army moving against heaven 'by force', on what is a futile attempt to oppose God himself. This army is composed of men in 'pieces'; shot to pieces spiritually, but still hopelessly trying to do the impossible in terms of fighting against God. This is very reminiscent of Dylan's 'Cross The Green Mountain' (the soundtrack for the US Civil War film, 'Gods And Generals'), and the foe that 'never dreamed of surrendering, they fell where they stood.'

Dylan can also see an 'unknown rider' and the 'pale white horse', again reminiscent of the book of Revelation (6:7-8). 'I heard the voice of the fourth living creature saying, "Come." I looked, and behold, an ashen [pale] horse; and he who sat on it had the name Death; and Hades was following with him. Authority was given to them over a fourth of the earth, to kill with sword and with famine and with pestilence and by the wild beasts of the earth.' If Angelina can only tell Dylan 'in God's truth' what she wants, then she can have it, but the sense is very similar to 'Jokerman' - 'but with truth so far off, what good will it do?' Early Christians were frequently killed in Roman gladiatorial arenas; Angelina is going to have to resist the forces of evil she has become subject to as a result of her childhood abuse.

Dylan's advice is for her to 'beat a path of retreat' using 'spiral staircases', surely a reference to the temple of Solomon in 1 Kings 6:8. 'The doorway for the lowest side chamber was on the right side of the house; and they would go up by winding stairs to the middle story and from the middle to the third.' She will pass an 'angel with four faces', as in the Hebrew prophet Ezekiel's vision of God's throne. [xxxviii] Angelina really needs to 'beg' God for his 'mercy' and forgiveness, with tears of remorse, but will she?

'Tell Me', also on Disc 3, carries a similar line of spiritual enquiry to that within 'Angelina'. An outtake from the 'Infidels' album (1983), it too points towards Dylan's concern for those lost; 'separated from Christ, excluded from the commonwealth of Israel, and strangers to the covenants of promise, having no hope and without God in the world.' (Ephesians 2:12). He asks whether that 'flame' (perhaps of a love for God) is still burning.

What is the subject of the song 'focused upon'? A 'glance or a sigh' is all Dylan needs to know (through his discernment) what the person's spiritual condition is. The person may indeed 'try to conceal' their state, but Dylan seems aware that everything is known to God. 'There is nothing concealed that will not be revealed, or hidden that will not be known.' (Matthew 10:26). Is the subject of the song's best friend

---

[xxxviii] Ezekiel 1:4-10: 'Storm wind was coming from the north, a great cloud with fire flashing forth continually and a bright light around it, and in its midst something like glowing metal in the midst of the fire. Within it there were figures resembling four living beings. And this was their appearance: they had human form. Each of them had four faces and four wings. Their legs were straight and their feet were like a calf's hoof, and they gleamed like burnished bronze. Under their wings on their four sides were human hands. As for the faces and wings of the four of them, their wings touched one another; their faces did not turn when they moved, each went straight, forward. As for the form of their faces, each had the face of a man; all four had the face of a lion on the right and the face of a bull on the left, and all four had the face of an eagle.'

someone with whom Dylan too has had an 'acquaintance'; someone not terribly good for one spiritually? Their 'rock and roll dreams' are a false reality; the artificial light of fame blinds them. Dylan asks where their 'treasure' lies hidden, knowing the truth of Jesus' words; 'Where your treasure is, there will your heart be also.' (Matthew 6:21, KJV).

Is the person just playing a 'game' with Dylan's heart? And if they are for real, just 'how deep' does he have to go in order to get through to them? For a start, do they 'have any morals?' - any compass that might still point them towards God?

One version of the song asks whether they wish to 'ride on that old ship of Zion?' (Zion being the city of God where God's people dwell.) 'Beautiful for situation, the joy of the whole earth, is Mount Zion, on the sides of the north, the city of the great King.' (Psalm 48:2, KJV). Dylan's verse asks whether the listener prefers a 'lapdog' or a 'dead lion', probably a reference to the scripture that likens the devil to a defeated lion. 'Your adversary, the devil, prowls around like a roaring lion, seeking someone to devour.' (1 Peter 5:8). Dylan asks for 'truth', and questions whether they are the object of anyone's spiritual concern; are they someone anybody 'prays for' or 'cries for' (as in, cries out to God for in prayer?)

Another song from the period in question was the heartfelt 'Lord Protect My Child'. This was another outtake from the 'Infidels' recording sessions held in the 'Power Station' studio in New York in April 1983. 'Lord Protect My Child' carries echoes of 'Forever Young' as a father's heartfelt prayer for his child. Bob and Sara Dylan had four children, three boys and one girl. This song, addressed to a son, could have been sung, as Jewish father's blessings are, over any or all of their boys - Jesse, Samuel and Jakob. For millennia, the Jews have sung prayers of blessing over their children. This particular child is to Dylan 'wise' beyond his years, but is also 'wild', and Dylan asks that God be there to protect him when Dylan is unable to be there for him. In the words of Psalm 41:2, 'The Lord will protect him and keep him alive, and he shall be called blessed upon the earth; and do not give him over to the desire of his enemies.'

While smiling at the sight of his child playing (peacefully oblivious to life's stresses and strains), Dylan reflects on both of their destinies, ones that have already been seen by God and so are 'centuries old'. God 'weeps' over the state the 'world' is in ('raped and defiled') not of his wish but as a result of men and women's free, but poorly directed, choices. 'Few things', Dylan sings, are truly 'worthwhile'; he does not ask God for 'material things to touch', only that God (the 'Lord') watch over and protect his children. Dylan may 'fall' on the path of life, he may not live to 'see another day', but he knows that God will be faithful to care for and protect his child in answer to his prayers.

The song goes on to speak of 'a time... when all will be well', 'when God and man will be reconciled.' These are not exactly 'post-Christian' sentiments, but rather ones reflecting the words of the Apostle Paul in his letter to the Ephesians: 'For he *[Christ]* is our peace, who has made both one, and has broken down the middle wall of partition between us *[Jew and Greek]*; having abolished in his flesh the enmity, even the law of commandments contained in ordinances *[the Jewish Law]*; for to make in himself of the two one new man *[as the church of Jews and Greeks together]*, so making peace; and that he might reconcile both unto God in one body by the cross, having slain the enmity thereby.' (Ephesians 2:14-16, KJV). Dylan concludes that this will only happen when 'men lose their chains and righteousness reigns', echoing yet another end-time scripture. [xxxix] Until then, Dylan will continue to pray for his children.

Yet another 'Infidels' outtake (from 1983) was 'Foot Of Pride', again a very Christian song for someone who was supposedly moving away from his faith. Commentators have sometimes struggled with the song's meaning, but the spiritual nature is apparent to anyone with even a

---

[xxxix] 2 Peter 3:11-13: 'Since all these things are to be destroyed in this way, what sort of people ought you to be in holy conduct and godliness, looking for and hastening the coming of the day of God, because of which the heavens will be destroyed by burning, and the elements will melt with intense heat! But according to his promise we are looking for new heavens and a new earth, in which righteousness dwells.'

rudimentary grasp of the Bible's contents. Just like 'Jokerman', the song is about the sin of pride that brought about the downfall of the devil, aka 'Satan' or 'Lucifer' ('the prince of this world' - John 12:31) and his work of corruption of all that God has made. The song's content was covered in chapter 3; also briefly here for chapter completeness' sake.

The song opens with a reference to an attribute described as a 'lion' that can tear man's flesh, just as 1 Peter 5:8 (ANIV) describes: 'Your enemy the devil prowls around like a roaring lion looking for someone to devour.' This is also likened to a woman impersonating a man, again a biblical allusion to a bad spiritual scene. The Old Testament book of Deuteronomy (also mentioned in 'Jokerman'), states that 'A woman must not wear men's clothing, nor a man wear women's clothing, for the Lord your God detests anyone who does this.' (Deuteronomy 22:5). God had purposely given gender-specific design and forbade it being blurred.

An empty, man-made form of religion is very much in evidence; the sentimental 'Danny Boy' ('Oh Danny boy, the pipes, the pipes are calling...') is being sung at a funeral, the 'Lord's Prayer' gets a mention, and we hear of a preacher 'talking 'bout Christ betrayed'. The betrayal of Christ was brought about through Judas, whose very name has come to be synonymous with treachery. 'Satan entered into Judas who was called Iscariot, who belonged to the number of the twelve *[the apostles]*. And he went away and discussed with the chief priests and officers how he might betray him to them.' (Luke 22:3-4).

The earth opening and swallowing somebody is a reference to Korah's rebellion in the Old Testament book of Numbers. [xl] The 'devil' theme continues. 'He reached too high, was thrown back to the ground' is a reference to the book of Isaiah and also to Revelation (12:9 - 'The great dragon was hurled down - that ancient serpent called the devil or Satan, who leads the whole world astray. He was hurled to the earth and his angels with him.') The reference is to the fate of the angel Lucifer, who

---

[xl] See page 39

fell from heaven following his act of deliberate rebellion, bring many similar 'fallen angels' (demons) with him. [xli]

Whereas the first verse speaks of the devil, his history and his works, the second switches direction to address Christ. Dylan has heard that he has 'a brother named James, don't forget faces or names.' As the Apostle Paul wrote: 'I did not see any other of the apostles except James, the Lord's brother.' (Galatians 1:19). The person the verse describes has blood that is 'mixed' (divine and human); the trauma and sleeplessness in the garden of Gethsemane and the (illegal) night-time trial and subsequent beatings have left Christ's face haggard and 'sunken' with pain, loss of blood and lack of sleep. He is then described as looking directly into 'the sun'. The gospel's record that Christ's death coincided with a solar eclipse (when it is possible to look directly at the obscured sun). 'It was now about the sixth hour, and darkness fell over the whole land until the ninth hour, because the sun was obscured; and the veil of the temple was torn in two. And Jesus, crying out with a loud voice, said, "Father, into your hands I commit my Spirit." Having said this, he breathed his last.' (Luke 23:44-46).

'Revenge is mine' may be a reference to the prophet Jeremiah. 'For that day belongs to the Lord God of hosts, a day of vengeance, so as to avenge himself on his foes.' (Jeremiah 46:10). Dylan then remarks that 'drinks can be fixed'. When Jesus was crucified 'they brought him to the place Golgotha, which is translated, 'Place of a Skull'. They tried to give him wine mixed with myrrh *[which had anaesthetic properties, hence 'fixed']*; but he did not take it.' (Mark 15:22-23).

Dylan then comments on the times we live in, ('Conformity's in fashion'), for example, the type of political correctness that says that

---

[xli] Isaiah 14:12-15: 'How you have fallen from heaven, O star of the morning, son of the dawn! You have been cut down to the earth, you who have weakened the nations! But you said in your heart, "I will ascend to heaven; I will raise my throne above the stars of God, and I will sit on the mount of assembly, in the recesses of the north. I will ascend above the heights of the clouds; I will make myself like the Most High." Nevertheless you will be thrust down to Sheol, to the recesses of the pit.'

'compassion' can be preached but not practiced; people may be left in their state of sin because others do not wish to be 'judgemental'. He challenges his audience to 'say one more stupid thing to me before the final nail is driven in'; another crucifixion reference. The song then reverts from Christ back to describing the devil; 'a retired businessman named Red'. The book of Revelation (12:3) comments, 'Then another sign appeared in heaven: and behold, a great red dragon having seven heads and ten horns, and on his heads were seven diadems.' The devil has been 'cast down from heaven'. 'How you have fallen from heaven, O morning star, son of the dawn! You have been cast down to the earth, you who once laid low the nations!' (Isaiah 14:12, ANIV).

Satan will use anything he can for his own purposes of mindless destruction ('sells tickets to a plane crash'). Dylan follows this up with a reference to the notorious Delilah of the book of Judges (chapter 16); she played a part in the downfall of the Hebrew judge, Samson. [xlii] Delilah stands for deception and betrayal; the Philistines being traditionally enemies of God's people Israel. She will certainly affect your 'fate' if you let her, and lead you astray, as (sexually and treacherously) she did with Samson. Dylan's line is 'spice buns in your bed'. This is fine, unless you happen to prefer not to sleep 'with your head face down in a grave'!

The devil is quite happy to use the 'beautiful people' to be a 'terror' to us. The fact that they have ''Mystery' written all over their forehead' is a

---

[xlii] Judges 16:18-21: 'When Delilah saw that he had told her all that was in his heart, she sent and called the lords of the Philistines, saying, "Come up once more, for he has told me all that is in his heart." Then the lords of the Philistines came up to her and brought the money in their hands. She made him sleep on her knees, and called for a man and had him shave off the seven locks of his hair. Then she began to afflict him, and his strength left him. She said, "The Philistines are upon you, Samson!" And he awoke from his sleep and said, "I will go out as at other times and shake myself free." But he did not know that the Lord had departed from him. Then the Philistines seized him and gouged out his eyes; and they brought him down to Gaza and bound him with bronze chains, and he was a grinder in the prison.'

sign that they are under the devil's influence, with his power to subdue our resistance and so try to control behaviour in just the same way that they accuse 'religion' or 'God' of doing, but to their own negative ends. This line (''Mystery' on the forehead') is another reference to the book of Revelation and the vision it describes of an adorned but evil woman sitting on the beast. ('On her forehead a name was written, 'Mystery, Babylon the Great, the Mother of Harlots and of the Abominations of the Earth'.) These beautiful people quote Billy Joel ('Only The Good Die Young'), and (still worse) commit infanticide ('kill babies'). They have no use for 'mercy', and will not accept any judgements or criticism of themselves. They can make you become 'anything that they want you to be', manipulating and using others for their own purposes.

The last verse of the song reverts again to describing Christ. Dylan sings that he 'loved him too', and can 'see him in his mind climbing that hill', surely of Calvary, the place of crucifixion, 'where he made it to the top, and dropped.' Christ was 'struck down' in accordance with God's will, as the Hebrew prophet Isaiah had foretold some 750 years earlier. [xliii]

So what is left? Only the 'dust of a plague'; a plague of sin and the 'fear' of impending judgement that will follow unless forgiveness is received into our lives in trust in God's provision of Jesus' sacrifice at Calvary. 'Let the dead bury the dead' is a quotation from the gospel of Matthew (8:22), something that Jesus said to a man who wished to delay indefinitely following him. The good news is that Jesus 'raised the shade'; this being the place of Sheol (Hebrew for 'shadow'), where the Hebrews believed the dead resided before the final judgement. Christ's death opened up Sheol.

Another absolute classic from this period surfaced on 'The Bootleg Series Volumes 1-3'. 'Blind Willie McTell' (another 'Infidels' outtake from 1983) is a sheer masterpiece of poetry and poignancy. The song is

---

[xliii] Isaiah 53:4-5: 'Surely our griefs he himself bore, and our sorrows he carried; yet we ourselves esteemed him stricken, smitten of God, and afflicted. But he was pierced through for our transgressions, he was crushed for our iniquities; the chastening for our well-being fell upon him, and by his scourging we are healed.'

named after one William McTear (born in Thomson, Georgia, May 5, 1901, died August 15, 1959), a blues singer and twelve-string guitarist. The track stands as a lament against the futility of life lived in a state of rebellion or indifference to God; a disposition that the Bible calls 'sin'. Sin is described in scripture as a form of spiritual slavery, every bit as real as plantation labour or the chain gang road crews the song depicts. As in 'Caribbean Wind', Dylan takes slavery and portrays it as a state of bondage approximated to men and women's spiritual condition when separated from a life-giving relationship with God.

Tramping hobos would traditionally leave signs signifying something useful to those who came after them in their travels. The song opens describing one; an 'arrow' drawn on a house doorframe. To those with the eyes to see and understand it (fellow hobos) its message is that the surrounding country is 'condemned'; presumably under God's curse. In the language of the Old Testament Bible, to 'condemn' an area of land was to impose a fine or penalty upon its inhabitants for an act of rebellion. [xliv] Dylan describes the land as being under condemnation. As the Apostle John said (1 John 5:19), 'The whole world lies in the power of the evil one', in other words, under his direct influence.

Dylan sings that this is true all the way from the slave town of 'New Orleans, to Jerusalem', or as he would very tellingly sing in concert, 'to new Jerusalem', thus completing the spiritual imagery. As the book of Revelation (3:12) records Jesus as saying, 'He who overcomes, I will make him a pillar in the temple of my God, and he will not go out from it anymore; and I will write on him the name of my God, and the name of the city of my God, the new Jerusalem, which comes down out of heaven from my God.'

[xliv] For example, 'Jehoahaz was twenty and three years old when he began to reign, and he reigned three months in Jerusalem. And the king of Egypt put him down at Jerusalem, and condemned the land in an hundred talents of silver and a talent of gold [tax, as an act of judgement]. And the king of Egypt made Eliakim his brother king over Judah and Jerusalem, and turned his name to Jehoiakim. And Necho took Jehoahaz his brother, and carried him to Egypt.' (2 Chronicles 36:2-4, KJV).

'Martyrs' falling in East Texas may refer to the many African slaves who worked and died in the plantations there; it may also stand for Dylan's fellow Messianic Jewish and musician friend Keith Green who died with family members in a plane crash there in July 1982. 'Martyr' is the Greek word for 'witness'; someone who tells what they have heard and seen. 'The blues' then stand for a song of lament to God for our poor spiritual condition. The next verse describes a carnival, part of the mid-West rural tradition that Dylan would have had exposure to growing up in the days before TV helped undo the more traditional forms of entertainment. The trees around are 'barren', reflecting the same condemnation that the land is under; no one is bothering to listen to the 'hoot owl' singing its mournful tones; possibly no one is listening to God's message either.

Dylan's mind can picture the large Southern 'plantations', made profitable by Negro slave labour 'burning' (more judgement); and he can hear the sound of 'whips'. Slavery is still alive and well and is called sin. Indeed, he can 'see the ghosts of slavery ships' - the ships that brought the African slaves to the southern states of America. Their 'tribes' can be heard 'moaning' under the cruelty of their affliction, along with the sound of the 'undertaker's bell' ringing for their dead. Meanwhile, down at the riverbank, a 'fine young handsome man' stands clothed after the manner of a land owning 'squire'. No English gentleman this; he is drinking 'bootlegged whiskey' as he surveys his plantation's ill-gotten gains. Dylan then hears another type of slave labour, this time a 'chain gang' of convicts out building roads; the links of chains that bind them being a scriptural metaphor for sin.

Dylan concludes by reflecting that while 'God is in his heaven', the problem is that mankind is after getting what is God's; usurping his power and authority for their own ends, such that all they end up with is 'power and greed and corruptible seed' - mankind gone wrong under sin and Satan's influence. As the Apostle Peter wrote, 'Seeing you have purified your souls in obeying the truth through the Spirit unto unfeigned love of the brethren, see that you love one another with a pure heart fervently; being born again, not of *corruptible seed, but of incorruptible,* by the word of God, which liveth and abideth for ever.' (1 Peter 1:22-23, KJV, *italics mine*).

The melody for 'Blind Willie McTell' appears to have been based in part upon a traditional folk piece entitled 'The St James Infirmary Blues'. This was itself based on the traditional English folk song called 'The Unfortunate Rake', a sad song about a sailor who dies of a venereal disease. It was fitting therefore that Dylan closed his reflections about the spiritual and physical consequences of sin 'gazing out the window of the St James Hotel'. Maybe a spiritual infirmary was needed after all. McTell himself wrote many faith-based songs; for example, 'Ain't It Grand To Be A Christian' (1935) and 'Lord Have Mercy, If You Please.' (1949).

The last song on 'The Bootleg Series Volumes 1-3' written post-1983 was 'Series Of Dreams', an 'Oh Mercy' outtake from March 23, 1989. Producer Daniel Lanois, wrote Dylan (in Chronicles Volume 1), "Liked the song... *[but]* liked the bridge better; and wanted the whole song to be like that. I knew what he meant, but it just couldn't be done. Though I thought about it for a second, thinking that I could probably start with the bridge as the main part and use the main part as the bridge... the idea didn't amount to much and thinking about the song this way wasn't healthy. I felt like it was fine the way it was; I didn't want to lose myself in thinking too much about changing it."

The song has a haunting, whimsical quality to it; things are 'wounded', coming 'to a permanent stop'. There is an 'exit', but it cannot be 'seen with the eyes'. The only 'cards' that are worth 'holding' come 'from another world'; presumably a spiritual world with which Dylan seems very familiar.

The year 1994 saw the release of another 'Greatest Hits' album, this one being 'Volume 3'. It was possibly an attempt by Columbia Records to profit one more time from their departing prodigy. (The following year Sony released another 'Best Of' album, 'MTV Unplugged', a collection of hits recorded 'live' in studio.) This particular offering contained one song from the post-1983 period, that being 'Dignity', an outtake from the 1989 'Oh Mercy' album.

The song was inspired by Dylan hearing of the death of US basketball legend 'Pistol' Pete Maravich, on January 5th 1988, aged 40. Maravich, forced to stop playing by a recurring knee injury, had arrived at a personal faith in Christ having gone through yoga, transcendental meditation and Hinduism, in a fruitless search for peace and freedom from alcoholism. He was widely quoted as saying he wanted to be remembered as a Christian rather than as a basketball player. [62] Dylan later wrote in his autobiography 'Chronicles Volume 1': "My aunt was in the kitchen and I sat down with her to talk and drink coffee. The radio was playing and the morning news was on. I was startled to hear that Pete Maravich, the basketball player, had collapsed on a basketball court in Pasadena; just fell over and never got up. I'd seen Maravich play in New Orleans, when the Utah Jazz were the New Orleans Jazz. He was something to see - mop of brown hair, floppy socks - the holy terror of the basketball world - high flyin' - magician of the court. The night I saw him he dribbled the ball with his head, scored a behind-the-back, no-look basket; dribbled the length of the court, threw the ball up over the glass and caught his own pass. He was fantastic. Scored something like 38 points. He could have played blind. I started and completed the song 'Dignity' the same day I'd heard the sad news about Pistol Pete. I started writing it in the early afternoon, about the time the morning news began to wear away and it took me the rest of the day and into the night to finish it."

And no wonder; the song is long and contains a huge variety of images that describe what 'Pistol' Pete had spent his life searching for, and had eventually found, in the life of a Nazarene teacher from first century Judea. Dignity is the state of being that is inherently worthy of esteem, and that can be respected because of inbuilt qualities of nobility and worth. From a scriptural perspective, this ultimately come from having been created, as the Bible puts it, in God's own image and likeness.

'Dignity' opens with a brutal comparison of two men, one 'thin' and one 'fat'. The former is facing his final meal, the latter is seeing his reflection in a 'blade', that is possibly about to be utilised in the former's execution. Next come the 'wise', the 'young' and the 'poor', all of whom are engaged in a relentless search for dignity; for a sense of their own meaning and self-worth amidst life's bigger picture. The poor man is looking 'through painted glass' (presumably therefore in a church setting) for dignity. Some of Dylan's other versions of the song liken dignity to various types of women and to the movement of a tropical wind.

Then there is a murder, and the song's search briefly becomes a detective hunt. Someone has been killed, and dignity was allegedly the 'first to leave'. (On the album 'Tell Tale Signs', Dylan puts it as 'last to leave'.) Man's depravity has apparently forced dignity out of the picture. The 'blind' are depicted as looking for dignity in 'the pockets of chance', a classically Dylanesque line; this leads into a verse about a wedding where Dylan's enquiry leads to the bride telling him that she could 'get killed' if she told him 'what she knew about dignity'.

Thus stonewalled, Dylan diverts to the place that 'vultures feed' (presumably the place of the dead); and finds that he has gone deep enough to find what he wants, where there are 'tongues of angels and men'. This is a direct quotation from St Paul's first letter to the Corinthians (13:1). 'If I speak with the tongues of men and of angels, but do not have love, I have become a noisy gong or a clanging cymbal.' To Dylan there is nothing to choose between them, indicating that neither has love, or that he is able to understand both; to him they have 'no difference'. The scene deteriorates with pictures of 'fire' and 'debts unpaid', then a bar-room scene where the mirrors are 'covered' and where the drinkers are trying to recover 'lost forgotten years' where, once upon a time, dignity dwelled.

Next comes an esoteric reference to a meeting with the British Queen Elizabeth II's husband Prince Philip, (or else someone with that nickname), who offers news of dignity if Dylan can give some 'money up front'. The idea of Prince Philip, a notoriously rude man, saying that he was being 'abused by dignity' is surely an enormous joke, and rather a good one at that. The detective imagery of 'footprints' leading downward to 'tattoo land' where Dylan meets some 'sons of darkness and light', is again classically Dylanesque. It is a quotation regarding the second coming of Christ, from St Paul's first letter to the Thessalonians (5:4-5). 'But you, brethren, are not in darkness, that the day would overtake you like a thief; for you are all sons of light and sons of day. We are not of night, nor of darkness.'

The song then progresses through a type of dream, where Dylan has nowhere to hide, and is coat-less in a 'boat' attempting to read a 'note' about dignity, then into a doctor's clinic where the search for the elusive character trait moves from palm reading to classic literature. It then switches to describing an unidentified 'stranded Englishman' biting the bullet, no doubt complete with courage and stiff upper lip, looking inside himself for dignity. Dylan then heads via the 'red' and the 'black' to 'the valley of dry bone dreams', another biblical reference, this time from the Old Testament prophet Ezekiel. 'The hand of the Lord was upon me, and he brought me out by the Spirit of the Lord, and set me down in the midst of the valley which was full of bones, and caused me to pass by them round about: and, behold, there were very many in the open valley; and lo, they were very dry. And he said unto me, "Son of man, can these bones live?" And I answered, "O Lord God, thou knowest." Again he said unto me, "Prophesy upon these bones..."' (Ezekiel 37:1-4, KJV).

The line, 'So many roads, so much at stake', has a distinctly biblical ring to it, where eternity in heaven or hell depends on whether it is the broad road or the narrow road that is taken. As Jesus said, "Enter through the narrow gate; for the gate is wide and the way is broad that leads to destruction, and there are many who enter through it. For the gate is small and the way is narrow that leads to life, and there are few who find it." (Matthew 7:13-14). There are 'so many dead ends' that Dylan is left wondering 'what it's gonna take to find dignity'. For 'Pistol' Pete Maravich, it took a career ending injury, and a journey through alcoholism and Eastern religion, before he found the dignity that Christ offers through faith and trust in him. Dylan often writes songs involving people of faith (Patton, Keys, Lewis...). Maravich is clearly in good company.

Chapter 11

'Time Out Of Mind'

'Time Out Of Mind', a synonym for 'time beyond memory', or 'time immemorial' was released in 1997, 7 years after the previous album of original material ('Under The Red Sky'). What all the critics and reviewers missed was the inference in adding a possessive article - time 'out of **my** mind' would sum up the reason for the intervening period's state of creative drought. One very good reason for his creativity drying up may have been the final dissolution in 1992 of his marriage to Carolyn Dennis. Filed in 1990 (the year of release of 'Under the Red Sky' with its nursery rhyme songs and cover-sleeve dedication reference to their young daughter Gabrielle), the years of pain seem to have taken a heavy emotional toll on Dylan's mental well-being.

'Time Out Of Mind' provides evidence of the emotional distress associated with the couple's parting. Only someone who has experienced new spiritual life as a Christian and then been divorced by his Christian wife can know what that feels like, especially when they have a young child. These personal circumstances were not publically known at the time of the album's release. Christians understand that 'God hates divorce' (Malachi 2:16), and self-questioning and recriminations are somewhat inevitable psychological consequences.

The album's content is loaded with depressive language, well recognizable to any physician who works with clinical depression. Every single one of the album's eleven songs contains some language symptomatic of moderate to severe depression. There are other themes too, but when listed consecutively, the prevailing mood is crystal clear.

'Sometimes I feel like I'm being plowed under' - 'Love Sick'.

'I've been pacing around the room hoping maybe she'd come back... I'm gonna have to put up a barrier to keep myself away from everyone' - 'Dirt Road Blues'.

'You left me standing in the doorway crying, I got nothing to go back to now... Sick in the head... All the laughter is just making me sad... Suffering like a fool... 'You left me standing in the doorway crying, blues wrapped around my head' - 'Standing In The Doorway'.

'I keep asking myself how long it can go on like this... You left me standing out in the cold... Feel like talking to somebody but I just don't know who... There's voices in the night trying to be heard, I'm sitting here listening to every mind-polluting word' - 'Million Miles'.

'You broke a heart that loved you... I've been walking that lonesome valley... I'm just going down the road feeling bad... They tell me everything is gonna be all right but I don't know what 'all right' even means... I'll close my eyes and I wonder if everything is as hollow as it seems' - 'Tryin' To Get To Heaven'.

'My nerves are exploding and my body's tense... I feel like I'm coming to the end of my way... My eyes feel like they're falling off my face... I'm tired of talking; I'm tired of trying to explain' - 'Till I Fell In Love With You'.

'Feel like my soul has turned into steel... I just don't see why I should even care... Sometimes my burden seems more than I can bear... Every nerve in my body is so vacant and numb' - 'Not Dark Yet'.

'I'm beginning to hear voices, and there's no one around... I'm all used up... It's almost like I don't exist... It's sadder still to feel your heart torn away... I thought some of 'em were friends of mine, I was wrong about 'em all... You can't see in and it's hard lookin' out... I'm twenty miles out of town in cold irons bound' - 'Cold Irons Bound'.

'The storms are raging on the highway of regret' - 'Make You Feel My Love'.

'Your loveliness has wounded me; I'm reeling from the blow... Skies are grey, I'm looking for anything that will bring a happy glow... That's how it is when things disintegrate... I'm strolling through the lonely graveyard of my mind' - 'Can't Wait'.

'I'm gonna go there when I feel good enough to go... Same ol' rat race, life in the same ol' cage... Feel like a prisoner in a world of mystery... Insanity is smashing up against my soul, you could say I was on anything but a roll... Feel further away than ever before... I'd trade places with any of them in a minute if I could... Everything looks far away' - 'Highlands'.

Hyperacusis (exceptionally sensitive hearing) is a sign of severe depression. [63] Dylan can hear 'the clock tick'; even hear people's 'hearts beating'. Equally he is 'beginning to hear voices when no one is around'; the words he hears are 'mind polluting'. All real artists suffer for their creativity to some degree ('behind every beautiful thing there's been some kind of pain' - 'Not Dark Yet'). It is to be hoped that someone close to Dylan at the time was able to offer some kind of real help. Carolyn Dennis filed for divorce on August 7 1990; [64] the ten years until the more up-beat and even jokey material of 'Love And Theft' (September 2001) is a long time for anyone to be in severe emotional and mental pain.

The 'Time Out Of Mind' sessions also contained other material released later on 'Tell Tale Signs'. These tracks tell a similar story. For example, 'Feel further away than I ever did before, feel further than I can take... it's driving me insane.' ('Dreamin' Of You'). 'Lord have mercy - feel heavy like lead. I've been hit too hard...' ('Marchin' To The City'). Severe depression is associated with muscle pain and fatigue; the limbs feel 'heavy', 'like lead', as Dylan says.

Of the album as a whole Dylan said, "Environment affects me a great deal. A lot of the songs were written after the sun went down. And I like storms; I like to stay up during a storm. I get very meditative sometimes, and this one phrase was going through my head: 'Work while the day lasts, because the night of death cometh when no man can work.' I don't recall where I heard it. I like preaching, I hear a lot of preaching, and I probably just heard it somewhere. Maybe it's in Psalms, it beats me. But it wouldn't let me go. I was, like, what does that phrase mean? But it was at the forefront of my mind, for a long period of time, and I think a lot of that is instilled into this record." [65] The quote is a paraphrase of Jesus' words: 'I must work the works of him that sent me while it is day; the night cometh, when no man can work.' (John 9:4, KJV). Dylan listens to 'a lot of preaching', and is clearly very familiar with scripture.

'Time Out Of Mind' was another collaborative effort with producer Daniel Lanois ('Oh Mercy') and was a huge critical success, winning three Grammy awards including being the 1998 Album of the Year. It was widely regarded as being somewhat 'sad' or 'dark'. Clinical depression does not seem to have been on the critics' radar; Dylan's marriage to Carolyn Dennis and subsequent divorce was still a well-kept secret.

The reviewers failed also to recognise the spiritual nature of some of the songs and their interpretations certainly did not sit well with Dylan. In a 'Rolling Stone' interview in September 2001, Dylan said, 'People say the record deals with mortality - my mortality for some reason. Well it doesn't deal with my mortality. It just deals with mortality in general. It's one thing we all have in common, isn't it? But I didn't see any one critic say; "It deals with my mortality" - you know, his own. As if he's immune in some kind of way - like whoever's writing about the record has got eternal life and the singer doesn't. I found this condescending attitude toward that record revealed in the press quite frequently, but, you know, nothing you can do about that." The comment about 'eternal life' is a telling one, as this chapter will show.

The opening number, 'Love Sick' must rank as one of Dylan's best but most misunderstood songs. No reviewer or commentator seems to have recognised the lyric, yet it is based on direct quotations from the love story recounted in the 'Song of Solomon' (aka 'Songs of Songs') in the Old Testament. This relates in romantic, even erotic, tones King Solomon's wooing of and marriage to a Shunammite woman. He is not sick and tired of love; rather he is sick with ('of') love, in other words, love-sick, as he in fact says in the second chorus. Love-sick with whom? His second wife whose divorce he is starting to come to terms with? Or with someone of an altogether higher nature and being? Dylan's song draws together this great passage about God's love with the greatest from the New Testament (1 Corinthians 13). It is an honest song about a disciple trying to come to terms with the enormity of God's love for him personally, and for everyone else. The song opens with him walking in the rain through 'dead' streets, presumably meaning spiritually dead. As he walks, he is aware that a third person ('you') is in his head, presumably God, who is speaking to him. His feet are 'so tired', yet the spiritual energy inside his skull means that his 'brain is so wired'. He has a spiritual sensitivity that comes from the Holy Spirit, and seems aware of it when someone is lying or crying; very little evades him.

The next line, 'I spoke like a child' is a direct quotation from St Paul's first letter to the Corinthians (13:11-13). 'When I was a child, I spoke like a child, thought like a child, reasoned like a child; when I became a man, I did away with childish things. For now we see in a mirror dimly, but then face to face; now I know in part, but then I will know fully just as I also have been fully known. But now faith, hope, love, abide these three; but the greatest of these is love.' This love appears to have 'destroyed' Dylan simply with 'a smile' (reminiscent of a later song 'Cry Awhile' - 'All you gave me was a smile'). This happened while he 'was sleeping' indicating that, if not already apparent, he is not speaking of human emotional or romantic love. There is no working or striving involved. All he needed to do was to accept God's love for him.

The Old Testament prophet Joel describes what will happen when God's Holy Spirit is poured out over his people (which occurred at the Feast of Pentecost as described in Acts chapter 2). 'It will come about after this, that I will pour out my Spirit on all mankind; and your sons and daughters will prophesy, your old men will dream dreams, your young men will see visions.' (Joel 2:28). Dylan's 'sleeping' implies that this revelation of what was presumably God smiling upon him came in a dream; something older men of faith can expect to experience.

'I'm sick of love' is also a direct quotation from the Song of Solomon (3:5), meaning 'love-sick', not sick and tired of love. Verses 3-7 (KJV) read, 'As the apple tree among the trees of the wood, so is my beloved among the sons. I sat down under his shadow with great delight, and his fruit was sweet to my taste. He brought me to the banqueting house, and his banner over me was love. Stay me with flagons, comfort me with apples: for I am sick of love. His left hand is under my head, and his right hand doth embrace me. I charge you, O ye daughters of Jerusalem, by the roes, and by the hinds of the field, that ye stir not up, nor awake my love, till he please.' There then follows a vision of 'lovers in the meadow' because this is where King Solomon walks with his beloved (7:11), who stands figuratively for the people of God: 'Come, my beloved, let us go forth into the field.' (7:11, KJV). In chapter 2 verse 3, the beloved sits under her lover's shadow, and at the end of the verse that is what Dylan is left hanging onto.

Dylan seems caught up in love for God and a depth of appreciation of God's love for him. He is 'love-sick'; a helpful clarification for those reviewers who say he is expressing that he is somehow tired of love. Dylan meditates on this love and asks himself (rhetorically) if it is what he thinks it is, because it seems too good to be true. He has been experiencing it for over 20 years now and there is no sign of it abating. Dylan 'thinks of', i.e. meditates on God, and 'wonders', as in awe and wonder, because he knows that this depth of God's love towards him really is true.

He just 'doesn't know what to do', but the song culminates with a wonderful expression of the love that he feels - he'd 'give anything' to be with 'you' (presumably God, the one who has been true to him). Soon afterwards Dylan went from this expression of faith to a hospital bed and a near-death experience with a rare form of fungal pericarditis. It may have been this brush with death that brought the spiritually beautiful gospel-folk song 'Hallelujah, I'm Ready To Go' into Dylan's stage show, first performed in June 1999. 'Hallelujah, I'm ready… I can hear the voices singing soft and low… Dark was the night, not a star was in sight, a highway heading down below. I let my Saviour in and he saved my soul from sin. Hallelujah, I'm ready to go. Sinner don't wait before it's too late, he's a wonderful Saviour to know…' There can surely be no doubt as to where Dylan's trust lies; he is ready to go and stand before his 'Saviour'.

'Dirt Road Blues' is the second track on 'Time Out Of Mind'. The song appears to describe life as a long journey with God. The good news is that though we have to walk, he walks alongside us and will even carry us if necessary. 'Walking' is scriptural language for living daily life. 'This I say, and affirm together with the Lord, that you walk no longer just as the Gentiles also walk, in the futility of their mind, being darkened in their understanding, excluded from the life of God because of the ignorance that is in them, because of the hardness of their heart.' (Ephesians 4:17-19). Like the prophet Elijah, Dylan will walk until someone comes to collect him for the ride home to heaven. [xlv]

The song also appears to touch on the pain of Dylan's divorce from his second wife. Dylan hopes that someone referred to as 'she' will come back. He is 'praying for salvation', which is an ongoing process with a beginning, a middle and an end, and continues until death. Dylan will keep on with his 'walk' until 'the chains' are 'shattered' and he experiences the ultimate freedom ('I've been freed'), presumably meaning in the next life in the Kingdom of Heaven. There, all will experience complete freedom from sin. 'Jesus answered them, "Truly, truly, I say to you, everyone who commits sin is the slave of sin. The slave does not remain in the house forever; the son does remain forever. So, if the Son makes you free, you will be free indeed."' (John 8:34-36).

Dylan has 'been watching the colours up above', in other words in the heavens. As the Hebrew prophet Isaiah said, 'Who is this who comes from Edom, with garments of glowing colours from Bozrah, this one who is majestic in his apparel, marching in the greatness of his strength? "It is I who speak in righteousness, mighty to save."' (Isaiah 63:1).

[xlv] 2 Kings 2:9-12: 'When they had crossed over, Elijah said to Elisha, "Ask what I shall do for you before I am taken from you." And Elisha said, "Please, let a double portion of your spirit be upon me." He said, "You have asked a hard thing. Nevertheless, if you see me when I am taken from you, it shall be so for you; but if not, it shall not be so." As they were going along and talking, behold, there appeared a chariot of fire and horses of fire which separated the two of them. And Elijah went up by a whirlwind to heaven. Elisha saw it and cried out, "My father, my father, the chariots of Israel and its horsemen!" And he saw Elijah no more.'

At the end of the 'dirt road', he will be 'right beside the sun'. Psalm 84:11 tells us that 'the Lord God is a sun and shield; the Lord gives grace and glory.' As he would later sing on 'Thunder On The Mountain', 'Some sweet day I'll stand beside my king' - by his throne in heaven.

The song 'Standing In The Doorway' also seems to recount the pain emanating from the divorce from his Christian wife Carolyn. This was likely to have been exacerbated by the fact that both Christians and Jews understand that marriage is supposed to be for life. The track seems to describe how he was trying to hang on to a faith perspective ('God's mercy') despite all the grief he is suffering. The 'jukebox' in the background carries the sense of old melodies being evocative of past memories. Things are now at a pace that seems 'too slow'; Dylan has nowhere to go. The sense is that he is at the end of his tether, with 'nothing left to burn'. He seems to be emotionally spent, and his feelings towards the lady of the song are mixed; his heart is on his sleeve with the ambivalence of whether he wants to 'kiss' her or to 'kill' her. Because Dylan has been left behind feeling sad, 'standing in the doorway, crying.'

The gloom of the song is summed up beautifully by the concept of its 'bad light' that is causing Dylan to feel 'sick'; he can't see clearly and he doesn't feel right, just 'sad'. He is depressed alright, ('sick in the head'), and even playing on his guitar doesn't lift his spirits. He is still haunted by the phantom of their 'old love'. He could say things in his defense but he is not going to bother trying to fight his corner, reassuringly, he is aware that the 'mercy of God must be near', as St Paul had said. [xlvi] The Bible promises that all can 'come boldly to God's throne of grace and may obtain mercy, and find grace *[unearned favour from God]* to help in time of need.' (Hebrews 4:16).

[xlvi] Ephesians 2:4-7: 'God, being rich in mercy, because of his great love with which he loved us, even when we were dead in our transgressions, made us alive together with Christ - it is by grace you have been saved. And God raised us up with him, and seated us with him in the heavenly places in Christ Jesus, so that in the ages to come he might show the surpassing riches of his grace in kindness toward us in Christ Jesus.'

The line about 'flesh falling off of my face', but still knowing that 'someone will be there to care', is reminiscent of the Old Testament book of Job (19:25-27). 'As for me, I know that my Redeemer lives, and at the last he will take his stand on the earth. Even after my skin is destroyed, yet from my flesh I shall see God; whom I myself shall behold, and whom my eyes will see and not another.' Being left 'Crying, blues wrapped around my head', sums up a severe state of depression; but nevertheless he is still hanging on to his faith.

The pain of the divorce from Carolyn Dennis seems still to be taking its toll on Dylan emotionally in 'Million Miles'. 'You' (probably meaning Carolyn) have gone away with something of Dylan's that he says he greatly misses; presumably part of his heart, but also surely their young daughter Gabrielle. He asks himself how long the situation, with its attendant emotional pain, can go on for, noting that while she 'told herself a lie', he did the same thing to himself. Perhaps what occurred seemed like the right thing to do. If so, it appears that his emotions seem to have been spending a long time telling him the opposite. He is 'trying to get closer', but is still a very long way off.

Dylan's divorce settlement was presumably generous; she did indeed take away 'silver' and 'gold', but it has still left him 'in the cold' emotionally and that is always going to effect the creative side of an artist of such sensitivity. When 'people ask' him about her, he doesn't 'tell them everything' that he could, because he is using his discretion in order to protect her reputation. For a Christian, speaking against someone is defined as slander; even if the negative things being said have some truth to them. The Bible teaches that it is wrong to wound someone's reputation in the eyes of others.

Dylan is burying his 'memories' of her in a 'deep ditch', and appears to be regretting some of his past actions (actions that he did not 'intend to do', but which might have contributed to their break-up). He still badly 'needs' her love, especially as it seems to sustain him in the 'places' that his work takes him. His giving of himself creatively is surely a very draining experience both emotionally and physically. Not daring to 'close his eyes', lest he misses something he needs to know to help him comprehend matters, he hopes that he will be better off 'in the next life'. In heaven, he will have the time and ability to be in touch with his thoughts in a better way.

The comment on their parting that she was going to 'find a janitor to sweep her off her feet' is telling, witty and painful all at the same time. Dylan's gruelling touring and recording schedule must have taken its toll on the relationship given their infant daughter's needs, and the demands of motherhood upon his new wife. It can't have been easy for either of them. Dylan's brave (yet humourous) optimism shines through with the African-American title of 'Mama' that reassures her that she can do whatever she has to do. Dylan is being troubled by 'voices in the night', but seems to know that they are not God's voice; the 'mind polluting' things he hears just leave him in an unhappy and depressed state of self-pity. He has many good friends who would accommodate him, but really what he wants to do is 'get closer' to 'you' - the one he loved then lost or perhaps even the one that had made them both.

'Tryin' To Get To Heaven' continues the theme of tired self-reflection; the heat and noise of thunder that Dylan describes indicates that there is a storm on the way. The state of the 'high muddy' flood water raises the question of whether the river's levees are going to stand up to it. Day by day the 'memory' of his ex-wife fades; what she meant to him is not as 'haunting' now, but still Dylan seems to be going 'nowhere', attempting to reach 'heaven' before the gates shut and it is too late. Jesus had said: 'Strive to enter through the narrow door; for many, I tell you, will seek to enter and will not be able. Once the head of the house gets up and shuts the door, and you begin to stand outside and knock on the door, saying, "Lord, open up to us!" Then he will answer and say to you, "I do not know where you are from."' (Luke 13:23-25). Not a pleasant reflection; 'heaven's door' seems again to be on Dylan's mind. He may have not succeeded in his marriage, but that fades into less significance when compared to life's greater journey.

Dylan appears to have been harassed by people who would not 'let him be'. He has a 'broken heart' and he needs time to heal up. It may be all right for his ex-wife to 'not write anymore', but his creative journey is not yet at its end. That journey may indeed have brought him into a 'lonesome valley', but his heavenward journey carries on while the 'door' is still open.

Trains are a frequent theme in Dylan's compositions, and the sight of fellow-travellers waiting on their trains' arrival causes him to be aware of their heartbeat as well as his own. This can come from a heightened state of spiritual sensitivity. He reflects that he seems to have 'lost everything' that was important to him (his wife and their child); he must keep his eye on the main goal of life (heaven) if he is not to lose that as well. In the meantime he will keep on walking, while 'feeling bad'.

Empty platitudes of reassurance ('everything is going to be alright') don't work; he is not sure whether he is even clear what 'all right' actually means anymore, he feels so low in himself. Life seems to be 'hollow', and without God it most certainly is. Shaking 'sugar down' may be a reference to the folk/blues singer Elizabeth Cotton song 'Shake Sugaree' that was an outtake from the 'Time Out Of Mind' sessions, or possibly a reference to 'Shake The Sugar Tree' by Pam Tillis. ("I'll shake the sugar tree 'til I feel your love fallin' all around me.") If so it is love that Dylan still, like all of us, seems to need.

''Til I Fell In Love With You' continues in this vein; reflecting on his feelings for a woman he loved but who left him, but apparently at the same time on the God who has never left him. The song opens by describing a state of mental anguish, with nerves 'exploding' amidst a general state of acute tension, even to the point of feeling being 'pinned' to the 'fence' by nothing less than the 'whole world'. Everyone it seems is against him; he is experiencing being 'hit too hard'. Only 'your touch' can heal him now. But whose touch is it? The woman's, who has left him, or God's? Dylan is at a loss to know what to do. He was 'all right' until something called love happened.

Part of him seems to be still in love, and hence he is in pain because she has left. Dylan feels as if he is 'coming to the end' of his path, but knows (with the Psalmist) that God is 'his shield' who will not lead him 'astray'. 'But you, O Lord are a shield about me, my glory, and the one who lifts my head. I was crying to the Lord with my voice, and he answered me from his holy mountain.' (Psalm 3:3-4). Dylan's ancient Hebrew patriarch Abraham was similarly told: 'Fear not, I am thy shield and thy exceeding great reward.' (Genesis 15:1, KJV).

When Dylan has gone, we are told that she 'will remember' his name; it would belong to their child when she came of age. But 'junk' is building up (presumably recriminations are mounting) and Dylan still seems 'downcast' ('staring at the floor') reflecting on the one who wouldn't be coming back. Dylan has tried to 'please', but his efforts came to naught. He is 'Dixie bound', to Delta-blues territory; 'blues' sums up his thoughts, standing metaphorically for a depressed state of mind.

'Not Dark Yet' is a song that stands out as a sign of Dylan's artistic resilience. From a psychological perspective, the lyrics also clearly indicate severe clinical depression. The divorce from Carolyn Dennis took him to a low place emotionally, lower than may have been widely recognised. 'Shadows' and darkness are recurring themes. The opening line communicates a state of weariness and non-accomplishment, diagnostically indicative of depression. Time is being wasted ('running away', like sand in an hour glass). Dylan's soul, he says, has become like 'steel'; the pain he has endured having hardened him emotionally. 'Scars' remain that the 'sun' (or is it 'Son' - the one he still has faith in?) 'didn't heal', (yet, at any rate), and he finds himself feeling emotionally confined without enough space to 'be anywhere'. Darkness is coming, possibly what the sixteenth century Spanish mystic St John of the Cross referred to as the 'dark night of the soul'.

Depression changes one's view of one's own and others' natures in a negative way; for Dylan it is now whirling around in sewage pipework ('down the drain'). Life, even in beauty, seems full of pain. This is another sign of severe depression. The (presumably 'Dear John') letter received from her was no doubt couched 'kindly', but as Dylan recalls it he asks himself whether he really cares either way anymore; again, a feature of depression. He is in pain, and the song communicates this. Dylan has been all over the world, even to the 'bottom', which he has found to be full of deceit, and he has (temporarily anyway) lost his sense of hope and confidence in others, having long since stopped looking for anything positive in 'anyone's eyes'. He says he feels worn out and hung out to dry, his 'burden' of sorrow too much for him to carry.

Dylan's Jewish heritage comes through in the line about being 'born here and I'll die here against my will'. This is a quotation from the Talmud (ancient Jewish rabbinic writings) tractate Pirkei Avot 4:29. Any internal spiritual activity is not being accompanied by externally visible signs; he feels anaesthetized and numbed to sensation, which is the body's defense against chronic emotional pain. He is experiencing loss of concentration and memory (again, features of stress and depression), losing focus even on a spiritual level; unaware even of the 'murmur' of 'prayer'. All he is aware of is impending darkness.

Anyone hoping for a more cheerful theme would have to wait a little longer; the next track 'Cold Irons Bound' provides no let up from the emotional and somewhat spiritual melee of depressive imagery. Still in post-divorce mode, Dylan is emotionally hurting and feels spiritually chained to unhappy memories. In addition to the emotional trauma, there is a spiritual question too - has he broken God's commands? There is nothing like unnecessary condemnation to drag someone down spiritually. The song's title is a reference to Psalm 107 verses 10 and 11: 'Some sat in darkness and the deepest gloom *[the misery of death's shadow]*, prisoners suffering in iron chains, for they had rebelled against the words of God and despised the counsel of the Most High.' 'Bound in iron chains' sums up depression robbing sufferers of the ability to move.

The song opens with 'voices' that Dylan is hearing when he is alone. Are they voices of recrimination or encouragement to press on? He feels spent ('used up') - scorched, like the surrounding countryside. Strangely enough, for someone who was (wrongly) said to have 'renounced' Christianity, he is still attending church; only on this particular Sunday 'she' passed him by. Did he see his ex-wife (a fellow believer) in church? Or was this a memory? Whichever, it is real to him, coming from a love that he is still very definitely experiencing. He feels as if he is wading up to his 'waist' in 'mist', such that it is hard to move or to see clearly spiritually. He feels as if he has ceased to 'exist' - almost as if he has lost his reason for living, a long way from home, and trapped in 'cold irons', feeling like the chained up prisoners of Psalm 107.

But he still has a great deal of spiritual insight, and, most happily of all, the humility to name his problem for what it is related to - 'walls of pride'. The New Testament book of James (4:6) says that God gives grace (unmerited favour) to the humble; Dylan can see 'walls of pride' that are 'high and wide', caging him in a spiritual prison; he 'can't see over to the other side'. He feels trapped, unable to see out, aware of a sense of 'decay' and an almost overwhelming sadness from sensing his 'heart' having been 'torn' away. He still, it seems, has feelings for her; being reminded of her can still cause him to be 'out of control'.

Like all trials, this one has brought to him an awareness of who is genuinely a true friend to him ('I was wrong about 'em all'). This is reminiscent of 'My so-called friends, have all fallen under a spell' ('Precious Angel', from 'Slow Train Coming'). His 'road' now seems full of rocky obstacles. Above him are 'clouds of blood', surely standing for the pain and mental suffering he is experiencing. He thought that he had 'found' himself in her, but now her 'love' has not been 'proved true' (partly because only God's love really does satisfy). If other people's love is unintentionally put in its place, we will always be let down and risk being left feeling abandoned.

Powerful 'winds' have left him 'torn to shreds' and in tatters, feeling like Hercules, who in Greek mythology had to fight the Lernaean Hydra, a many-headed monster that simply grew more when one was cut off. This is how 'reality' seems to Dylan, (it has 'too many heads'). Dealing with the intensely painful types of reality (such as a divorce and separation from your wife and child) often takes 'longer than you think'. Hercules could kill most things (with a bit of help); Dylan however may find it a little harder to erase the things that are troubling him. She is still very much on his mind, but cut off by prison walls that hamper Dylan's vision as much as impeding others' access to him.

The next verse brings the enormously personal line: 'I tried to love and protect you because I cared.' Dylan has every material benefit, but some

156

things, such as the happiness of one's wife and child, cannot be purchased with money. The 'joy they had shared' together will always remain with him, and is now founded upon prayer ('bended knee'). Soon, because God hears every heartfelt prayer, the bonds of iron chains will be released.

Dylan is still able to offer love, as the next number 'Make You Feel My Love' relates. When things are not going well, everybody seems to be 'on your case' (and not for good). When circumstances are adverse (the wind-driven rain is against you) and opposition is being experienced, Dylan can now offer a 'warm embrace'. The darkness is still there ('evening', and 'stars' above), but whereas previously an overwhelming sense of sadness (associated with clinical depression) was all that there was, there is now the offer of being held for an eternity ('a million years'). Dylan provides reassurances that he will 'never do wrong', and, if necessary, will undergo further hardship ('go hungry' and 'black and blue') to prove it. His love is willing to show the extent it will go to if needed, in the same sort of way that Christ's love did.

There are still 'storms raging', and he still has his regrets about choices that have been made, but the storm's winds are now 'winds of change'. They can lead to freedom and a new beginning; a new and previously unseen opportunity to take hold of, and move forward, out of stagnation. Dylan's comment about going to 'the ends of the earth' echoes St Paul (himself quoting Psalm 19 verse 4). The Psalm describes the angelic servants of God. 'Their voice has gone out to all the world, and their words to the ends of the earth.' (Romans 10:18). Dylan's song emphasises that love is meant to be experienced, not simply rationalised.

'Can't Wait' seems to plot Dylan's recovery from a depressed state of mind. His feelings for his ex-wife Carolyn Dennis still seem to be glowing; but the song seems to also carry a message of another love, one associated with the 'end of time', hence a love for God. Should he wait for his ex-wife to think again, or should he carry on with his life with the greater backdrop of love for God? The song is, once again, set at night. There are people around some of whom are 'on their way up', some 'down', journeying to their individual, eternal destinies. Dylan needs to think clearly to figure out what to do; part of him seems to want to wait for her to come back to him, and part seems to want to get going on a new path.

Wanting to get back the 'sweet love' of the former days is reminiscent of Jesus' words to the church at Ephesus. 'I have this against you, that you have left your first love.' (Revelation 2:4). Dylan has not given up on love, he still needs its 'happy glow' and sees himself 'doomed' to carry on loving, which although painful from time to time, brings with it the promise of an eternal reward into the 'ends of time'. The 'lonely graveyard' of his thoughts remind him of an earlier time when he, through God's mercy, 'left his life', presumably to journey with the God who is still there at 'the end of time.' Dylan may not know how much longer he can pause for, but he is still aware of a love that will go on forever.

'Time Out Of Mind' closes with the longest of recorded Dylan songs, the sixteen and a half minute 'Highlands'. The song is a type of ramble through Dylan's poetic mind, evidently influenced by the Scottish poet Robert Burns who wrote 'My Heart's In The Highlands' in 1789 in tribute to the beauty of the Scottish countryside. Ten years later Dylan, with his brother David, would purchase his own home there in Nethy Bridge, Inverness-shire. In the song, Dylan will be there 'when he feels good enough to go'; right now he doesn't feel good enough - another feature of depression.

The song is vintage Dylan, an epic after the manner of 'Brownsville Girl', describing a journey, presumably symbolic of life, towards heaven. In this track, Dylan looks forward into eternity, musing about life's emptiness without God, and seems to come to a new sense of assurance regarding God's faithfulness in seeing him to his life journey's end. There is a splendid description of the Scottish Highlands ('gentle and fair'), where 'honeysuckle' blossoms amidst the bluebells and other beautiful native flora. We seem to be inside a dream. Everything appears normal, but somehow mundane; life is likened to a cooped-up monotonous existence on an endless treadmill. 'Same 'ol rat race... same 'ol cage'.

Dylan has everything he needs, and seems to have abandoned sexual relations since his divorce; 'telling a real blonde' from a 'fake' might involve comparing the colour of the hair of the head with that of the pubic region. He still feels locked up (a 'prisoner'), and wants to go back in time (pushing 'back the clock'). But at the same time he can look forward to where he would like to be 'when he gets called home' (to the glory of an even better heavenly kingdom). 'Buckeye trees' are common in the Mississippi region, the home of blues music. Dylan's 'heart is in the Highland' (singular, which seems to stand figuratively for heaven), towards which he is moving one step at a time.

Neil Young gets a shout-out; apparently Dylan thinks he sounds better played 'loud', and we find Dylan mentally drifting from place to place, with 'insanity' (related to depression but in any event always a close relation of creativity) 'smashing up against his soul'; the part of him into which God has breathed his own spiritual life. He is 'on anything but a roll', still being in a state of depressed mind. Despite his condition Dylan can still crack a joke, even one about trading in his 'conscience' in a 'pawn shop'. He would deal with more such humour in his next round of new material, in the album 'Love And Theft'. We are then treated to a fabulous description of dawn in the Highlands, where 'big white clouds, like chariots swing down' (rather like the low-swinging chariot of Negro spiritual fame, based on the chariot that the prophet Elisha saw coming to take Elijah to heaven. [xlvii]

Dylan then switches from Scotland to a dreamland closer to home, with seven verses illustrative of the type of empty promises that fame makes. You can't even get proper service in an empty restaurant! This one is in Boston, with Dylan in an almost trance-like state of indecisiveness that his waitress tries to break through, with her recognition of him as being an 'artist'. She is not happy with the napkin pencil sketch that Dylan obliges her with, and he resorts to proving his knowledge of female

---

[xlvii] 2 Kings 2:11-12: 'As Elijah and Elisha were going along and talking together, suddenly a chariot of fire and horses of fire appeared and separated the two of them, and Elijah went up to heaven in a whirlwind. Elisha saw this and cried out, "My father! My father! The chariots and horsemen of Israel!" And Elisha saw him no more.'

authorship in the form of Erica Jong. (Jong is a feminist writer of whom it has pertinently been said that 'the only salve she offered over her books was that of interminable adultery.') [66] When the waitress goes away Dylan takes the opportunity to exit outside where 'nobody's going anywhere'; no progress is being made in any direction.

Then it is back to the Highlands, with Dylan feeling 'further away than ever before' (yet another feature of depression), having 'made a few bad turns', presumably a reflection of his feeling being out of touch with God. Is it really a case of 'too late to learn?' He can see 'people in the park' enjoying life without being weighed down with the cares of the world. The problem is that, despite wishing he could 'trade places with any of 'em', he is unable to, so he will cross 'the street to get away from a mangy dog' (depicted in scripture as standing for uncleanness and disease, as in Philippians 3:2, but also possibly the 'black dog' of depression). The sun that is 'beginning to shine' on him again is not quite the same as previously, because he is not in the same place he was then, having since been wounded emotionally. He has 'new eyes', which can maybe see things differently because of the pain he has been through, indeed now 'everything looks far away' (another feature of a depressive illness).

Dylan's heart is 'in the Highlands', he just has to 'get there', when he 'feels good enough to go' (right now he does not). But he is 'already there in his mind' (indicating an assurance that God's faithfulness is going to see him through). Which is 'good enough for now'.

Dylan's apparent bout of reactive depression did not last forever. After another four years had passed, the more upbeat, even jocular material of 'Love And Theft' appeared. Some reviewers commented that it was almost music you could dance to. Dylan's creative powers had perhaps yet to fully recover, if the 'Theft' element of the album's title and the amount of material borrowed from other sources is any guide. But it was a step back up, and a very welcome step too.

Chapter 12

'Love And Theft'

Released on the ill-fated day of September 11th, 2001 [67] after a live album and another 'Greatest Hits' offering, the music critics greeted 'Love And Theft' with almost unanimous acclaim as a great mixture of style, from blue-grass to rock. One influence the reviewers omitted to note was faith.

As Dylan told Dave Herman, "They're born again by the spirit from above. Born once is born with the spirit from below. Which, when you're born is the spirit that you're born with. Born again is born with the spirit from above, which is a little bit different." [68] The problem is that the old nature ('with the spirit from below'), with its old habits has a tendency to hang around, though diminished substantially in influence. It is this internal spiritual conflict that Dylan seems to be describing in the opening song, 'Tweedle-dee Dum And Tweedle-dee Dee', Lewis Carroll's characters from his 1871 novel 'Through The Looking-Glass'.

Both are described as 'dead man's bones', but one, Tweedle-dee Dum, seems to have become regenerated. While both place their fates into 'the hands of God', Tweedle-dee Dum can hear 'His Master's voice calling' but Tweedle-dee Dee apparently cannot, implying a spiritual deafness that is part of him being 'obnoxious' to Tweedle-dee Dum. Both work in their own individual ways, in the 'Land of Nod' - the place Cain was exiled to after murdering Abel. [xlviii] Nod therefore stands for our world, from which we will one day awaken into eternity, just as the song's two main characters do, trusting their destiny into God's hands.

[xlviii] Genesis 4:13-16: 'Cain said to the Lord, "My punishment is too great to bear! Behold, you have driven me this day from the face of the ground; and from your face I will be hidden, and I will be a vagrant and a wanderer on the earth, and whoever finds me will kill me." So the Lord said to him, "Therefore whoever kills Cain, vengeance will be taken on him sevenfold." And the Lord appointed a sign for Cain, so that no one finding him would slay him. Then Cain went out from the presence of the Lord, and settled in the land of Nod, east of Eden.'

The reference to a 'Streetcar Named Desire' recalls the 1947 play written by American playwright Tennessee Williams, which represents life's complexities - who people really are versus who they appear to be. The two characters are depicted as walking together within one person inexorably moving towards life's ending (the 'sun'), or even 'in and through eternity' (to quote from Dylan's 'In The Summertime').

The image of the pair being called to in a garden (where the 'stately trees' are found) is reminiscent of Genesis (3:8, KJV) where Adam and Eve 'heard the voice of the Lord God walking in the garden in the cool of the day: and Adam and his wife hid themselves from the presence of the Lord God amongst the trees of the garden.' In scripture, 'stately trees' can stand for eternal things, such as those represented in the book of Revelation. 'On either side of the river was the tree of life, bearing twelve kinds of fruit, yielding its fruit every month; and the leaves of the tree were for the healing of the nations.' (Revelation 22:2). The 'breeze' that they 'know the secrets of' may be a reference to the Holy Spirit, described in scripture as a wind that 'blows where it wishes and you hear the sound of it, but do not know where it comes from and where it is going; so is everyone who is born of the Spirit.' (John 3:5-8).

If Tweedle-dee Dee stands for the old nature's earthly desires, which is offensive to both God and the new nature, and which is supposed to be put to death and buried (in baptism); then it is clear why it is 'obnoxious' to Tweedle-dee Dum. Love for him is 'in vain'; sin needs to be put to death, not simply tolerated. Tweedle-dee Dee gets to his knees, imploring to be fed and so kept alive to carry on his 'obnoxious' ways, despite the comment that what is good for Tweedle-dee Dum is good for him too.

The imagery then shifts to a New Orleans carnival-type scene, with a 'parade permit' for the characters that are both 'determined' to carry on in their different ways, although the old is destined to end. Tweedle-dee Dee can be seen for what he is, 'a lowdown, sorry old man', which is a scriptural term for the old sinful nature, which needs to be 'put off' in baptism. 'Knowing this, that our *old man* is crucified with him, that the body of sin might be destroyed, that henceforth we should not serve sin.

For he that is dead is freed from sin.' (Romans 6:6-7, KJV, *italics mine*). Tweedle-dee Dum acts with a knife to hasten the demise of the old nature, saying "I've had too much of your company." Sin's company gets old and tiring after a while; it needs to be put to death through faith.

The second track, 'Mississippi', is an outtake from 'Time Out Of Mind'. The Mississippi delta stands musically for the blues, the melancholy music of the African-American communities of the Deep South. Spiritually it can stand for depression (which Dylan seems now largely to have emerged from) or even the old ways of doing things. Possibly coincidentally, on June 4th 1997, the body of fellow-Columbia recording artist Jeff Buckley was washed up by the Mississippi River at the foot of Memphis' Beale Street, the home of the blues. Swollen by having been in the water for 6 days, his body was identified based on a navel piercing and the clothes he was wearing at the time of his freak drowning in the Wolf River, a channel of the Mississippi. His body had stayed in the Mississippi 'a day too long', 'clothes tight' on his skin. Dylan described Buckley as 'one of the great songwriters of this decade'; his death was a huge loss to music-lovers and mourned by many.

Dylan sings of walking 'the line'. 'To walk' is a biblical term meaning to 'live your life'. For example, 'He who walks righteously and speaks with sincerity, he who rejects unjust gain, and shakes his hands so that they hold no bribe... his refuge will be the impregnable rock.' (Isaiah 33:15-16). He also takes up the biblical idea that our days are all 'numbered'. 'As for the days of our life, they contain seventy years, or if due to strength, eighty years, yet their pride is but labour and sorrow; for soon it is gone and we fly away... So teach us to number our days, that we may present to you a heart of wisdom.' (Psalm 90:10-12). As for all of us, Buckley's days had been numbered; his had come to an end.

For Dylan, life can become a series of 'games' that are played out; you can be 'trapped' in it as someone who does not really belong there. Of himself, he has 'nothing' to give, and seems empty even of things 'for himself'. 'Pain', not rain, pours down; presumably the pain of great loss or the awareness of a distance from God and the experience of his love. Dylan knows that there is 'nothing' of value that the world can give or 'sell' him. He has 'sublime' thoughts, ones that come to him from a higher spiritual place, but which he knows could never do the subject of his song justice.

Dylan has 'heard it all'. People can say what they like; criticism does not affect him much anymore. The song moves into the season of autumn, and he seems to be looking back on his life; things he can't undo, and expressing sorrow and remorse for them. Some reconciliation is possible ('some offer their hand'), but not all. Dylan needs something 'strong' to think on, to 'look at' until his 'eyes go blind'.

Dylan has 'crossed that river' to be 'where you are', reminiscent of the Israelites crossing of the River Jordan. Following the 'southern star' is the opposite of the journeys escaped Negro slaves made. They followed the northern star on their way to freedom in the northern states, often across the Rappahannock River in Falmouth, Stafford County, Virginia, which represented a dividing line between slavery and freedom. Despite feeling that he has been 'drowning in poison' (rather than the Mississippi River), his 'heart is not weary', but is now 'light and free', reminiscent of the freedom that Christ offers. As Paul wrote to the Galatians (5:1): 'It was for freedom that Christ set us free; therefore keep standing firm and do not be subject again to a yoke of slavery.' This sense of freedom allows Dylan the confidence to keep 'moving' with 'affection' for those around him, knowing that when the Spirit starts to move then things do indeed 'start to get interesting'.

Dylan acknowledges that he had 'painted himself' in a 'corner' (almost certainly the 'corner' of post-divorce depression). Now the one he has faith in can 'give him their hand' and so lead him. The future will be 'kind' to him, despite him having stayed in the (Mississippi) blues 'a day too long'.

'Summer Days' is an altogether more cheerful number. Even though summer has gone (i.e. we are in autumn), Dylan still knows where some action may be found, 'Where there is still something going on.' Where is it? It seems connected to a wedding party - we find Dylan proposing a toast to 'the King' (with a capitalised K). Could this be a reference to the marriage feast of the King of kings? 'Blessed are those who are invited to the marriage supper of the Lamb.' (Revelation 19:9). The 'Lamb' here is Christ, the King of kings; 'The Lamb shall overcome them: for he is Lord of lords, and King of kings.' (Revelation 17:14).

It seems there is a fog about; things are not always easy to see, and spying out the land is impossible. This is yet another biblical concept, dating from Israel's exodus into the land of Canaan. Numbers (13:17-18) records that 'Moses sent them to spy out the land of Canaan, he said to them, "Go up there into the Negev; then go up into the hill country. See what the land is like."' Then Dylan asks a rhetorical question, 'What good are you anyway if you can't stand up to some old businessman?' This seems to be a paraphrase from Dr Saga's 'Confessions Of A Yakuza' (page 141) where the Yakuza gangster Ijichi Eiji says, "D'you think I could call myself a Yakuza if I couldn't stand up to some old businessman?" The 'businessman' theme is also rather reminiscent of 'Foot Of Pride' and the line 'There's a retired businessman named Red, cast down from heaven and he's out of his head', where the 'businessman' in question is the devil.

Then we are back to the wedding theme, this time with a choir singing, again reminiscent of what would seem to be one of Dylan's favourite books, Revelation (19:7). "Let us rejoice and be glad and give the glory to him, for the marriage of the Lamb has come and his bride has made herself ready." The cryptic remark about things looking different at night to the 'good' that they looked during the day is not so cryptic if placed alongside Jesus' comment that 'we must work the works of him who sent me as long as it is day; night is coming when no one can work.' (John 9:4-5). Jesus is referring to the time before his return when the devil would have a temporary form of authority after being thrown down the earth from heaven. It is a passage Dylan knows well (see page 145).

The line about being able to 'repeat the past' is a quote from 'The Great Gatsby', where the narrator, Nick Carraway, says in chapter six to the confident extrovert Jay Gatsby 'You can't repeat the past', to which Gatsby replies 'You can't repeat the past? Of course you can!' Some of Dylan's life is personal enough to be off-limits, being things we don't 'need to know'. Creatively it would be fair to say that his 'back has been to the wall', but he seems to have regained his (Jewish) sense of humour when he says his back feels as if it is 'stuck' (to the wall), and offers to have his heart broken once more 'just for good luck'.

We are then transported to the world of the hotshot cars of the 1950's and 1960's, whose intake manifolds had up to eight carburettors. Dylan is 'using them all' so it seems any depression has lifted and he is able to enjoy life once more, even though such a powerful engine means that he will run 'short on gas' once in a while. He knows the effort cannot be all his though (he needs help from above), because 'hammer' as hard as he will, the 'nails' aren't always 'goin' down'.

There is another burst of humour in the line about politicians 'running for office' in their 'jogging shoes', and certainly Dylan doesn't feel he can hang around indefinitely; his 'soul is beginning to shake', indicating that he can sense God's power at work in the place where God's Spirit resides within him. Dylan knows that the 'dark clouds' will soon 'lift'; the depression has gone and he will have to be on his way, but not without one more burst of humour. He is not overly enamoured with where he has been spiritually (in a state of depression), and so will burn down 'the place as a parting gift'.

Next came 'Bye And Bye', a country-blues style number with a title evocative of Negro spiritual music, meaning 'over yonder' - in the next life. Dylan has frequently cited Johnny Cash's influence in his life, and Cash's version ('In The Sweet Bye And Bye') makes the meaning plain. 'The Father waits over the way, to prepare us a dwelling place there, in the sweet bye and bye'. Dylan's version too is replete with spiritual content and meaning.

He opens with telling us that he is 'breathing a lover's sigh'. So who is it he is in love with at this stage in his life? Could it still be God? More Jewish humour appears with the picture of him wanting to be 'on time' and achieving that by having sat down 'on his watch'. There is a double entendre here, as in many good Jewish jokes; the 'watch' can also mean to keep a lookout for someone's return. Jesus had told his followers to

'Watch therefore, for you know neither the day nor the hour in which the Son of man is coming.' (Matthew 25:13, NKJV).

Like Christ did, Dylan is packaging the truths he is delivering in a way that will make them easier for his audience to swallow. He sings 'love's praises' (surely those of his Lord) with a rhyming that is 'sugar-coated', just as Jesus taught in parables - stories that left behind a spiritual message. As he would later sing in 'Spirit On The Water', he can have a 'whoppin' good time' with his 'partner'; even dancing, as the Bible encourages us to do. 'Let them praise his name with dancing.' (Psalm 149:3). He has come to know just 'who he can depend on' and 'trust', and his study of the 'dust' (that is, humanity. Genesis 2:7, KJV: 'And God formed man out of the dust of the ground') serves to confirm that there is only one who has proven utterly trustworthy.

His 'walk' with God may take him onto 'briars' (sometimes the ground underneath the dancer's feet can be uncomfortable to tread upon) but he has learned to distance himself from his 'own desires' and so not be too controlled by them. He seems more concerned with what somebody else wants for him. This is a 'dream that hasn't been repossessed' (another great line in its own right), where the future has already happened. Because God exists in a realm outside of time, to him everything that is future (to us) has already taken place. He can see and so declare the end from the beginning (Isaiah 46:10). The subject of the song is someone who was Dylan's 'first love' and will also be his 'last'. This is reminiscent of Christ's words to the church at Ephesus in Revelation (2:4), who they are told that they have left their 'first love'.

Who other than a believer, and a very committed one at that, would talk of 'baptizing you in fire so you can sin no more'? Dylan is surely a follower of Christ (who was a Jew) and is a Jew himself. He is not compromising in any way his faith, which is both Jewish and Christian. The two are not mutually exclusive, as the early church (which consisted almost entirely of Jews) showed. The Jewish prophet John the Baptist had predicted Jesus' ministry, saying, 'I baptize you with water for repentance, but he who is coming after me is mightier than I, and I am not fit to remove his sandals; he will baptize you with the Holy Spirit and fire. His winnowing fork is in his hand, and he will thoroughly clear his threshing floor; and he will gather his wheat into the barn, but he will burn up the chaff with unquenchable fire." (Matthew 3:11-12).

This sort of rule of God never comes without a struggle from the old nature, and so Dylan predicts a 'civil war'. In this internal struggle for supremacy, the 'new man' - we could call him Tweedle-Dee Dum - will win. Dylan will prove to his heavenly master just exactly how 'loyal and true' he is. He is going to be faithful to his Lord, just as would later sing on 'Thunder On The Mountain'. 'Some sweet day I'll stand beside my king. I wouldn't betray your love or any other thing'. He is continuing to propose 'a toast to the King'.

The next song was 'Lonesome Day Blues'. Having a spiritual direction for life does not exempt anyone from life's sad happenings; Dylan's mother Beatty Zimmerman had died the previous year, and he sings that he 'wishes' she was 'still alive'. 'Sad old lonesome days' happen, but Dylan's mind is in another place, 'a million miles away'. As one gets older, so the more one's friends and family die off, but Dylan knows that, as Psalm 27:10 (KJV) says, 'when my father and my mother forsake me, then the Lord will take me up.' He paraphrased this verse after the manner of the 19th century Rabbi Shimshon Rafael Hirsch at his Grammy acceptance speech on February 20 1991. "You know, it's possible to become so defiled in this world that your own father and mother will abandon you and if that happens, God will always believe in your ability to mend your ways."

Dylan still knows how to tease people in fun; the line about Samantha Brown living in his house for 'four or five months', and his boast that he 'never slept with her even once' is jocular indeed. Samantha Brown is a (married) host of an American TV travel show who has lived in other people's homes for TV documentary purposes. The line seems to be a reference to the Japanese novel 'Confessions Of A Yakuza', by Dr Junichi Saga. Dr Saga wrote about a Japanese Yakuza gangster's (one Eiji Ijichi's) dying disclosures, which he converted into a type of biography. His book contains the line: 'Just because she was in the same house didn't mean we were living together as man and wife... I don't know how it looked to other people, but I never even slept with her - not once.' ('Confessions Of A Yakuza', page 208). [69]

Dylan has learned that old habits die hard; the things that are really not important are sometimes the hardest to give up. The Bible encourages us to 'lay aside every encumbrance and the sin which so easily entangles us, and let us run with endurance the race that is set before us, fixing our eyes on Jesus, the author and perfecter of faith, who for the joy set before him endured the cross, despising the shame, and has sat down at the right hand of the throne of God.' (Hebrews 12:1-2).

We are told that sometimes Dylan's road has been 'washed out', and that he is closing on his final destination. His is the voice of experience that warns against the 'lover-man' who is a 'coward', a thief and 'rotten to the core'. Jesus too warned of one who came 'only to steal and kill and destroy.' (John 10:10). Dylan seems to be comparing this thieving devil-like figure to Christ when he goes on to sing of his own 'captain' who has been 'decorated' (presumably for bravery), as well as being educated sufficiently highly to hold the title 'Rabbi' and even 'Doctor' (of the Jewish Torah - John 3:2). [70] The line about his lack of concern for his 'pals' who 'have been killed' is another reference to the Japanese novel 'Confessions Of A Yakuza', which contains the line, 'There was nothing sentimental about *him* - it didn't bother him at all that some of his pals had been killed.' (Dr Saga, 'Confessions Of A Yakuza', page 243, in relation to the war between Japan and China).

Dylan sings that he listens at night to the 'wind whispering'; somewhat reminiscent of Mark Twain's 'Huckleberry Finn', who lay awake in Widow Douglas' house with 'the wind trying to whisper something to me and I couldn't make out what it was.' He may also be referring to the imagery that Christ used to describe the Holy Spirit. 'The wind blows where it wishes and you hear the sound of it, but do not know where it comes from and where it is going; so is everyone who is born of the Spirit.' (John 3:8). 'Nothing ever happens', but then God's timetable is not always the same as ours. 'The Lord is not slow about his promise, as some count slowness, but is patient toward you, not wishing for any to perish but for all to come to repentance.' (2 Peter 3:9).

The line about sparing the defeated is from the Roman poet Virgil. 'But yours will be the rulership of nations, remember Roman, these will be your arts: to teach the ways of peace to those you conquer, to spare defeated peoples, to tame the proud.' [71] Similarly Dylan is 'teaching peace' to those willing to allow God's love to conquer them, and to 'tame the proud', as God himself does. God will 'look on everyone who is proud, and make him low.' (Job 40:11-12). As Jesus' mother Mary sang, "He has brought down rulers from their thrones but has lifted up the humble." (Luke 1:52). The wind's effect can be seen in leaves rustling and items 'falling' from shelves. Ultimately God acts out of love, a love he calls all people to share in.

'Floater (Too Much To Ask)' again finds Dylan drawing on the Japanese gangster biography 'Confessions Of A Yakuza' by Dr Junichi Saga, in a song that paints a picture of intimidation and menace. 'If you ever try to interfere with me or cross my path again, you do so at the peril of your own life'. Dr Saga was writing based on the testimony of one of his patients (Eiji Ijichi, a dying Yakuza gangster), and the imagery resonates with the behaviour of the 'rotten to the core coward' of the previous track. The scene is set by a description of a 'back alley' room with the blinds kept down, and a description of cross-generational conflict. The line about 'The older men around here get on bad terms with some of the younger men' appears to be a paraphrase from Dr Saga (page 153), 'Some kind of trouble that put him on bad terms with the younger men'. The disclaimer that 'age doesn't matter in the end', paraphrases Dr Saga quoting the Yakuza gangster, 'age doesn't matter in that business... Age by itself just doesn't carry any weight.' ('Confessions Of A Yakuza', page 155). In eternity there is no such thing as age.

The line 'one of the boss' hangers-on' seems to be a paraphrase from page 192 of Dr Junichi Saga's book. 'The boss... would divide the rest among the younger men... ten or twenty hangers-on for a start.' 'My old man, he's like some feudal lord' reflects a line from page 6, 'My old man would sit there like a feudal lord.' 'Things come alive or they fall flat' is a paraphrase from page 154, 'A good bookie makes all the difference... it's up to him whether a session comes alive or it falls flat.' Dylan's variation on Shakespeare has Juliette responding to Romeo's criticism of her 'poor complexion, it doesn't give your appearance a very youthful touch', with 'Why don't you just shove off if it bothers you so much?' This compares well with Dr Saga (page 9). 'If it bothers you so much, why don't you just shove off?' 'I'm not quite as cool or forgiving as I sound' reflects Dr Saga (page 158), where the main gangster character recalls: 'I'm not as cool or forgiving as I might have sounded.' 'Not always easy kicking someone out' paraphrases Dr Saga (page 154), 'But even kicking him *[a rival]* out wasn't as easy as that'. Dylan then sings, 'Somebody wants you to give something up, tears or not, it's too much to ask.' Dr Saga's book (page 182) reads, 'Tears or not, though, that was too much to ask.' 'Interfering with me at the peril of your life' carries a message similar to Isaiah 41:11, where the prophet says, 'Those who contend with you will be as nothing and will perish.'

'High Water (For Charlie Patton)' is about the Mississippi river flood of 1927 when the levees broke, and according to Patton's account, 'The water done jumped through this town' [72] of Sumner, Tallahatchie County, Mississippi. The theme of Mississippi floodwater would recur in Dylan's portfolio of allegory as a symbol of judgement in the song 'The Levee's Gonna Break' ('Modern Times'). The poorer riverside towns' levees were ill equipped to withstand severe flooding. Such consequences were brought home in the New Orleans' flood of August 2005 caused by Hurricane Katrina, when 80% of New Orleans was flooded, with some parts under fifteen feet of water.

Dylan dedicated his 'High Water' to Charlie Patton (1891-1934), a black Blues singer/guitarist whose father was a preacher. Patton became a notorious womanizer and drunkard, but he allegedly died reciting scripture and his favourite sermon. [73] That being the case then Patton represents another type of 'Pistol' Pete Maravich, the great All-American basketball player who found faith in Christ after a fight with alcoholism. The line 'High Water Everywhere' is the title of a 1929 Patton song.

Dylan describes the water rising, in consequence of which 'the gold and silver are being stolen away'; possibly the richer people quietly removing their valuables before the water makes escape impossible. The song then introduces us to 'Big Joe Turner', a Kansas City Jazz Singer (born in 1911) who 'made it' as far as the jazz clubs in Kansas City located in the area of 'Twelfth Street and Vine' (Street). But 'nothing' is 'standing' because the flood has swept it all away, and especially the poorer black folks' houses (the 'shacks'). People are losing everything, and being forced to leave. The song then turns to 'Bertha Mason'. Patton's wife was named Bertha Lee, a woman noted for her violent temper; the song's given-name of Mason perhaps hails from the madwoman in the attic of Charlotte Bronte's novel Jane Eyre. Dylan paraphrases Patton's own song 'Shake It And Break It (But Don't Let It Fall Mama' (1929), which starts 'You can shake it, you can break it, you can hang it on the wall'. Dylan depicts Bertha who 'shook it, broke it, then she hung it on a wall'; she is not however sufficiently affected to stop her bossily dictating who can dance with whom!

Patton lived his life at a fast pace, referenced by 'blazing speed' and a 'hopped-up Mustang Ford' with the rhyming 'panties overboard' fittingly describing (in modern terms) Patton's lifestyle. Patton wrote songs ('poems') reflecting spiritual influences that were not all positive, including premonitions of his demise. The 'pig without a wig' reference hails from a traditional old-English nursery rhyme ('Upon my word and honour, as I was going to Bonner, I met a pig without a wig, upon my word and honour!'),[74] as does the later 'cuckoo' line.

Flood water 'six inches' over people's heads signals their imminent demise, described by 'coffins droppin' in the street'. Vicksburg (a town on the Mississippi where the Confederates surrendered to the Unionists in the American Civil War) gets a mention. People, especially black folk like Patton, drowned in the flooding, being too poor to leave easily.

George Lewis, a jazz clarinettist in the Great Depression in the USA during the 1920's, is then referred to (by an odd coincidence he was also a committed Christian). Dylan supplies a jokey line about not having your mind wide open 'to every conceivable point of view', while, at the same time, presumably, keeping it firmly closed to God. There is still more humour in the image of Charles Darwin (symbolic of agnosticism and atheism) being 'trapped' 'on Highway Five', and wanted 'dead or alive'. The jump from natural selection to what most Messianic Jews regard as an impossibly ridiculous series of evolutionary flukes, is to contradict God's creative role. It would be a good example of a 'conceivable point of view' which it may be unhelpful to uncritically 'open up one's mind' to.

The line the 'cuckoo is a pretty bird, she warbles as she flies' is from a nursery rhyme ('The Cuckoo's A Fine Bird') and also 'The Cuckoo', a traditional English folk-song. 'The cuckoo is a fine bird, he sings as he flies; he brings us good tidings, he tells us no lies.' Our poetic lyricist now tells us that he is 'preaching the Word of God'; which is fairly obvious to those with ears to hear. 'Putting out the eye' was a common judgement on prisoners in Old Testament times. For example, in 2 Kings 25:7, 'They slew the sons of Zedekiah before his eyes, and put out the eyes of Zedekiah, and bound him with fetters of brass, and carried him to Babylon.' The Word of God that Dylan says he is 'preaching' has power to judge as well as to save.

'Dust my broom' is another jazz reference from the period, this time to Robert Johnson. He was a Delta Blues singer (1911-1938) who wrote 'I Believe I'll Dust My Broom', meaning 'leave for good.' We also learn that Dylan has now resolved to keep out of trouble with women (just in case anyone was worrying). 'Thunder' can be heard in the skies over Clarksdale; Clarksdale Mississippi is widely held to be the birthplace of the Blues and is where Highways 61 and 49 intersect. The 'thunder' signals that another storm is coming - more rain - all indeed looks 'blue' for the home of the blues. The outlook is 'getting darker'; and the message is spiritual as well as meteorological.

'Moonlight' is a love song - no two ways about it - but towards whom are his feelings directed? 'Love Sick' saw Dylan take his relationship with God and turns it with consummate skill into a love song, in the manner of the Song of Solomon. 'He has brought me to his banquet hall, and his banner over me is love.' (Song of Songs 2:4). We hear Dylan sing of 'seasons turning' and his 'sad heart yearning' for times when he is visited 'out in the moonlight alone'. As Psalm 17:3 puts it, 'You have tried my heart, you have visited me by night, you have tested me and you find nothing, I have purposed that my mouth will not transgress.'

Dylan is out in the 'dusky' evening air, sweet with the scents of wild flowers, witnessing the heavens 'melt with flesh and bone'. Evening time represents the hour of meeting with the beloved; Dylan would later relate ('Ain't Talkin'' on 'Modern Times') how he 'walked out tonight in the mystic garden', when 'someone hit me from behind'. He seems to be describing a spiritual encounter in a similar way as depicted in 'Moonlight'. The image of the skies melting 'with flesh and bone' is a wonderful description of the incarnation, when God became human flesh in the incarnation of Christ. 'And the Word became flesh, and dwelt among us, and we saw his glory, glory as of the only begotten from the Father, full of grace and truth.' (John 1:14). Dylan, it appears, has a moonlight rendezvous with his beloved.

Consequently, he tells us that he is 'preachin' peace and harmony', just as the angels did at the birth of Christ, when the incarnation became visible. The angels sang, 'Glory to God in the highest, and on earth peace among men with whom he is pleased.' (Luke 2:14). This 'peace on earth' is the 'tranquillity' that Dylan finds so blessed. But it isn't all about peace; he knows that there is a battle raging for men's and women's souls, and he will work in accordance with God's timetable; 'when the time is right', and so is going wherever he has to go.

In the 'mystic' beauty of the garden Dylan's 'tears keep flowing', presumably in prayer; he knows that 'it takes a thief to catch a thief', and that the devil is the ultimate thief. He comes 'to steal and kill and destroy', whereas Christ 'came that they may have life, and have it abundantly.' (John 10:10). The 'bell' eventually tolls for everyone - but who will respond?

'Honest With Me' finds Dylan being frank with his audience about the difficulties he faces. He is staying away now from 'the Southside', possibly a reference to that part of Chicago notorious for prostitution; the women there just give him 'the creeps'. He has a past, that is for certain; its memory, if he lets it, will willingly 'strangle' him. He has

174

come 'ashore' (and figuratively crossed over Jordan) into God's promised land, but things 'can get in the way', especially if, like him, you have made a decision to do 'what's right' in God's sight.

Dylan has 'feelings', presumably for his fans, and knows that they would 'be honest' with him if they knew what he was really saying to them. When Dylan had been 'honest' in plain speech about his faith in the late 1970's and early 1980's, he had been rejected. Now he seems to be explaining himself in a more indirect and often allegorical manner. He is 'not sorry for nothing', the double negative implying that he may have some regrets, but is 'glad' that he 'fought' and at least gave it a shot. He just wishes that he had been more successful, perhaps that more people had been able to accept his message and not reject it out of hand.

The song then moves to a country fair's freak show (conjoined/Siamese twins would be a huge attraction at any fair), and people often seem more interested in any form of aberration rather than being exposed to truth. Women's beauty) is no longer so important ('a face like a teddy bear'). He seems to prefer a willingness to fight for truth, rejecting life's false images ('advertising boards') by driving into them 'trunk first'.

His sense of humour is still very much intact; he will sell his 'pretty eyes and smile at a reduced price', but also knows 'some things' that he'd rather not have to tell his audience; such as some unpalatable spiritual truths concerning their eternal destiny. 'I won't come here no more if it bothers you' is another quotation from Dr Saga's 'Confessions Of A Yazuga' (page 189), 'I won't come any more if it bothers you.' There is then one of Dylan's trademark train references - 'the Southern Pacific' train is departing. It connected east and west coasts of the USA; it may represent 'a slow train' of the final judgement at Christ's second coming. The spiritual language continues with Dylan 'having a hard time believin' some people were ever alive' (presumably meaning alive spiritually).

Dylan feels 'naked' (probably spiritually and emotionally), exposed to God's all-seeing eye, but again his sense of humour comes through with a joke about 'huntin' bare'. He is about the creation of a hitherto unseen 'imperial empire', the same one he referred to on his CBS 'Sixty-Minute' interview (with Ed Bradley) as being ruled by the 'commander in chief - of this earth and the one unseen'. [75] Dylan is prepared to do whatever is necessary to bring that empire's rule into visible reality in people's lives. Why? Because he 'cares so much' for his audience. Dylan's mother and father may have counselled him not to squander his time in unfruitful activities; if so their words of advice are still with him.

'Po' Boy' finds Dylan once more in country blues mode, with the time-honoured theme of the poor black man, often opprobriously referred to as 'boy' by the rich white plantation owners. Dylan himself is the 'poor boy', only one who seems to be serving a much more munificent master, one with a sense of humour (a Jewish one) similar to his own. The song opens with a rhetorical question regarding his previous whereabouts; 'Where you been?' Dylan answers with a terse statement to the effect that the question has already been answered, and that Dylan is not about to repeat himself for the umpteenth time ('Won't tell you again'). As such, the message is the same as in 'Ain't Talkin' from 'Modern Times'.

Dylan feels he has explained his position regarding his spirituality enough times already. There is always someone who wants to ask the same question again and again, the problem being that they are never satisfied with his answer. People witnessed Christ's miracles and still were not prepared to believe, so what chance does Dylan have? In the end their persistent rejection is just making their state worse, and throwing 'pearls before swine' does the one throwing them no good either. 'Do not throw your pearls before swine, or they will trample them under their feet, and turn and tear you to pieces.' (Matthew 7:6).

The exchange in the store where Dylan offers four dollars in place of the asked-for three is an amusing illustration of the tension between the simplicity of the 'poor boy' and the generosity of a man who keeps giving artistically long after others might have said goodbye. 'Alright bye and bye' is a common Negro-Spiritual allusion to heaven. Dylan's 'game' is the same as before - communicating spirituality - but it has gone to a different 'level' of communication under God's inspiration.

Another train reference describes Dylan as being careful to avoid 'fallin' between the cars', and laying out 'straight' what he has to say, even with a joke about Shakespeare's play 'Othello'. Othello's wife Desdemona is in fact innocent of the sexual wrongs that Othello suspects her of. But that does not prevent him poisoning himself with jealousy and doubts, which then lead to him murdering his wife. 'Time and love has branded' Dylan; love will last forever, whereas time's changes will be lost when human mortality is exchanged for immortality, as St Paul described. [xlix]

In Christ, Dylan is no longer under the Law of Moses. Small wonder then to find him 'dodging' the laws of Georgia, a euphemism for laws that make no sense. For example, if a charity registered as 'not for profit' fails to register their fund-raising raffle with the local sheriff, they risk paying up to 10,000 dollars in fines or spending five years in jail for commercial gambling under the Georgia statutes.

The scene then shifts to a hotel 'The Palace Of Gloom' (a fitting name for the abode of most of mankind, when cut off from God's love and joy by indifference or rebellion towards him). Dylan cuts through the gloom though with another joke, one about the hotel's room service being asked to 'Send up a room', as in Groucho Marx's line, 'Room service - send up a larger room' (from the 1935 Marx Brother's film 'A Night At The Opera'). Dr Saga's book pops up again with the line about Dylan's 'family'. Dylan: 'My mother was a daughter of a wealthy farmer, my father was a traveling salesman, I never met him. When my mother died, my uncle took me in... He did a lot of nice things for me and I won't forget him.' Saga's reads: 'My mother... was the daughter of a wealthy

---

[xlix] 1 Corinthians 15:51-57: 'Behold, I tell you a mystery; we will not all sleep, but we will all be changed, in a moment, in the twinkling of an eye, at the last trumpet; for the trumpet will sound, and the dead will be raised imperishable, and we will be changed. For this perishable must put on the imperishable, and this mortal must put on immortality. But when this perishable will have put on the imperishable, and this mortal will have put on immortality, then will come about the saying that is written, "Death is swallowed up in victory. Oh Death, where is your victory, Oh Death where is your sting?" The sting of death is sin, and the power of sin is the Law; but thanks be to God, who gives us the victory through our Lord Jesus Christ.'

farmer... I heard that my father was a traveling salesman who called at the house regularly, but I never met him... *[My uncle]* was a nice man, I won't forget him...' ('Confessions Of A Yakuza', pages 57-58).

Dylan is still 'thrilled' by his beloved's 'kiss', again reminiscent of the 'Song of Solomon' (1:2) which says, 'May he kiss me with the kisses of his mouth. For your love is better than wine.' This is all he really needs to know. There is time for one last joke before the song ends; this time a 'knock knock' joke around the name 'Freddy' where 'Freddy or not here I come', replaces the conventional 'Hide and Seek' line of 'Ready or not, here I come'. The last line about 'feeding swine' is reminiscent of the story of the prodigal son (Luke chapter 15), who wasted his father's money and ended up feeding pigs. Eventually he 'comes to his senses' and returns to his father, who receives him back as a son - a picture of God's willingness to take back any who will return to him.

'Cry A While' seems to recount some of the tensions between an artist motivated by spirituality and the recording industry motivated by the bottom line. The song's 'Mr Goldsmith' would clearly fall into this category; he has nothing in common with Dylan, and so Dylan will 'deal' with him according to his kind. Dylan is someone in touch with his feelings and not ashamed to weep when it is right to do so; 'Thunder On The Mountain' ('Modern Times') finds him 'crying' over the plight of (the then apparently lost) Alicia Keys. Christ too was very familiar with tears. 'In the days of his flesh, he offered up both prayers and supplications with loud crying and tears to the one able to save him from death, and he was heard because of his piety.' (Hebrews 5:7). Dylan has done his fair share of crying; part and parcel of intercessory prayer.

Dylan can appeal to his professional longevity; he is hardly a 'flash in the pan.' He also describes himself as a 'union man', probably a nod to those Unionists who fought under Ulysses S Grant to overturn slavery in the American Civil War; Dylan opposes the spiritual slavery that the indifference about (or rebellion against) God brings. There is a War of Independence reference about the condition of the 'Pennsylvania line'. The Pennsylvania line was a division of the American Continental Army lead by George Washington in the Revolutionary War against British rule. The poorer Pennsylvanian regiment had mutinied in search of a fair deal that they eventually were granted. 'The Denver Road' mentioned is the name of the Fort Worth and Denver Railway.

The next verse sees a clearly still believing Dylan going to church. He is certainly still living out his faith; 'Every day I go an extra mile', as Christ had taught his followers to do; 'Whoever forces you to go one mile, go with him two.' (Matthew 5:41). The Roman army could press people into service to carry their gear up to one mile; Jesus told his followers to go two miles.

There follows a humourous reference to the Italian comic opera figure Don Pasquale in relation to a nocturnal disturbance in a local alleyway. Pasquale got married in order to try and disinherit his nephew; Dylan suggests that the noise is the Italian making a 'booty call' (a phone call made for the purpose of obtaining a sexual act). Intercessory prayer appears to be getting another mention with Dylan again weeping 'on the fringes of the night' and 'crying to the Lord'. His message cannot get any clearer. He is doing God's work in prayer; interceding for people who have lost their humanity - 'They got no heart or soul.' All the while Dylan is doing his best to be 'meek and mild', as Christ was said to be, (that is, when he wasn't cleansing the temple or confronting the phony religious authorities).

'Preachers in the pulpits and babies in the cribs, I'm longin' for that sweet fat that sticks to your ribs' paraphrases a problem St Paul faced while working with the church in Corinth (in Greece). 'I, brethren, could not speak to you as to spiritual, but as to carnal, even as to babes in Christ. I have fed you with milk, and not with meat: for hitherto you were not able to bear it, neither are you yet now able.' (1 Corinthians 3:1-2, KJV). What Dylan is wanting is the meat of God's word that builds up even more than milk does; he is no spiritual 'baby'. He does not want to become 'senile'; drowning in 'whiskey' would be better than that. The song closes with an apparent return to the shortcomings of the recording industry. They had 'bet on' Dylan for commercial success, but he had turned around (in his statements of faith) and was running in the opposite direction to what they had envisioned - 'the wrong way'. If

179

their 'sorrow' was genuine, it might point them in the right direction, before it is too late

The final track's title, 'Sugar Baby', seems to have been derived from the folk banjo musician Moran Lee 'Dock' Boggs. Dylan would have been familiar with the song from his folk club days in New York City in the early 1960's. The line 'look up, seek your maker, before Gabriel blows his horn', comes from the Nathaniel Shilkret and Gene Austin song 'Lonesome Road' which was made popular by Frank Sinatra. 'Sugar Baby' seems to describe some features of Dylan's journey on his own lonesome road, which he has to walk looking away from the intensity of the sun's rays. Pilgrims to the Temple in Jerusalem would often have to look away from the gold plated structure as it caught the rays of the evening sun, and as Dylan turns his eyes back to the direction he has come from he can see what obstacles the others on the road are facing.

He certainly seems to feel unable and indeed unwilling to 'turn back', reminiscent of the passage in Luke's gospel (9:61-62) where 'another also said, "I will follow you, Lord; but first permit me to say good-bye to those at home." But Jesus said to him, "No one, after putting his hand to the plough and looking back, is fit for the kingdom of God."' That kind of disciple cannot plough a straight line, but Dylan also appears cognizant of the peril of running too far ahead. The chorus appears to address the mindless sycophants of the type described in 'Yonder Comes Sin', with their 'fifty dollar smiles' and their inability to recognize eternal truth. They have 'no brains', and have gone 'years without me'. Dylan encourages them to 'keep going'.

The next verse comments on the behaviour of 'ladies down in Darktown' who 'strut', presumably representing prostitution. Dylan knows the 'amount of trouble' such women bring; they have helped corrupt 'love', something never intended by its Maker.

The song then turns its attention to one whose charm has 'broken many a heart', Dylan counting himself among those thus afflicted. It is 'love' that he is addressing, but whose love? This love has torn 'a world apart'

180

- whose can it be? Some things it seems we can all be 'sure' of; we are advised to 'look up - seek your Maker - 'fore Gabriel blows his horn.' The person behind this love now becomes clear. The Apostle Paul had written, (1 Corinthians 15:51-52), 'Behold, I tell you a mystery; we will not all sleep, but we will all be changed, in a moment, in the twinkling of an eye, at the last trumpet; for the trumpet will sound, and the dead will be raised imperishable, and we will be changed.' This 'last trumpet', which the angel Gabriel will blow, signals the end of all things on this earth. Dylan often puts the song he particularly wants to be noticed at the end of his albums. 'Love And Theft' is no exception.

Faith-based messages were clearly present in 'Love And Theft'. They would be even clearer, and brought right up to date, in Dylan's next album, 'Modern Times'.

Chapter 13

'Modern Times'

Dylan fans waited five years (until 2006) for the next album offering original material following 'Love And Theft', with the intervening gap being plugged by two live albums (from 1975 and 1964), the soundtrack of the Martin Scorsese documentary, 'No Direction Home' detailing Dylan's rise to fame in the 1960's and another 'Best Of' album in 2006.

Once again the new album was met with a high degree of acclaim; once again it was replete with biblical content, and once again the reviewers either missed it or chose to ignore it. The opening track 'Thunder On The Mountain', which has figured very highly in Dylan's stage shows since its release, might as well be called a scripture-based song and have done with it.

The 'mountain' from whence comes the sound of thunder (as well as the music that Dylan receives) is reminiscent of Mount Sinai, where the Law was given to Moses with thunder and lightning. 'It came about on the third day, when it was morning, that there were thunder and lightning flashes and a thick cloud upon the mountain and a very loud trumpet sound, so that all the people who were in the camp trembled. And Moses brought the people out of the camp to meet God, and they stood at the foot of the mountain.' (Exodus 19:16-17). The moon is depicted ('fire on the moon'), i.e. glowing red with the light of an eclipse, which scripture associates with the return of the Lord Jesus Christ. 'The sun shall be turned into darkness, and the moon into blood, before the great and the terrible day of the Lord comes.' (Joel 2:31, KJV).

Day is breaking, a day that will see Dylan sound his 'trombone'. To blow on a wind instrument, such as a ram's horn (a Jewish 'Shofar'), is a way of announcing God's coming. (One of Dylan's record labels is named 'Ram's Horn Music'.) 'Hot stuff' appears to follow Dylan around. The song then refers to the black American singer Alicia Keys. To be 'thinking about' is a spiritual euphemism for praying for someone; it appears that Dylan has been praying for Alicia Keys, even to the point of tears ('Couldn't keep from crying'). Scripture associates tears with heartfelt intercessory prayer, and Alicia Keys is herself a committed Christian, someone about whom Dylan said 'There's nothing about that girl I don't like', [76] which would therefore include her faith. Keys is a Global Ambassador for the charity 'Keep A Child Alive', and was born in Hell's Kitchen, Manhattan on January 25, 1981. Dylan, a Christian by then, appears to also have had a residence in New York 'down the line'. Many reviewers noted the name-check. None surmised why.

At the time Dylan was writing the song, Alicia Keys had suffered a type of nervous breakdown following her grandmother's illness and subsequent death. Her grandmother had been closely involved in raising Alicia; the death hit her hard. Amid concerns for her well-being, Alicia simply disappeared, precipitating much disquiet about her personal safety. In 'Thunder On The Mountain', Dylan, a fellow believer and artist, communicates the fact of his prayers and regard for her health at that time. 'I was wondering where in the world Alicia Keys could be.' She eventually reappeared in Cairo, Egypt, where she had gone to be alone to recover her peace of mind and sense of direction. As she later said: 'My grandmother died and we were so close, I broke down. But you have to break down to build back up, to realise something had to change. No one's perfect - you can't be. I needed a break, so I went to Egypt.' [77] Dylan was 'wondering where in the world' she was; his search for her 'clear through Tennessee' is a phrase taken from the Lizzie Douglas (aka 'Memphis Minnee') song 'Ma Rainey'. It contains the lines: 'I was thinking about Ma Rainey, wonder where could Ma Rainey be, I been looking for her, even been in old Tennessee.' Dylan's care and concern for a fellow-artist shines through.

He can feel his soul, likened in biblical thought to the lungs, expanding. The soul is the place within us where we experience God's life. Rather like taking a deep breath, when we spiritually take in God's life-giving Spirit our souls expand. If we want to understand Dylan he invites us to look into his heart, to see where his priorities lie. They are clear for all who wish to discern, as clear as 'the writing on the wall' was to the Old Testament prophet Daniel. A disembodied hand has appeared in the dining room of Belshazzar, King of Babylon, and Daniel was called to read it. Daniel (5:5) records that the king was holding a feast when 'Suddenly the fingers of a man's hand emerged and began writing opposite the lamp stand, on the plaster of the wall of the king's palace, and the king saw the back of the hand that did the writing.'

Dylan is inspired by the drum-like noise of the thunder, so much so that he will 'sleep over there'; the place where the music is emanating from. How will he get there? Well, he tells us he won't be in need of a guide, 'he already knows the way.' Jesus had said, 'I am the way, the truth and the life, and no one comes to the Father but through me.' (John 14:6). Dylan then appears to be addressing God with the words, 'Remember this, I'm your servant both night and day.' Jesus had said: 'Whoever serves me must follow me; and where I am, my servant also will be. My Father will honour the one who serves me.' (John 12:26, ANIV). Dylan has spent a lot of time 'serving' in his own unique way.

The song then describes what appears to be a time of civil disturbance and uncertainty, to which Dylan's response it to 'forget about himself', and instead 'go out and see what others need'. He appears to be saying: 'I will take on the attitude of a servant (like Christ) and look to the needs of others first.' Jesus had said to his followers, "You know that those who are recognized as rulers of the Gentiles lord it over them; and their great men exercise authority over them. But it is not this way among you, but whoever wishes to become great among you shall be your servant; and whoever wishes to be first among you shall be slave of all. For even the Son of Man did not come to be served, but to serve, and to give his life a ransom for many."' (Mark 10:42-45).

We learn that Dylan has been 'studying the art of love'; perhaps the Roman poet Ovid's (43BC-17/18AD) 'Ars amatoria', or equally possibly the Apostle Paul's treatise on love found in 1 Corinthians chapter 13. Love fits Dylan well; 'like a glove'. The road down from the mountain where he has been spending the night is 'hard'. Jesus had said, 'Small is the gate and narrow the road that leads to life, and only a few find it.' (Matthew 7:14, ANIV). There is an especially strong spiritual message in the lines, 'Some sweet day I'll stand beside my king, I wouldn't betray your love or any other thing'. Dylan has a 'king' that he serves (and even stands on tables to toast - 'Summer Days', from 'Love And Theft'); he has even made 'religious vows', and cites St Herman, who brought Russian Orthodoxy to North America via Alaska. The reference to the milk of 'a thousand cows' may refer to the Orthodox Church's Lenten holy days in which their congregations abstain from milk.

Dylan seems to be saying that he is done with traditional religious forms which fail to provide a living and dynamic relationship with God in an on-going way. After all, what would a good Jewish boy be doing with 'pork chops' otherwise? He certainly condemns 'greed' and 'wicked schemes'; people's 'dreams' are the last thing he is concerned with.

The song then switches to what appears to be an impending disaster of some sort; a 'twister' (a tornado) is coming and there is a panic to get out of town. Dylan has come too far to 'take a chance with somebody new'; he has found the truth and is sticking with it. He did all he could; 'right there and then', back when he gave his life over to Christ and spent time at his concerts sharing about it. He has 'already confessed' (his faith); there is no reason to repeat the confession in such direct terms, especially to deaf ears, for which an indirect style of allegorical communication works better. He is still able to 'make money', but 'plants and harvests' with it, like the Apostle Paul, [1] rather than using it frivolously. The song ends with a heartfelt plea ('for the love of God') that his audience 'take pity on themselves' while there is still time.

'Spirit On the Water' is another piece that draws upon biblical imagery. The very first words of the Bible are: 'In the beginning God created the heavens and the earth. Now the earth was formless and empty, darkness was over the surface of the deep, and the Spirit of God was hovering over the waters.' (Genesis 1:1-2, ANIV). When Dylan sings, 'Darkness on the face of the deep', he is going way back in time to before the

---

[1] 1 Corinthians 3:6-8: 'I planted, Apollos watered, but God was causing the growth. So then neither the one who plants nor the one who waters is anything, but God who causes the growth. Now he who plants and he who waters are one; but each will receive his own reward according to his own labour.'

185

creation of light. Apparently there is a 'baby' about whom he cannot stop thinking. Who is this 'baby'? Orthodox Christian art frequently depicts Christ in the arms of Mary as a baby with mature adult features.

Is Dylan using this depiction as a basis for spiritual metaphor? His 'baby' keeps him awake; many of his songs refer to nocturnal times of spiritual interaction. For example this album's 'Ain't Talkin'' ('As I walked out tonight in the mystic garden'), and the 'Lonesome Day Blues from 'Love And Theft.' ('Last night the wind was whisperin', I was trying to make out what it was.') As Dylan travels, this 'baby' is 'always on his mind', such that he cannot 'stay away'. Apparently Dylan had 'forgotten about' this 'baby' but then his 'baby' 'turned up again'. This is somewhat reminiscent of the Francis Thompson poem of 1907, 'The Hound of Heaven', in which God is likened to a bloodhound who never gives up seeking us in the pursuit of our souls.

Dylan 'always knew' that their relationship was deeper than friends; in Christ we become adopted into the very family of God as one his sons and daughters. Being 'near' him has communicated spiritual truth 'plainly', because the Holy Spirit reveals it, as Jesus had promised. John 16:12-13: "I have much more to say to you, more than you can now bear. But when he, the Spirit of truth comes, he will guide you into all truth. He will not speak on his own; he will speak only what he hears, and he will tell you what is yet to come."

Dylan carries a 'hidden pain' that he cannot fathom the source of, apparently drawing inspiration from Henry Timrod (1828-1867), a US Civil War poet who wrote 'Two Portraits'. 'How then, O weary one! Explain, the sources of that hidden pain', becomes to Dylan, 'Can't explain, the sources of this hidden pain.' This pain of Dylan's seems to come from a sense of spiritual concern, or perhaps a sense of separation, that has been 'burned into his heart'. St Paul wrote to those he watched over in the church at Corinth that 'you yourselves are our letter, written on our hearts, known and read by everybody. You show that you are a letter from Christ, the result of our ministry, written not with ink but with the Spirit of the living God, not on tablets of stone but on tablets of human hearts.' (2 Corinthians 3:2-3).

The 'mud' of life, which Dylan has had to push through, has been made easier by his 'praying to the powers above'. The plurality may indicate the tri-unity of Father, Son and Holy Spirit, and like the second person of that Godhead he is 'sweating blood'; the phenomenon that Jesus experienced before his arrest in the garden of Gethsemane. There Jesus grappled in prayer with the enormity of the spiritual task that lay ahead; to be the sin-bearer, sacrificed for all humanity. While his closest friends slept, Jesus 'in an agony prayed more earnestly: and his sweat was as it were great drops of blood falling down to the ground.' (Luke 22:44, KJV). In extreme traumatic states the blood pressure in the scalp rises to a point causing bleeding into the sweat glands, a recognised medical condition known as haematidrosis.

Without his 'baby', Dylan says his existence is meaningless; his love worthy only of being cast 'into the deep blue sea'. His life has not been easy (not treated 'right'); his own nocturnal experiences seem to do him 'wrong' (perhaps they are painful), yet the relationship somehow surpasses that leaving him 'a thousand times happier', and willing to pay any 'price' for it personally. He may get tired ('feel like laying down'), and this may come across in his appearance; he is as 'pale as a ghost', like the Jewish prophet Daniel after his spiritual encounter. ('Have you ever seen a ghost?' asks Dylan; ghosts being another term for spirit.) 'So I was left alone, gazing at this great vision; I had no strength left, my face turned deathly pale and I was helpless.' (Daniel 10:8, ANIV).

Like Daniel (10:6), Dylan can 'see' the subject of the song. He is 'blinded by the colours', like he sang in 'Dirt Road Blues' ('watching the colours up above'), and rather like the Apostle John was when he received a heavenly vision in the book of Revelation (often quoted by Dylan). 'At once I was in the Spirit, and there before me was a throne in heaven with someone sitting on it. And the one who sat there had the appearance of jasper and carnelian. A rainbow, resembling an emerald, encircled the throne.' (Revelation 4:2-3). The content communicated is not just visual; Dylan can 'hear' this person's name 'ringing up and down the line'. So he will tell it 'plain'; his connection ('ties') are powerful ones that will not let him go, as the prophet Hosea said of God, who 'led them with cords of human kindness, with ties of love.' (Hosea

11:4, ANIV). God (who else could it be?) 'calls' to him from an 'old familiar shrine'; perhaps Calvary, the place where Christ was crucified.

There is a reference in the line 'Can't believe these things would ever fade from your mind', to the Roman poet Ovid ('Black Sea Letters', Book 2, Section 4, Line 24: 'I cannot believe these things could fade from your mind.'). Dylan's revelations are never going to 'fade', and he knows that he will 'live forever' (with God) 'perfectly' (i.e. in heaven).

Everything in the relationship has been meant 'for the best'; even if sometimes it has led to being in 'a brawl'. When Dylan's back is against 'the wall' he will take a break, but he will always 'be back'. The place where Dylan's friend carries his 'thoughts' is 'high on the hill', again a probable reference to Calvary, the place of execution referred to in 'Foot of Pride.' 'I can still see him in my mind climbin' that hill. Did he make it to the top? He probably did, and dropped.' Dylan, like one of the crucified thieves on either side of Christ's cross, wants to 'be with you in paradise' [li] but it seems there is a 'paradise' (perhaps of past experience) that is clearly in the past and which there is no way back to, because he has 'killed a man back there'.

When someone comes to faith and trusts in Christ to save them, there is always a certain 'putting to death' that occurs. [lii] Dylan's spiritual partner has still 'got' a lot for him and to show him; God never retires anyone. Dylan's audiences certainly think he has a few miles left in him; live shows frequently feature the song's lyrics interacting with them in a

---

[li] Luke 23:39-43: 'One of the criminals who were hanged there was hurling abuse at him, saying, "Are you not the Christ? Save yourself and us!" But the other answered, and rebuking him said, "Do you not even fear God, since you are under the same sentence of condemnation? And we indeed are suffering justly, for we are receiving what we deserve for our deeds; but this man has done nothing wrong." And he was saying, "Jesus, remember me when you come in your kingdom!" And he said to him, "Truly I say to you, today you shall be with me in Paradise."'

[lii] Colossians 3:5: 'Put to death whatever belongs to your earthly nature: sexual immorality, impurity, lust, evil desires and greed, which is idolatry.' (ANIV).

type of call and response: 'You think I'm over the hill?' - 'No-o!!' 'You think I'm past my prime?' - 'No-o!!'

The album's third track 'Rollin' And Tumblin'' shares a title and the first two lines ('crying all night') with a Muddy Waters song from 1950, itself derived from Gus Cannon's 'Minglewood Blues' (1928). Dylan sings about his 'troubles', particularly it seems relational ones (a 'slut' charming him). Truly, troubles come to us all, and all the more to the famous. Jesus had said, 'In this world you will have trouble, but take heart! I have overcome the world.' (John 16:33). There is a hint of this optimism in the next line; the countryside 'glows' in the dawn of a new morning that has arrived with a sunrise that makes everything look new and a little different. He is not going to hold anything back, he has 'paid' the price and his 'sufferin'' heart is always on the line', presumably because the heart can only be at rest in God's presence, and it objects when we try and turn away from him.

Both Jesus and the Apostle Paul practiced celibacy, which Dylan's relational problem seems to be leading him towards. ('I swear I ain't gonna touch another [woman] for years.') The theme of seeing 'The rising sun return' seems to remind him of the forthcoming judgement - 'Sooner or later you too shall burn.' Scripture teaches that we will have to give an account of what we have done. ('If any man's work is burned up, he will suffer loss; but he himself will be saved, yet so as through fire.' 1 Corinthians 3:15.) If we are without faith, we will have to give an account of ourselves, with nothing other than our own flawed 'good deeds'. ('Death and Hades were thrown into the lake of fire. This is the second death... And if anyone's name was not found written in the book of life, he was thrown into the lake of fire.' Revelation 20:14-15).

This theme of an impending judgement continues in the next line, with 'the night's shadows', and years that are 'filled with early doom', probably referring to those people who are dying without knowing God, represented by 'long dead souls from their crumblin' tombs'. Mutual forgiveness is encouraged ('Let's forgive each other darlin''), as Jesus had taught. 'If you forgive others for their transgressions, your heavenly father will also forgive you. But if you do not forgive others, then your

Father will not forgive your transgressions.' (Matthew 6:14-15). Forgiveness enables past wrongs to be put behind one, with the effect of releasing the person who has been wronged and bringing them to a place of inner peace. Holding on to the wrongs done only leads to a bitterness that poisons the one wronged, causing the affliction to self-perpetuate.

'When The Deal Goes Down' is yet another spiritually focussed piece. Dylan has walked a long road, and, after a lot of searching, found the hope of eternal life (Titus 1:2), a hope that sustains him on the rest of life's journey. The song opens with another nocturnal setting; the 'ancient light' of the moon is illuminating one of Dylan's nocturnal meditations about the state of a world where 'Wisdom grows up in strife'. The book of Proverbs records that 'Through insolence comes nothing but strife, but wisdom is with those who receive counsel.' (Proverbs 13:10). Sometimes Dylan's paths have been dark and 'bewildering', but he surely knows that God's 'word is a lamp to my feet and a light to my path.' (Psalm 119:105). His 'invisible prayers' gather like a 'cloud', helping the guidance when 'tomorrow' appears uncertain. Proverbs 27:1 reads, 'Do not boast about tomorrow, for you do not know what a day may bring forth.' Many things happen without the reason being apparent, but what Dylan is certain of is that he will be with the one who is guiding him 'when the deal goes down', most likely at his death or when Christ returns, whichever occurs first.

Dylan has flesh and blood like everyone else, and emotions too, even regrets for times when he has 'strayed', presumably away from God's purposes for him. These can 'haunt' him like a raincloud. Sorrow is a part of human life, in which Christ himself shared, albeit on a much deeper spiritual level. The 'thorny crown' is a reference to the physical abuse Christ suffered at the hands of the Roman soldiers who crucified him. 'And after twisting together a crown of thorns, they put it on his head, and a reed in his right hand; and they knelt down before him and mocked him, saying, "Hail, king of the Jews!"' (Matthew 27:29).

Although some of these reflections come to Dylan at night under moonlight, the 'glow' of it is barely palpable; it seems insignificant compared to the light of the spiritual sunlight that Dylan has experienced. He has learned to 'live' and to 'forgive' (as in the previous song) because life is fragile enough without the additional baggage of unforgiveness. There then appears to be another reference to the US Civil War poet, Henry Timrod's 'A Rhapsody Of A Southern Winter Night.' His line 'A round of precious hours… with logic frailer than the flowers' compares with Dylan's 'frailer than the flowers, these precious hours'. This sense of life's fragility is reminiscent of the Apostle James' words: 'What is your life? You are a mist that appears for a little while and then vanishes.' (James 4:14). We are all 'tightly bound' by our experience of our common humanity, but Dylan has revelations that come 'like a vision from the skies', like those of the Apostle John. [liii]

Life's 'noise' and 'joys' do not endure, and Dylan seems determined to rise above the 'disappointment and pain' that inevitably follows sin and human frailties. He won't give in to self-pity, he truly does 'owe his heart' to someone, with whom he will be 'when the deal goes down'.

Until then though, life goes on, with its attendant struggles, including the one with what the Bible describes as the 'old nature', or the 'flesh'. This stands for the patterns of behaviour that recur; trying to re-take territory previously surrendered to the rule of God. The Apostle Paul encouraged the church at Ephesus to 'Put off, concerning the former conversation, the old man, which is corrupt according to the deceitful lusts; and be renewed in the spirit of your mind.' (Ephesians 4:22-23).

The album's fifth song, 'Someday Baby', appears to address, in the third person, this issue of the all too human sinful nature whom we all, with Dylan, 'born to love' but whose neck he wants to 'wring' (not 'ring' as per the official lyrics site). He knows that 'someday' it will cease to

---

[liii] Revelation 1:13-16: 'I saw one like a son of man, clothed in a robe reaching to the feet, and girded across his chest with a golden sash. His head and his hair were white like white wool, like snow; and his eyes were like a flame of fire. His feet were like burnished bronze, when it has been made to glow in a furnace, and his voice was like the sound of many waters. In his right hand he held seven stars, and out of his mouth came a sharp two-edged sword; and his face was like the sun shining in its strength.'

'worry' or be concerned at all 'po'' me' (in the version on 'Tell Tale Signs', Dylan sings 'about me' and ''bo me') any longer, because by then the struggle will be over.

This is what the Apostle John promised (1 John 3:2). 'Beloved, now we are children of God, and it has not appeared as yet what we will be. We know that when he appears, we will be like him, because we will see him just as he is.' This transformation, which starts when a person commits their life to Christ, is concluded when he returns or when he is met when they die, whichever comes first. Then, the 'self doubt' and wasteful behaviour will end, and relief given from what is currently 'driving' him to his 'grave'. Dylan's youthful behaviour was perfectly natural from a human perspective, as the Old Testament prophet Isaiah says: 'We all like sheep have gone astray, each of us has turned to his own way.' (Isaiah 53:6, ANIV). Similarly Psalm 49:14 tells us, 'Like sheep they are destined for the grave, and death will feed on them.'

The only creative input this nature gives is 'the same old thoughts', which keep his cognitive processes 'knotted up', unable to recognize goodness even when it is under his nose - 'Good things I overlooked.' The problem is that he is 'hooked'. There are echoes here of the Apostle Paul's cry, a combination of frustration and revelation. 'Who will set me free from the body of this death? Thanks be to God through Jesus Christ our Lord! So then, on the one hand I myself with my mind am serving the law of God, but on the other, with my flesh the law of sin.' (Romans 7:24-25). The 'flesh' here stands for the old nature, which is put to death through faith in Christ's sacrificial death, and buried in baptism.

'Self-respect' is cited as a motivator for spiritual change. Being a slave to a corrupted human nature is not an attractive idea, but it afflicts all humanity aside from the intervention of God's grace and mercy perfectly demonstrated in Christ's sacrificial offering at Calvary. Dylan is determined to evict this unwanted person, and all their belongings. He knows that their eviction is not a 'natural thing to do'; it goes against our instincts. As St Paul said: 'The man without the Spirit does not accept the things that come from the Spirit of God, for they are foolishness to him, and he cannot understand them, because they are spiritually discerned.' (Corinthians 2:14, ANIV). Loving the old is natural; we are born in that condition. But 'someday', or as the Negro Spirituals say, 'bye and bye', we won't be troubled by it anymore.

'Workingman's Blues #2' is yet another of Dylan's classics, sharing a title with country singer Merle Haggard's 1969 number one hit 'Workin' Man Blues'. Haggard had toured with Dylan in 2005, and this song shares a line 'Sing a little bit of these working man's blues' with Haggard's original.

Dylan's song has a number of spiritual references, and he also appears to have drawn some of his lyrical inspiration from the Roman politician and poet Ovid's (43BC-17AD) poems 'Tristia' ('Sadness') and 'Black Sea Letters'. In scripture, work is a product of the fall of man. As a consequence of sin, God cursed the ground thus making man work hard for a livelihood. In the song Dylan appears to compare the need to take responsibility for spiritual life (with its work of serving God), with the need to take responsibility for working life as an integral part of human life. Neither are as they were intended to be. Because of sin's negative effects there are problems to face, including economic downturn. Dylan may have had the poor economic state in the USSR in mind with his comment about the strength of the proletariat (a Marxist term for the class of industrial workers who do not possess independent capital and have to earn their livelihood from providing labour). The proletariat's purchasing ability has been diminished. The song weaves back and forth between spiritual conflict and the oppressive economic conditions.

Dylan reflects back on a 'place' that he loves the most, presumably the place he met his 'friend' in whom he 'finds no blame', and with whom he is now treading a 'new path'. We are then back to economic oppression that seeks to find any reason to keep wages low and profits high. The poet Ovid now makes an appearance, as we learn that 'cruel weapons have been put on the shelf.' (From Ovid's 'Tristia', book 2. 'Show mercy, I beg you, shelve your cruel weapons.') The one Dylan is singing to is 'dearer' to him than he himself is (another line from Ovid, 'Tristia', book 5), 'as you yourself can see', and so could easily be seen as being Christ, who can 'see' spiritual love when it is present.

Trains feature prominently in Dylan's Northern Minnesotan outlook, and we find him 'listenin' to the steel rails hum' (maybe 'a slow train' is coming?) with his eyes closed, as in prayer and meditation answering a spiritual 'hunger'. We are invited to 'meet' him, bringing his 'boots and shoes'. Only one set of shoes can be worn at a time so this may be a reference to the shoes God provides; 'Having your feet shod with the preparation of the gospel of peace.' (Ephesians 6:15, KJV). There is a spiritual battle going on, which is part of the spiritual work we have to do. We are invited to join in and 'fight your best.'

Dylan has been a keen sailor in the Caribbean, and the next verse finds him settling down for the 'long haul', but no matter how stormy it gets, he will fulfill his mission and see judgement come upon his spiritual enemies. To recuperate, he 'feeds his soul with thought' in meditation, a lot of which happens at night, meaning he needs to sleep during the daytime. It is not always so easy to fulfill God's purposes; he laments that 'sometimes no one wants what you got.' They ignore the message, even though the good news comes free of charge - 'given away'. We are then back to warfare and Ovid again with 'the place is ringed with countless foes', or, as Ovid put it, 'I'm barred from relaxation, in a place ringed by countless foes.' (Tristia 5.12.19-20). There is also an echo of Psalm 22:12 and its prediction of the crucifixion: 'Many bulls surround me; strong bulls of Bashan encircle me.' 'Bulls' here is a metaphor for evil spirits, and Dylan adds that 'some of them may be deaf and dumb', as evil spirits are sometimes referred to as being. [liv] No one knows when this 'sorrow' will come to pass. As Jesus said, 'But of that day or hour no one knows, not even the angels in heaven, nor the Son, but the Father alone.' (Mark 13:32).

Then it is back to night-time and the birdsong, with Dylan still in touch with somebody. He 'can feel *[not 'hear' as on the official lyrics site]* a

---

[liv] Mark 9:25-27: 'When Jesus saw that the people came running together, he rebuked the foul spirit, saying unto him, "Thou dumb and deaf spirit, I charge thee, come out of him, and enter no more into him." And the spirit cried, and rent him sore, and came out of him: and he was as one dead; insomuch that many said, "He is dead." But Jesus took him by the hand, and lifted him up; and he arose.' (KJV).

lover's breath... sleep is like a temporary death.' This is another paraphrase from the Civil War poet Henry Timrod (from 'Two Portraits'). ''Ere they feel a lover's breath, lie in a temporary death.' In the Old Testament (Song of Solomon 2:10-12), Christ is portrayed as a lover. 'My lover spoke and said to me, "Arise, my darling, my beautiful one, and come with me. See! The winter is past; the rains are over and gone. Flowers appear on the earth; the season of singing has come."'

Then we are back again to economic pressures with arson, theft, and a different type of night approaching as the sun begins to go down. 'Am I wrong in thinking, that you have forgotten me?' is another line reminiscent of Ovid. 'May the gods grant... that I'm wrong in thinking you've forgotten me!' ('Tristia', Book 2, page 179). The good news is that God does not forget his children. 'Can a mother forget the baby at her breast and have no compassion on the child she has born? Though she may forget, I will not forget you! See, I have engraved you on the palms of my hands; your walls are ever before me.' (Isaiah 49:15-16).

'Them I will forget' is also from Ovid's 'Black Sea Letters'; 'Them I'll forget, but you I'll remember always.' 'Wounded me with your words' is reminiscent of Shakespeare ('Titus Andronicus'), 'These words are razors to my wounded heart.' Dylan sings of a 'friend' in whom he 'finds no blame', reminiscent of Christ, his king. 'You know that he appeared in order to take away sins; and in him there is no sin.' (1 John 3:5). This friend can read Dylan's soul anytime; he knows that Dylan has never set out to oppose him. This is also taken from Ovid's 'Tristia', book 2. 'My cause is better; no-one can claim that I ever took up arms against you.' The battle will rage across earth's 'sacred fields', but opposition will be in vain. 'Those who contend with the Lord will be shattered; against them he will thunder in the heavens. The Lord will judge the ends of the earth; and he will give strength to his king, and will exalt the horn of his anointed.' (1 Samuel 2:10).

Dylan seems to be sore with the conflict, but is still ready for more. 'Expecting you to lead me off in a cheerful dance' is another line from Ovid, 'Tristia', Book 5. 'Niobe, bereaved, lead off some cheerful dance.' Dylan has a 'brand new suit'; Haggard's version has a 'brand new pair of shoes'. He is ready to live in simplicity if necessary ('rice and beans'). He is not yet ready to stop working. As he has said, electricians don't have to stop work, so why should he? (See page 239).

'Beyond The Horizon' draws melodic inspiration from the Kennedy and Williams' song 'Red Sails In The Sunset' (1935), and is about as clear a Christian message as you can get without flatly stating it. In fact, 'my repentance is plain' is just about as flat as you can get. A clearer statement of Dylan's spiritual position would be hard to envisage.

The track finds Dylan looking forward to the day when he will be in the presence of perfect love, in heaven, where the one he experiences transiently now will be fully known by him. Heaven is 'behind the sun', the place where life, real life, actually starts. Eternal life, with a new spiritual body, begins after this life has finished. Yet again Dylan's night-time meditations come through with the 'long hours of twilight'. He is looking towards the place where the main character trait of God (love) comes easily, without the interference of any sin-stained nature. As the Apostle Paul said, 'For now we see in a mirror dimly, but then face to face; now I know in part, but then I will know fully just as I also have been fully known. But now faith, hope, love, abide these three; but the greatest of these is love.' (1 Corinthians 13:12-13).

Dylan has had some personal trials and tribulations; he has come 'through flame and through fire', and now seems to orientate his universe around his saviour, who is waiting for him on the other side of the 'divide' between life and death. When it is crossed, he knows that they will both be 'on the same side' and he will be permanently in God's presence.

That cannot be taken for granted though; there is a 'valley' where the 'water runs cold'. Valleys stand for places of spiritual darkness, as Psalm 23:4 relates, 'Even though I walk through the darkest valley, I fear no evil; for you are with me.' The song's hope is that 'someone prayed for your soul', so this place can be avoided. Revelation (5:8) describes the intercessory prayer in heaven where 'the twenty-four elders fell down before the Lamb. Each one had a harp and they were holding golden bowls full of incense, which are the prayers of the saints.'

Dylan can feel 'an angel's kiss', signifying God's love and acceptance of him; old reproaches fall away with the sense of 'mortal bliss' of his experience of God's love. He is now in step in his spiritual relationship - 'Walking the same.' 'The [church] bells of St Mary' remind him that he 'found' God 'just in time', before the destructive tendencies around him took hold. His night-time work continues with him 'pleading', presumably in intercessory prayer, and perhaps not getting the answers he wants. He can say hand on heart though that his 'repentance is plain'; he has turned back towards the God of his fathers through trusting in Messiah and his sacrificial death. Repentance is part of coming to God; 'changing one's mind' about what counts in life, or as Dylan had previously written (and would re-write), 'Gonna Change My Way Of Thinking'.

With the 'treacherous sea' of life's uncertainties, he still 'can't believe' that God has 'set aside' his love for him, as the Apostle Paul wrote. [iv] When daybreak comes Dylan will 'follow' with his 'eyes', as Psalm 123:2 relates, 'as the eyes of servants look to the hand of their master, as the eyes of a maid to the hand of her mistress, so our eyes look to the Lord our God, until he is gracious to us.' God has always cared about all his children, and regularly 'spares people's lives' that don't deserve it. He has a plan for everybody's life, even though not everyone finds it. In heaven, beyond this life, there is indeed 'more than a lifetime to live lovin' you'; there is all eternity 'knowing that you have a better and an enduring possession for yourselves in heaven.' (Hebrews 10:34, KJV).

[iv] Ephesians 2:4-9: 'God, being rich in mercy, because of his great love with which he loved us, even when we were dead in our transgressions, made us alive together with Christ - it is by grace you have been saved. And God raised us up with him, and seated us with him in the heavenly places in Christ Jesus, so that in the ages to come he might show the surpassing riches of his grace in kindness toward us in Christ Jesus. For by grace you have been saved through faith; and that not of yourselves, it is the gift of God; not as a result of works, so that no one may boast.'

'Nettie Moore' was the subject of an 1857 song ('Gentle Nettie Moore', by Marshall Pike and James Lord Pierpont). She was a black house slave who was sold on into a life of misery, as the original song recounts. 'One sunny morn in Autumn, 'ere the dew had left the lawn, came a trader up from Louisiana bay, who gave to master money, and then shackled her with chains, and then he took her off to work her life away.' The oppression of the Negro race (well documented and in the UK described by Charles Dickens in his 'American Notes' of 1842), provides a rich source of analogies with man's spiritual condition.

The song opens with a character called 'Lost John', a reference to another black slave, as in the song 'Lost John' by Van Morrison. Something is wrong ('out of whack'); there is a sense of depression about, described as 'blues' that descend like 'hail'. Dylan is going to continue to 'travel' and 'struggle'; it would appear that his mission is meeting with opposition. As he says, he has 'a pile of sins to pay for'. Dylan seems to believe and takes seriously the idea that he can make some form of reparation for past wrongdoing by serving God in the here and now. He is willing to 'walk through fire' if need be for his 'baby', a term he seems to use occasionally as a euphemism for Christ, the baby of the Bethlehem manger.

The chorus takes lines from the original song: 'Oh, I miss you Nettie Moore, and my happiness is o'er', and contrasts the coming of spring, as reflected in the rising of the river water, with the emptiness experienced after the tragedy of Nettie Moore's enforced slavery. Humankind in general appears to be in a poor state ('research has gone berserk'); indicating that men's knowledge had got ahead of their moral capacity to apply that knowledge responsibly, as nuclear issues illustrate. 'They are raising hell'. 'Albert' (now dead - 'in the graveyard') may be Albert Einstein of nuclear physics fame; apocalyptic images so familiar to Dylan from his studies of the book of Revelation may be behind the line about him 'believing what the scriptures tell'.

Dylan will head for the location of Moorhead, Mississippi, where the 'Southern' (the railroad track out of New Orleans) intersects with the 'Yellow Dog' (also known as the Yazoo Delta railroad). This represents the heartland of Mississippi Delta blues music. The dangers of excess alcohol and 'bad luck women' get a mention before we get back to Dylan's baby whose 'cooking' (perhaps standing for the spiritual food Dylan receives) takes 'all night' to digest. We then turn to the 'Judge' with a capital 'J', before whom all mankind will eventually 'rise'. Dylan tells us, 'Lift up your eyes', presumably to God, before whose 'judgement seat we will all stand'. (Romans 14:10). We all have freewill as a gift from God and so can do as we please, but wrongdoing like slander ('calling dirty names') has consequences, so 'think twice'.

The 'steady lights' (of heaven) make everything we see down here seems darker ('dimmed'), more so by the tears that fall when Dylan's 'grief gives way' and he can express how he feels toward the one about whom 'a lifetime with is like some heavenly day'. As the Apostle Peter wrote: 'Beloved, do not forget this one thing, that with the Lord one day is as a thousand years, and a thousand years as one day.' (2 Peter 3:8, NKJV). He is confident that he will 'stand in faith, and raise the voice of praise', because he stands 'in the light', presumably of God's love. Soon 'night' will come, when no man can work' (John 9:4), followed by Christ's return; Dylan 'wishes to God' that it will come.

'The Levee's Gonna Break' is another song with floods as a symbol of judgement, along the lines of 'High Water (For Charlie Patton)'. The springtime rise in the Mississippi water tests the levee flood barriers, vital for survival in the low-lying southern US states bordering the mighty river. (This was brought home in 2005 when New Orleans was flooded following Hurricane Katrina.) Africans brought to New Orleans on slave ships in the 1700's were usually sold as agricultural slaves, and many worked building the flood barriers to protect the farmland from river flooding. Dylan draws the comparison with the spiritual slavery that sin causes people to live in; people 'sold into bondage to sin'. (Romans 7:14). God's eventual judgement will be 'a day only the Lord could make'.

The song starts with a scene of a slave gang of forced labourers working around the clock to secure the river's flood barrier, but then seems to switch to an escape. Dylan makes is as far as a river where he throws his 'clothes away', presumably so that any pursuing dogs could not pick up the scent and track him down. Crossing a river is also symbolic of baptism; candidates would receive a change of clothes symbolic of making a new start. This is reinforced by Dylan saying he has become 'good as new'; paying for 'his time' can be seen as buying his freedom from the plantation owner - he is now a free man.

That does not mean everything is wonderful; for some, greed is the motivating factor (they will 'strip all they can take'), but that's not going to worry Dylan for whom 'salvation can be waiting behind the next bend in the road' in a heavenly kingdom. There seems to be a change of speaker in the next verse, which describes the ingratitude commonly displayed by those who have received significant help. ('I pick you up from the gutter and this is the thanks I get.') God doesn't 'quit' on us; after he has taken us from the spiritual rubbish heap and adopted us into God's family. 'Never will I leave you; never will I forsake you.' (Hebrews 13:5, ANIV). Jesus said: 'I am with you always, even to the end of the age.' (Matthew 28:20). When Dylan looks into this person's eyes he sees, tellingly, 'All that I am and all I hope to be', and presumably all he will become. This is because God both shows us our present state (of spiritual need) and also what is possible for us when he comes to work in us - a great source of hope.

There is always the choice in life of which 'road to take'; the broad or the narrow way. As Jesus said, "Enter through the narrow gate; for the gate is wide and the way is broad that leads to destruction, and there are many who enter through it. For the gate is small and the way is narrow that leads to life, and there are few who find it." (Matthew 7:13-14). When Dylan is with the one he is singing to, he 'forgets he was ever blue' (the depression and the memory of it lifts right off him). But when he feels they have drawn apart, 'there's no meaning in anything he does'; presumably because it is his faith-relationship that gives his life meaning and direction.

The need to leave town due to the impending flooding means that some folk are travelling 'carrying everything that they own.' The poorest slaves are practically only skin and bones. Not all are in that condition;

'Mama' has her 'camp clothes'. ('Camp' being a slang term based on the French 'se camper' - 'to pose in an exaggerated fashion; in this case referring to evening dress.) Otherwise the 'cat clothes' (clothing worn once by a fashion model on a catwalk and then sold to rich clients to wear) can be worn for a 'few more years'. After that is the millennium after Christ's return ('a thousand years of happiness'), yet another reference to the book of Revelation. [lvi]

In the meantime life goes on, mistakes and all, such as being overly motivated by the desire to please people who are really only interested in the 'cheap stuff'. He finds that 'butter and eggs' (a North American noxious weed called 'toadflax', noted for its showy flowers) gets 'in his bed'. This weed can choke him out if he is not careful. Jesus had said: "'Good seed' stands for the sons of the kingdom. The 'weeds' are the sons of the evil one." (Matthew 13:38, ANIV). Some may be asleep to the spiritual realities that exist, but to those who are 'wide awake', Christ brings a spiritual relationship that he will maintain without 'ever more parting'.

The album closed with 'Ain't Talkin', a song that appears to say a lot about where Dylan was coming from in regards to his faith. Walking is a scriptural term for living out the Christian life. 'This I say, and affirm together with the Lord, that you walk no longer just as the Gentiles (non-Jews) also walk, in the futility of their mind, being darkened in their understanding, excluded from the life of God because of the ignorance that is in them, because of the hardness of their heart.' (Ephesians 4:17-18). Dylan has stopped 'talking' openly about his faith and now speaks about it, in the language of parables and allegory, as Christ often did.

The song opens, as is usual in Dylan's more meditative pieces, with a night time excursion to a place of intimacy and spiritual fellowship in a

---

[lvi] Revelation 20:1-3: 'I saw an angel coming down from heaven, holding the key of the abyss and a great chain in his hand. And he laid hold of the dragon, the serpent of old, who is the devil and Satan, and bound him for a thousand years; and he threw him into the abyss, and shut it and sealed it over him, so that he would not deceive the nations any longer, until the thousand years were completed; after these things he must be released for a short time.'

201

'mystic garden', reminiscent of Adam and Eve walking with God in the Garden of Eden. 'The man and his wife heard the sound of the Lord God as he was walking in the garden in the cool of the day.' (Genesis 3:8, ANIV). Dylan is making his journey through a 'world of woe' and is 'weary'. He has stopped openly 'talkin'' about his faith, but he still living it out ('walkin''). His heart burns as he yearns; almost certainly in relation to God, just as the disciples that Jesus met on their way to Emmaus found. They said to one another, "Were not our hearts burning within us while he was speaking to us on the road, while he was explaining the scriptures to us?" (Luke 24:32).

Dylan quotes that 'prayer has the power to heal', and asks for prayer for himself. He is aware that demons ('evil spirits') are for real and can enter ('dwell in') the hearts of men and women causing great oppression. He is doing his best walking out his faith, 'trying to love his neighbour and do good unto others', as the Bible teaches. "'Love the Lord your God with all your heart and with all your soul and with all your mind and with all your strength.' 'Love your neighbour as yourself', there is no commandment greater than these." (Mark 12:30-31, ANIV). Unfortunately things are not going as well as he would like ('Oh mother, things ain't going well'), so 'talking' will have to wait a while until he has walked his walk for a little longer.

He is 'worn down by weeping' perhaps in sorrow or possibly from intercessory prayer, as in 'Thunder On The Mountain', for Alicia Keys. Dylan has real spiritual enemies too, that he is determined to overcome. He will not allow his thinking to be 'torn away from contemplation' by idle 'speculation' and various philosophies that lead nowhere. As he sings on 'High Water (For Charlie Patton)'; 'You can't open up your mind boys, to every conceivable point of view.' The delta blues get another nod with the reference to 'hog eyed grease in a hog eyed town'; a 'hog-eye' being the slang term for the Mississippi River barges.

Fame can work negatively, like a curse ('wealth and power can crush'). Dylan will 'make the most' of whatever time that he has left in God's plan for his life in 'practicing his faith that's been long abandoned', presumably the spirituality of his Messianic Judaism. There are 'no altars on that road' because a once-for-all sacrifice has already been made. His 'not talking' may be because 'the fire's gone out', 'but the light is never dying'; Christ's light still shines even when zeal wanes. Dylan can get 'heavenly aid'; it is always available to him through the Holy Spirit and angelic help. [lvii] He knows that all is 'bright in the heavens'; 'the flying wheels' are reminiscent of Ezekiel's vision of the throne of God and the accompanying angelic beings that the prophet described.

Dylan is 'carryin' a dead man's shield'; the shield of faith of Ephesians 6:16 ('...taking up the shield of faith'). This 'man' had been 'dead' for three days, then raised to life in bodily form; albeit a new type of body, one that could appear and disappear. He is 'walkin' with a toothache in his heel', surely a reference to the devil who struck at Christ's heel. The book of Genesis contains the prophecy that 'He [Christ] will crush your [the devil's] head, and you [the devil] will strike his [Christ's] heel.' (Genesis 3:15, ANIV). He is 'sufferin'', right enough, like the Apostle Paul who could say, 'I rejoice in my sufferings for your sake, and in my flesh I do my share on behalf of his body, which is the church, in filling up what is lacking in Christ's afflictions.' (Colossians 1:24). He will keep walking until 'clean out of sight' (in heaven, which the eye can't see).

The song ends back in 'the mystic garden', only this time it seems to be the garden of Jesus' burial, where Mary Magdalene confused the risen Christ for the local gardener. 'Jesus said to her, "Woman, why are you

---

[lvii] Ezekiel 1:16-21: 'The appearance of the wheels and their workmanship was like sparkling beryl, and all four of them had the same form, their appearance and workmanship being as if one wheel were within another. Whenever they moved, they moved in any of their four directions without turning as they moved. As for their rims they were lofty and awesome, and the rims of all four of them were full of eyes round about. Whenever the living beings moved, the wheels moved with them. And whenever the living beings rose from the earth, the wheels rose also. Wherever, the spirit was about to go, they would go in that direction. And the wheels rose close beside them; for the spirit of the living beings was in the wheels. Whenever those went, these went; and whenever those stood still, these stood still.'

weeping? Whom are you seeking?" Supposing him to be the gardener, she said to him, "Sir, if you have carried him away, tell me where you have laid him, and I will take him away." Jesus said to her, "Mary!" She turned and said to him in Hebrew, "Rabboni!" (which means, Teacher). Jesus said to her, "Stop clinging to me, for I have not yet ascended to the Father; but go to my brethren and say to them, 'I ascend to my Father and your Father, and my God and your God.'" (John 20:15-17). Or as Dylan puts it: 'Excuse me, ma'am, I beg your pardon, there's no one here; the gardener is gone.' Gone up into heaven, 'the last outback at the world's end'.

'Modern Times' saw Dylan clearly setting out his stall of faith, bringing his audience right up to date with his spiritual journey. The fact that so few people seemed to 'get it' may have contributed to his choice of title for the next album (after the compilation CD set 'Dylan' in 2007). 'Tell Tale Signs' there were aplenty. But would they be recognized?

Chapter 14

'Tell Tale Signs' and 'Together Through Life'.

2008 saw another set of outtakes and rare recordings of hitherto unpublished material, in the form of a 2 CD (and a limited edition 3 CD) collection, entitled 'Tell Tale Signs: The Bootleg Series Vol. 8 - Rare and Unreleased 1989-2006'. Most of the material has been commented on under the albums from the sessions in which they were originally recorded, but there are some previously unreleased post-1983 numbers (the main subject matter of this book), as follows.

'Red River Shore' (from disc 1) was dropped from the 'Time Out Of Mind' sessions, much to the disbelief of sessional musician Jim Dickinson, who said, 'They left the best song off the record.' [78] (And presumably also Sean Curnyn, who has called it 'Just maybe the greatest thing this Bob Dylan guy has ever done'.) [79] The song shares a title with one performed by the 'Kingston Trio' (an American folk band from the 1950's), but that is about all; Dylan's traditional folk-style leaves lesser artists behind with his poetry.

The identity of the 'Girl From The Red River Shore' has been the subject of some debate. At points she seems to be a real person: 'I sat by her side and for a while I tried, to make that girl my wife'. Yet at other times it is clear that she is not: 'Everybody that I talked to who had seen us there, said that they didn't know who I was talking about.' The song has a very definite spiritual content. Dylan sings of being 'where angels fly' at the end of the first verse, and of himself as a 'stranger in a strange land', which is Moses' description while in Midian (Exodus 2:22). To cap it off the final verse is dedicated to the Messiah of Isaiah 53. 'Now I heard of a guy who lived a long time ago, a man full of sorrow and strife, that if someone around him died and was dead, he knew how to bring him on back to life.' Isaiah's prophecy reads: 'He was despised and forsaken of men, a man of sorrows and acquainted with grief; and like one from whom men hide their face. He was despised, and we did not esteem him. Surely our griefs he himself bore, and our sorrows he carried; yet we ourselves esteemed him stricken, smitten of God, and afflicted. But he was pierced through for our transgressions, he was crushed for our iniquities; the chastening for our well-being fell upon him, and by his scourging we are healed. All of us like sheep have gone astray, each of us has turned to his own way; but the Lord has caused the iniquity of us all to fall on him.' (Isaiah 53:3-6). Jesus' ability to raise the dead (and not simply resuscitate people) is recorded in Matthew 9:18 (the synagogue ruler's daughter), in Luke 7:15 (the widow of Nain's son) and in John 11:44 (Lazarus, who had been dead for three days).

The theme of the 'girl' seems to be related to the Jewish scripture's use of the concept of the feminine personification of wisdom, as in 'Seek her as silver, and search for her as for hidden treasures' (Proverbs 24), and 'Does not wisdom call, and understanding lift up her voice?' (Proverbs 8:1). This would tie in with the line: 'She gave me her best advice, she said: "Go home and lead a quiet life."' This is a typically Jewish and wise piece of advice, quite in keeping with that which the Jewish Apostle Paul gave to his disciple Timothy, in relation to prayer. 'Pray for all... that we may lead a quiet and peaceable life in all godliness and honesty.' (1 Timothy 2:2). Spiritual wisdom is to be found in the word of God; something that is seen but often not fully comprehended: 'They didn't know who I was talking about.'

'Tell Ol' Bill' was part of the soundtrack for the 2005 film 'North Country', about a woman facing harassment while working as a miner in Dylan's region of origin, Northern Minnesota. The movie's theme only obliquely impacts the lyrics (Dylan sings of 'bleak rocks' and 'iron clouds'), and does not detract from an underlying spiritual content. The first verse's lyrics, 'The heavens never seemed so near, all of my body glows with flame', is reminiscent of Jesus' 'transfiguration' as recorded in Matthew chapter 17. [lviii] 'Glowing with flame' aptly summarises Jesus' post-ascension bodily state as witnessed by the apostle John on the Isle of Patmos. 'His eyes were like a flame of fire. His feet were like

---

[lviii] Matthew 17:1-3: 'Six days later Jesus took with him Peter and James and John his brother, and led them up on a high mountain by themselves. And he was transfigured before them; and his face shone like the sun, and his garments became as white as light. And behold, Moses and Elijah appeared to them, talking with him.'

burnished bronze, when it has been made to glow in a furnace.' (Revelation 1:14-15). Dylan then sings of being tortured by someone who has 'come down from your high hill'. In scripture the 'high hill' is linked with the practice of pagan idol worship, e.g. 'Solomon built a high place for Chemosh the detestable idol of Moab, on the mountain which is east of Jerusalem, and for Molech the detestable idol of the sons of Ammon.' (1 Kings 11:7). And, 'They set for themselves sacred pillars and Asherim on every high hill.' (2 Kings 17:10). The song then moves on to the one who has 'left the coldest kiss upon his brow' and ends with the rather more hopeful, 'I look at you now and I sigh. How can it be any other way?' There seems to be an underlying spiritual relationship at work, one that supports Dylan in his statement, 'All the world I would defy.'

'Dreamin' Of You' hales from the 'Time Out Of Mind' album sessions. It is another song bearing the hallmarks of the depression (e.g. 'Feel further away than I ever did before, feel further than I can take'), that followed Dylan's divorce from Carolyn Dennis, a fellow Christian. At this point in his life he may have experienced various forms of recrimination. But in this song he seems to have a new vision for moving forward spiritually with the one he has never stopped 'dreamin' of'. Many of the lyrics (e.g. 'Flesh falling off his face") are shared with 'Standing In The Doorway' from the 1997 album 'Time Out Of Mind', such as the opening line about the 'bad' quality of the light with which he is working. He feels it is like being in a (bad) 'dream'. It has caused him much emotional trauma and spiritual disturbance, even identifying himself with the death of a 'child' who never had the opportunity to weep or to smile; in other words, an autistic child existing somewhat beyond the reach of human emotions. He 'ponders his faith in the rain'; thinking on it despite the adverse circumstances of post-divorce depression.

But he is not without hope; a new day ('dawn') is coming, representing a new start with God, about whom it is written, 'The Lord's loving kindnesses indeed never cease, For his compassions never fail. They are new every morning; great is your faithfulness.' (Lamentations 3:22-23). The concept of making a fresh start with God is a common biblical one that is echoed in 'Thunder On The Mountain' ('Modern Times'). 'For the love of God you ought to take pity on yourself.' Dylan reflects this idea again in his late 2009-2011 stage show version of 'Gonna Change My Way Of Thinking', to which he has added a new line: 'Every day you've got to give yourself another chance.'

Back in the song, 'church bells' can be heard, causing Dylan to reflect on their message; for whom are they ringing? In 'Ring Them Bells' ('Oh Mercy'), they ring 'so the world will know that God is one'. Bells also figure in Dylan's 'Standing In The Doorway.' ('Time Out Of Mind'). 'I can hear the church bells ringing in the yard; I wonder who they're ringing for.' Dylan still has his 'pain', because some emotions last for a longer time than he thought they would, but most importantly he still has his dreams.

Eating when 'hungry' and drinking when 'dry' are lines that appear in the traditional folk song 'Rye Whiskey'. 'I'll eat when I'm hungry, I'll drink when I'm dry, and when I get thirsty I'll lay down and cry.' Dylan appears to be focussing on the present ('living life on the square'), which he knows will go well, so long as 'you're there', and 'care'. God fulfills both being there and caring. The description of Dylan as a 'ghost in love, underneath the heavens above' could be equally well replaced by 'spirit.' Dylan's spirit is still 'in love' with God, despite the emotional trauma that has led to him feeling 'further away'.

'Everything in the way' is reminiscent of the term applied to the early followers of Christ. As the Apostle Paul said (Acts 24:14), 'I admit to you, that according to the Way which they call a sect I do serve the God of our fathers, believing everything that is in accordance with the Law and that is written in the Prophets.' Dylan's 'way' appears 'so shiny today'; possibly his spiritual eyes can detect the shining of God's reflected glory in what he sees around him; things look different when seen from the perspective of God's kingdom. The 'spirals of golden haze in a blaze' is scriptural language also signifying God's glory. Revelation (8:3-5) describes 'smoke of incense' from a golden censor; an offering at an altar before God's throne, being accompanied by peals of thunder, with lightning flashes blazing.

Also on disc 1 was 'Huck's Tune', a song written as part of the soundtrack for the 2007 film 'Lucky You' (and so qualifies as part of Dylan's so-called 'post-Christian' works). This was a drama about a poker player by the name of Huck Cheever. The first verse finds Dylan in a 'desert of stone', which surely stands for a dry barren place of unresponsiveness; the condition of many human hearts. From Dylan's perspective, 'death' can in truth be referred to as 'life', in so far as our lives on earth prepare us for the moment of death, which is the point of entry into eternity and everlasting life. Where we spend eternity depends on us and how we respond to God's invitation to enter a personal and spiritual relationship with him, which is what Christ's sacrifice made possible.

Dylan's 'plate' and 'cup' being 'straight up' appears to be a reference to Christ's criticism of the Jewish religious leaders whose outward show of pretentious piety hid their inner rottenness. "Woe to you, scribes and Pharisees, hypocrites! For you clean the outside of the cup and of the plate, but inside they are full of greed and self-indulgence. You blind Pharisee! First clean the inside of the cup, so that the outside also may become clean." (Matthew 23:25-26, italics mine).

Next is a reference to Dylan's often-quoted Old Testament book, the Song of Solomon. 'When I kiss your lips, the honey drips' is an image found in Song of Solomon 4:11. 'Your lips, my bride, drip honey; honey and milk are under your tongue.' The same text then describes an occasion where the bridegroom leaves the bride, temporarily. 'I opened for my lover, but my lover had left; he was gone. My heart sank at his departure. I looked for him but did not find him.' (Song of Solomon 5:6). This completes the idea of being 'put down for a while'.

There is a gambling theme (as per the movie) with the verse about pushing 'it all in' despite having 'no chance to win'. The stakes are loaded against winning in the game of life if you are separated from God's mercy and grace. But some folk carry on regardless, blind to their losing outcome, and so 'play 'em to the end'. He goes on to sing that his 'faith is cold' (it is nowhere near dead), but that he is 'not without proof'. His faith is based upon many evidences. ('Having overlooked the times of ignorance, God is now declaring to men that all people everywhere should repent, because he has fixed a day in which he will judge the world in righteousness through a man whom he has appointed, having furnished proof to all men by raising him from the dead.' Acts 17:30-31). 'Come see' and 'find no guile' are direct references to John's gospel (1:46-47, KJV) where Philip tells his friend Nathaniel about Jesus. 'Nathaniel said unto him, "Can there any good thing come out of Nazareth?" Philip saith unto him, "Come and see." Jesus saw Nathaniel coming to him, and saith of him, "Behold an Israelite indeed, in whom is no guile!"' If an expression of his faith has been 'put down for a while', it is only for a while.

'Marching To The City' is another outtake from the 'Time Out Of Mind' recordings, and it shares some of the lyrics of 'Till I Fell In Love With You'. In common with much of this album's material, this too chronicles Dylan's recovery from post-divorce depression ('Feel heavy like lead'), and his moving onwards and upwards towards the celestial city which is the subject of the song. The song opens with a reflection on life's direction, and starts with Dylan 'Sitting in church' (an unlikely place for a Jew who was not a Messianic Jew), knowing that this is the last place many of his fans will think to look for him!

'Loneliness' (especially post-relationship breakup depressive loneliness) is not easy to snap out of, and is not helped by having a crowd about you ('the more people around you, the more you feel alone'). Dylan feels 'chained' to this earthly sphere of existence, unable to connect well with heaven, and compares himself to a 'silent slave' bound up in life's negative consequences, but all the while 'trying to break free'. Jesus promised, "If you continue in my word, then you are truly disciples of mine; and you will know the truth, and the truth will make you free." (John 8:31-32). When that happens we can exit the 'dark cave' of life's futility and an existence apart from God (which the Bible describes as spiritual death) and into newness of life, 'buried with him through baptism into death, so that as Christ was raised from the dead through the glory of the Father, so we too might walk in newness of life.' (Romans 6:4). Dylan, we learn, is 'thinking about paradise, wondering what it might be'.

The old 'wrong' of his divorce, presumably, is behind him and he can move onwards and upwards to that city that is now not all that far off from him in terms of his life's journey. He had hoped within his 'soul' that they would never split up; that together they would 'drink from life's clear streams', but it is not to be. His 'house' is on fire, burning towards heaven now ('the skies'), rather than burning down to the ground. The rain promised has passed him by, and the withholding of rain was seen by the Israelites as a judgement from God. ('You have polluted a land with your harlotry and with your wickedness. Therefore the showers have been withheld, and there has been no spring rain.' Jeremiah 3:3.) Dylan did not get re-married with the intention of getting divorced again, but it happened, and now it seems that it is 'time to get away' and sort out his depressed state of mind so that he will know what he is 'a-gonna do'.

'Can't Escape From You' is another previously unreleased number. Recorded in 2005, the track (no relation to the Hank Williams song of the same name) compares the gloom of earth with what is promised 'over the horizon'; it appears to lament the fact that many have not grasped faith in the way that it is possible to. The song opens describing life's 'evening train' taking Dylan home. His focus is the other side of 'the horizon'; presumably in heaven, and his 'dreams' seem to have been placed to one side allowing him to focus more closely on God's revealed purposes for him. Night is drawing in; the notion of 'stars' falling 'from above' is reminiscent of the Bible's use of that term for angels (as in Daniel 8:10 and Revelation 9:1.) The pleasures and happiness of life on earth, however good, are always going to fade when compared with heaven, where 'eye has not seen, nor ear heard, neither have entered into the heart of man, the things which God has prepared for them that love him.' (1 Corinthians 2:9, KJV).

In Dylan's post-divorce depressed state of mind, night is 'untouched by love'. The concept of the dark 'shroud' is reminiscent of St Paul's words that 'the wages of sin is death', which we all experience, but for those who have trusted in Christ, 'The free gift of God is eternal life in Christ Jesus our Lord.' (Romans 6:23). In his current condition he can only 'pretend' to be without sorrowful feelings. The 'bells' he can hear tolling are 'dead', and he seems to feel that his train 'is overdue' to be carrying him to his eternal heavenly home.

He is 'clinging' to the recollections of one from whom he 'can't escape'. The sound of a storm with its associated image of God's judgement ('thunder roaring loud and long') makes him 'wonder' what he has done to bring this particular judgement about. His strength seems to have been sapped away, like King David's who described himself in Psalm 31:10, 'My life is spent with sorrow, and my years with sighing; my strength has failed because of my iniquity, and my body has wasted away.' Somebody has thrown away the 'Christmas pie', which could easily stand for the blessing in this life that Jesus' (Christmas) incarnation into human form is supposed to bring us. Persistent sin and rebellion has caused a 'withering', and ignoring or rejecting the reality of God's existence will inevitably lead to spiritual death.

The song then cheers up somewhat with another reference to heaven ('the far off sweet forever') where the light of God's love is unstoppable. 'Shadows' (such as painful past memories) have congregated, and 'rain' is falling, bringing back a sense of the melancholy. Ahead of him his 'path' winds its way homeward towards eternity and heaven. There the angelic spirit-beings ('stars', as in Daniel 8:10) never grow old and die, and God's mercies are new every morning. 'The Lord's loving kindnesses indeed never cease, for his compassions never fail. They are new every morning; great is your faithfulness.' (Lamentations 3:22-23).

We then have a quotation from Shakespeare, 'All the world's a stage.' ('As You Like It' Act 2, 7: 'All the world's a stage and all the men and women merely players; they have their exits and their entrances.') A 'mystery of madness' has afflicted everyone; a likely reference to God sending confusion as a judgement on sin. 'The Lord will afflict you with madness, blindness and confusion of mind.' (Deuteronomy 28:28, ANIV). It is 'propagated in the air', as the Apostle Paul said, 'You were dead in your trespasses and sins, in which you formerly walked according to the course of this world, according to the prince of the power of the air, of the spirit that is now working in the sons of disobedience.' (Ephesians 2:1-3). Dylan had used this analogy ('spiritual airways') in his song 'Yonder Comes Sin.'

Dylan has 'ploughed the fields of heaven'; presumably seeking to share the gospel's good news and so bring a spiritual harvest into God's kingdom; and will do so 'to the end'. He hopes that he can 'be forgiven' if he has given any offence. Forgiveness is something God has accomplished for everyone (and which is received by faith and trust) through Christ's death. 'You were dead in your transgressions... he made you alive together with him, having forgiven us all our transgressions, having cancelled out the certificate of debt consisting of decrees against us, which was hostile to us; and he has taken it out of the way, having nailed it to the cross.' (Colossians 2:13-14).

Forgiveness is important to Dylan. "Peace, love and harmony are greatly important indeed, but so is forgiveness, and we've got to have that too." (His induction to the 'Rock and Roll Hall of Fame', New York City, January 20, 1988.)

As Dylan reflects on the many 'moments full of grace' that he has experienced (grace being the 'undeserved favour' of God), he is drawn back to 'looking' at this one who is so matchless.

Disc 2 of 'Tell Tale Signs' ended with 'Cross The Green Mountain', the soundtrack to the 2003 film 'Gods And Generals' (based on the novel by Jeffrey Shaara) about the American Civil War (1861-1865). The track finds Dylan in the 'Green Mountain' of Vermont, a place which provided many volunteers for the US Civil War, including a force of paramilitary infantry (known as 'Green Mountain Boys'); and the song opens with Dylan as the narrator; 'heaven blazing' in his head. God's thoughts are being revealed to him.

These thoughts come in the form of a 'monstrous dream', in which a monster appears, 'up out of the sea', yet another quotation from one of Dylan's favourite scriptural books, Revelation (13:1, KJV). 'I stood upon the sand of the sea, and saw a beast rise up out of the sea, having seven heads and ten horns, and upon his horns ten crowns, and upon his heads the name of blasphemy.' (Italics mine). The monster is able to roam in the 'rich and free' land, presumably the North American continent, and the song picks out the outworking of this demonic activity (a type of spiritual warfare [lix]) interweaving with the theme of the American Civil War; mingling the physical manifestations ('a gunshot wound to the breast') with the spiritual ones ('blasphemy on every tongue').

This vision or dream causes Dylan to connect with his 'merciful friend', who appears to stand for Christ, and ask 'is this the end?' as in signifying the coming of the 'end times' which herald Christ's return. His thoughts are heavenward, where the 'souls' of some that know God now reside, souls he knows that one day he will meet. Back on earth, someone has been setting fire to 'altars'; some of God's enemies seem to have 'crossed over from the other side'. No ordinary soldiers these; 'You can feel them come', not just see and hear them. This connects the theme of war with the idea of demonic forces released from hell, come to express defiance (in the 'tipping of their hats') and to 'spill' brave men's blood; an image of martyrdom. They leave a 'ravaged land' behind them.

The 'Atlantic line' was the Western and Atlantic Railroad, which ran supplies supporting the Confederate Army from Atlanta, Georgia, to Chattanooga, Tennessee during the US Civil War. The light of their destructive fire advances along 'broad streets', like those Christ described as leading to destruction. 'The gate is wide and the way is broad that leads to destruction, and there are many who enter through it.' (Matthew 7:13). But Dylan knows that all resistance to an 'avenging God' is futile - 'all must yield.'

Dylan is aware that time is moving on towards its completion. He also knows that life's 'lessons' cannot be learned in one day. From where he is standing, Dylan can hear with his spiritual ears 'music that comes

---

[lix] Ephesians 6:12: 'Our struggle is not against flesh and blood, but against the rulers, against the powers, against the world forces of this darkness, against the spiritual forces of wickedness in the heavenly places.'

from a far better land', i.e. paradise; again the lyric moves between earth and heaven using the image of warfare, both human and spiritual. He will 'watch and wait' as Christ had taught his followers in regard to the signs of his second coming. [lx]

In Dylan's song his 'Captain' dies, just as the Confederate General Thomas 'Stonewall' Jackson does, shot accidentally 'by his own men' at the Battle of Chancellorsville in May 1863. General Jackson was not, however, 'killed outright'. He recovered from post-injury surgery (the amputation of his arm) for long enough to anticipate a complete recovery, before succumbing to post-anaesthetic pneumonia eight days after incurring his wounds. He was able to reflect on the coming of his own demise (as the devout Christian that he was) commenting that he felt it a privilege to die 'on the Lord's day'. [80]

In Dylan's lyric, the Captain's 'long night is done'; in scripture 'night' can stand for the time between Jesus' arrest and death and his resurrection. 'When I was with you daily in the temple, you did not try to seize me. But this is your hour, and the power of darkness.' (Luke 22:53, NKJV). Jesus also said, 'We must work the works of him who sent me as long as it is day; night is coming when no one can work.' (John 9:4). The song's 'great leader' has been 'laid low', as Christ was. 'Being found in appearance as a man, he humbled himself by becoming obedient to the point of death, even death on a cross.' (Philippians 2:8). This is because the 'Captain' was 'ready to fall'. Christ gave up his life willingly to go to the cross, 'killed outright' (put to death) at the hands of 'his own men'. It was his disciple Judas and the Jewish priests (his own people) who conspired together to bring about Christ's execution with the aid of the Romans.

[lx] Mark 13:32-37: 'But of that day and hour no one knows, not even the angels in heaven, nor the Son, but only the Father. Take heed, watch and pray; for you do not know when the time is. It is like a man going to a far country, who left his house and gave authority to his servants, and to each his work, and commanded the doorkeeper to watch. Watch therefore, for you do not know when the master of the house is coming - in the evening, at midnight, at the crowing of the rooster, or in the morning - lest, coming suddenly, he finds you sleeping. And what I say to you, I say to all: Watch!' (NKJV).

The image of the end of time continues with the references to the 'last day's last hour of the last happy year.' The 'end' is approaching, and Dylan can sense that the 'unknown' (probably the spiritual realm that continues beyond this life) is 'near.' This is the place where all 'pride will vanish', along with every other sin. The Bible says that in heaven, 'God shall wipe away all tears from their eyes; and there shall be no more death, neither sorrow, nor crying, neither shall there be any more pain: for the former things are passed away.' (Revelation 21:4, KJV).

Man's transient 'glory' will not endure (it 'will rot'); 'virtue' on the other hand will 'live', and last forever. It 'cannot be forgot' by God, being marked in heaven with an eternal reward. As the Apostle Paul said, in 1 Corinthians 3:13-14, (KJV), 'Every man's work shall be made manifest, for the day shall declare it, because it shall be revealed by fire; and the fire shall try every man's work of what sort it is. If any man's work abides which he hath built thereupon, he shall receive a reward.'

'Blasphemy' is being spoken, another nod to the book of Revelation. [lxi] Dylan wants to be remembered as one who lived his life ('walked') in 'fair nature's light', and that he was 'loyal to truth and to right', and the ways of God in general. We are encouraged to 'serve God' in a 'cheerful' way, as the Bible says: 'A cheerful heart has a continual feast.' (Proverbs 15:15). 'Each one must do just as he has purposed in his heart, not grudgingly, or under compulsion, for God loves a cheerful giver.' (2 Corinthians 9:7). In the song, the (spiritual) enemies' opposition is implacable; 'surrendering' for them is not an option, they fall where they stand.

Individual 'stars' are to be seen 'falling' over Alabama, reminiscent of men falling in battle and also of the biblical imagery for angelic beings. Their 'fallen' state stands for demonic angels who inspire rebellion and a

---

[lxi] Revelation 13:1-6: 'I saw a beast coming up out of the sea... and on his heads were blasphemous names... There was given to him a mouth speaking arrogant words and blasphemies, and authority to act for forty-two months was given to him. And he opened his mouth in blasphemies against God, to blaspheme his name and his tabernacle, that is, those who dwell in heaven.'

pointless waste of life. The 'ground' has frozen solid; too hard to receive the seed of God's word, 'and the morning *[of opportunity]* is lost'.

The last two verses describe the death, presumably of the narrator, by a 'gunshot wound'. His mother is encouraged to believe he will survive. However the reality is that he is 'already dead', being 'lifted away' and illuminated by an 'ancient light'; a supernatural light that comes from God. In death there are no barriers in relationship; all are 'known', as the Apostle Paul said, 'For now we see in a mirror dimly, but then face to face; now I know in part, but then I will know fully just as I also have been fully known. But now faith, hope, love, abide these three; but the greatest of these is love.' (1 Corinthians 13:12-13).

The love of comradeship that has been shown on the battlefield does not end there; it continues in a much purer way into heaven beyond. Warner Brothers produced a video directed by Thomas Krueger to accompany the film 'God's And Generals' in which Dylan appeared; it closes with a shot of Dylan turning from the Civil War grave (of a Captain Jeter), towards (and silhouetted by) a large stone cross.

The inclusion of 'Things Have Changed' (written for the movie 'Wonder Boys' in 2000) on disc 3 meant it would figure on three out of four consecutive albums. The track appears to assess the allures of the world and to find them lacking in substance. The 'woman' of the first verse has 'assassin's eyes'; she is evidently up to no good, and fits the night-time image of the 'dark sapphire-tinted skies', with Dylan expecting the 'last train' (signifying the end of time) to arrive at any moment.

He has seemingly been condemned to die on the 'gallows', reminiscent of the Apostle Paul who wrote, 'We were burdened excessively, beyond our strength, so that we despaired even of life; indeed, we had the sentence of death within ourselves so that we would not trust in ourselves, but in God who raises the dead; who delivered us from so great a peril of death, and will deliver us, he on whom we have set our hope.' (2 Corinthians 1:8-10). Dylan expects the imminent spiritual opposition of 'all hell' breaking out, with 'crazy' folk and the 'strange' circumstances he finds himself in locking him 'in tight', possibly away from them and towards God. He may have previously been concerned ('care') about such issues as what people thought of what he did and said, but now 'things have changed'.

Where he finds himself is unprofitable for him spiritually; it does him no good. Perhaps because he feels he is not getting through to people. Maybe he should move somewhere they take anything seriously, such as Hollywood! He has nothing to prove, like Christ, who 'made himself of no reputation, taking the form of a bondservant, and coming in the likeness of men'. (Philippians 2:7, NKJV). He is 'only passing through' this life, a sojourner on the way to a different destination - heaven.

Dylan is aware of what the scripture teaches, 'If the Bible is right, the world will explode.' This is prophesied by Isaiah (34:4), 'The host of heaven will wear away, and the sky will be rolled up like a scroll; all their hosts will also wither away, as a leaf withers from the vine, or as one withers from the fig tree.' John the Baptist had said, 'He *[Jesus]* must increase, but I must decrease.' (John 3:30). This is echoed in Dylan's 'trying to get as far away from myself as I can'. Outside of God's providence, life holds a 'losing hand', one 'you can't win with'.

Dylan is sensitive to the effects of emotional trauma; he hurts 'easy', despite keeping it mostly hidden. The idea of 'sixty seconds' being like an 'eternity' echoes 2 Peter 3:8: 'With the Lord one day is like a thousand years, and a thousand years like one day.' Dylan also understands the importance of humility before God. Getting 'low down' will lead to him flying 'high', as in 1 Peter 5:6: 'Humble yourselves under the mighty hand of God, that he may exalt you.' The truth that the 'world' has to share is nothing more than 'one big lie', which can easily distort one's thinking and lead to 'mistakes' that Dylan is not at all 'eager to make'.

The bonus disc also featured a live version of 'Tryin' To Get To Heaven', recorded on 5th October 2000, at the Wembley Arena in North London. The editorial group that selected that particular (and somewhat atypical) rendering of the song might have listened more closely before deciding to include it. At the song's end this North Londoner can clearly make out the local dialect of a dissatisfied audience member shouting, 'F**king rubbish!' There's just no pleasing some folk.

Dylan's next album, 'Together Through Life', was released in April 2009. It was co-written with the Grateful Dead lyricist Robert Hunter with whom he had previously released two songs ('Silvio' and 'Ugliest Girl in the World') on his 1988 album 'Down In The Groove'. As Dylan said to Bill Flanagan, [81] 'I go back a ways with Hunter. We're from the same old school so it makes its own kind of sense.'

The album had part of its origin in a request from the French film director, Olivier Dahan, for Dylan to compose some songs for a film he was writing and directing, based around a 'journey of discovery' through the American South, from Kansas City to New Orleans. 'Together Through Life' reached number one both in the USA and in the UK, but being co-written with Hunter (to date none of the tracks have gained 'classic' status with any reviewer), it is harder to assess from a Dylan-based spiritual perspective than are songs that Dylan composed by himself alone.

The album opens with 'Beyond Here Lies Nothin''. Of this song Dylan told Flanagan, in answer to the question: "Is pain a necessary part of loving?" Dylan replied: "Oh yeah, in my songs it is. Pain, sex, murder, family - it goes way back. Kindness. Honour. Charity. You have to tie all that in. You're supposed to know that stuff." Asked whether the character in the song represented another from 'Across the borderline', Dylan answered, "I know what you're saying, but it's not a character like in a book or a movie. He's not a bus driver. He doesn't drive a forklift. He's not a serial killer. It's me who's singing that, plain and simple. We shouldn't confuse singers and performers with actors. Actors will say, "My character this, and my character that." Like beating a dead horse. Who cares about the character? Just get up and act. You don't have to explain it to me."

The first verse concludes, 'Beyond here lies nothing, nothing we can call our own.' That is presumably because in the realm beyond all belongs to God. Dylan has 'the mountains of the past' behind him and a 'pretty baby' to lay a 'hand upon his head', as the Jewish patriarchs did in blessing and prayer. (E.g. Jacob and Joseph's sons in Genesis 48: 9-20).

Next came 'Life Is Hard', written as the proposed soundtrack for Olivier Dahan's movie, in what Dylan said was to be a ballad for the main character to sing towards the end of the movie. The song describes the emptiness that is felt when a relationship with someone 'near and dear' is cut off. Since Dylan told Bill Flanagan that the songs are about him it is fair to conclude that he has felt an 'emptiness so wide' such that he 'doesn't know what's wrong or right'. He has gone 'astray', and is badly in need of the 'strength to fight that world outside'. All of which is spiritual language reminiscent of Paul's words to the Ephesians (6:12, KJV). 'We wrestle not against flesh and blood, but against principalities, against powers, against the rulers of the darkness of this world.'

'My Wife's Home Town', aka hell, is a jokey piece about where his wife was from (and not the town called 'Hell' located in Michigan). According to Dylan, 'The only person it could matter to gets a kick out of it. That song is meant as a compliment anyhow.' [82] Dylan sings, "Dreams never did work for me anyway." He told Flanagan that "Dreams can lead us up a blind alley. Everybody has dreams. We go to sleep and we dream. I've always thought of them as coming out of the subconscious. I guess you can interpret them. Dreams can tell us a lot about ourselves, if we can remember them. We can see what's coming around the corner sometimes without actually going to the corner." 'Don't be looking at me, with that evil eye,' sings Dylan; 'Keep on walking.' It seems he is practicing what he preaches.

'If You Ever Go To Houston' is the song with the clearest Christian or faith reference. 'Mary Anne's sister Betsy' is advised 'to pray the Sinner's Prayer'. In the Bill Flanagan interview, Flanagan asked Dylan "What's the 'Sinner's Prayer'?" "That's the one that begins with 'Father forgive me for I have sinned,'" replied Dylan. The prayer is based on the words of the 'Prodigal Son', a parable Jesus told to illustrate God's capacity to forgive. The son left home and wasted his inheritance; the father's gracious response to his return is contrasted in the story that Jesus told with that of the ungracious response of the older brother (who stands for the religious leaders of Jesus' day). [lxii] Dylan sings, "Boy, you better walk right." 'Walk' is the scriptural term for 'live', as in one's daily life. He has to 'keep ridin' forward'.

'Forgetful Heart' seems to sum up the melancholy blues mood of the album. According to Dylan, [83] it has a minor key modality like 'Little Maggie' which was recorded in 1946 by 'The Stanley Brothers' (an American bluegrass group comprising brothers Carter and Ralph Stanley). Dylan also said it was like 'Darling Cory' (a traditional folk song recorded, amongst others, by 'The Carter Family', a group of gospel and country singers that recorded between 1927 and 1956 and who were highly influential on the music of 1960's US folk singers, including Bob Dylan). 'Forgetful heart' remembers the 'good time' had with one who was 'the answer to my prayer'. But a sense of depression has arrived, summed up in the lines, 'I lay awake and listen to the sound of pain, the door has closed forevermore' - presumably the door his marriage.

The song 'Jolene', for whom 'I am the king and you're queen', helps to lift the mood somewhat. As Dylan said, he is 'not a playwright. The people in my songs are all me', from which we can gather that, like anybody else, Dylan's mood goes up and down ('It's a long old highway, don't ever end.') But he is still willing to 'lay his life on the line', just as a certain someone else did for him. Sure of life's lessons, Dylan has 'found out the hard way', but now life doesn't have to 'look so dark'.

'This Dream Of You' finds Dylan singing of a 'moment when all old things become new'. This is a straight quotation from the Apostle Paul's

---

[lxii] Luke 15:17-21: 'When he came to his senses, he said, "How many of my father's hired men have more than enough bread, but I am dying here with hunger! I will get up and go to my father, and will say to him, "Father, I have sinned against heaven, and in your sight; I am no longer worthy to be called your son; make me as one of your hired men." So he got up and came to his father. But while he was still a long way off, his father saw him and felt compassion for him, and ran and embraced him and kissed him. And the son said to him, "Father, I have sinned against heaven and in your sight."'

second letter to the Corinthians (5:17) 'If any man be in Christ, he is a new creature: old things are passed away; behold, all things are become new.' The deliberate use of 'all' here renders this no co-incidence. Yes, that 'might have come and gone', but something is still keeping Dylan 'living on'; and it is identified as a very particular 'dream of you'. Even though there are ups and downs, he will 'keep believing it'. The line 'I'll run this race until my earthly death' has a familiar scriptural ring about it too. 'Let us lay aside every weight, and the sin which doth so easily beset us, and let us run with patience the race that is set before us, looking unto Jesus the author and finisher of our faith; who for the joy that was set before him endured the cross, despising the shame, and is sat down at the right hand of the throne of God.' (Hebrews 12:1-2, KJV).

When he sings that he 'saw a star from heaven fall', we are back in the book of Revelation. 'The fifth angel sounded, and I saw a star fall from heaven unto the earth: and to him was given the key of the bottomless pit.' (Revelation 9:1, KJV). 'Stars' in scripture can stands for angels (Daniel 8:10); this particular one is charged with releasing a dark smoke and a plague of locusts upon those in rebellion to God.

'Shake, Shake Mama' is another song that carries a somewhat depressed air ('I get the blues for you' on 'heartbreak hill'). People who should be representative of God given authority are not to be relied upon; Judge Simpson 'shocks' Dylan, presumably by the abuse of his authority. In his Bill Flanagan interview, Dylan describes him as a 'possum hunting judge'; possum hunting is a common rural pastime in the American South, where the local people elect their county judges. Dylan feels orphaned (both his parents are dead), and 'almost friendless too'. The subject of the song is advised, 'Raise your voice and pray' for the 'shortest way home'; presumably to heaven.

In the album's penultimate song, 'I Feel A Change Comin' On', Dylan's 'baby' is 'walking with the village priest', implying that a faith-based relationship is established. He can feel that a 'change' is in the air. Given that the day is drawing to a close, we are moving towards what the Bible calls the 'end-times', when human history will be concluded. The phrase the 'fourth part of the day' appears in the Old Testament book of

Nehemiah, who oversaw the re-construction of the city of Jerusalem circa 430 BC. He spiritually purified the people who were living there, such that 'The descendants of Israel separated themselves from all foreigners, and stood and confessed their sins and the iniquities of their fathers. While they stood in their place, they read from the book of the Law of the Lord their God for a fourth of the day; and for another fourth they confessed and worshiped the Lord their God.' (Nehemiah 9:2-3).

Dylan seems to be still feeling a 'striving' within him for the 'same old ends', perhaps the desire to be fully one with his God. He has experienced 'dreams' becoming reality, but knows that they end up being empty. The Texan country music singer songwriter Billy Joe Shaver gets a mention; Shaver wrote the song 'Good Christian Soldier'. 'Lord, I want to be a Christian soldier just like you, and fight to build a new and better day.' The other shout-out is for James Joyce (1882-1941), the Irish writer and poet, who Dylan says he reads.

The album closes with 'It's All Good', a song (as Dylan told Flanagan) came 'from hearing the phrase one too many times'. The disgusting has become 'all good', from 'politicians' lies' to 'restaurant kitchens' flies'. Marriages break-up, people are drowning, and sickness abounds. The line, 'The widow's cry, the orphan's plea' reflects God's words to the Hebrew prophet Isaiah, 'Learn to do good, seek justice, reprove the ruthless, defend the orphan, and plead for the widow.' (Isaiah 1:17).

Isaiah appears again with a prophesy about the Messiah, 'I'll pluck off your beard.' Isaiah (50:6) reads, 'I gave my back to those who strike me, and my cheeks to those who pluck out the beard', a foresight of Christ's treatment at the hands of the Roman soldiers before the crucifixion. Murder is on the streets, but the sardonic Dylan 'wouldn't change a thing'. Why should anyone want to? After all, it's 'all good', isn't it?

Chapter 15

'Christmas In The Heart'

If there could still be a debate about the nature of Dylan's faith, speculation should surely end with this album. It would be hard to imagine a clearer way of stating his spiritual position in a non-threatening way. The concept of truth being 'in the heart' is a particularly Messianic/Christian one, and the particular festival of the 'Mass of Christ' (the Eucharist celebrating the incarnation of Jesus through Mary's virgin birth) is blatant while at the same time providing the convenient option of deflecting the faith question behind the social and cultural trappings of the modern holiday season.

Religious issues were deflected further by Dylan's decision to gift all profits from the US sales in perpetuity to the US charity 'Feeding America', which is estimated to help feed 1.4 million families during the holiday season. [84] International royalties went to the United Nations' World Food Programme and 'Crisis', the UK based charity in aid of the homeless. Dylan was reported as saying, "That the problem of hunger is ultimately solvable means we must each do what we can to help feed those who are suffering and support efforts to find long-term solutions. I'm honoured to partner with the World Food Programme and Crisis in their fight against hunger and homelessness." It was hard therefore for the hardened cynics to criticize the album's faith-based values too vehemently. The religious emphasis was further softened by the inclusion of a number of secular seasonal festive numbers, with the directly Christian ones making up just over one-third of the total songs.

Predictably, the album sent those who had pointed towards Dylan's apparent re-connection with his Jewish roots at the expense of his Christian faith into shock, with a series of responses emphasizing the nostalgic cultural American Christmas shaping the mid-west US society of Dylan's childhood. [85] They might have got away with that had it not been for the now expected Bill Flanagan interview, this time published in the North American Street Newspaper Association, which primarily addresses issues related to poverty and homelessness, and whose publications are distributed by the poor and particularly by homeless people (equivalent to the 'Big Issue' publication in the UK). Flanagan commented to Dylan that the conviction with which he sang 'O Little Town Of Bethlehem' was notable. While Flanagan 'didn't want to put Dylan on the spot', he thought that Dylan, when singing the words 'the hopes and fears of all the years are met in thee tonight' were 'sure delivered like a true believer'. Dylan replied, 'Well, I am a true believer.' Spin that how you like, the context is plain enough. Dylan also told Flanagan, 'I like all the religious Christmas albums. The ones in Latin. The songs I sang as a kid.' When asked about secular songs of a Christmas nature, Dylan replied, 'Religion isn't meant for everybody.' [86]

The album opened with the Gene Autry and Oakley Haldeman song 'Here Comes Santa Claus', with lines such as 'hang your stockings and say your prayers', and 'let's give thanks to the Lord above' setting the tone. Santa Claus, an abbreviated form of 'Saint Nicholas' (Saint-Ni-Claus), was a third century Christian from Southern Turkey who followed Christ's command to the rich young ruler. 'Sell all that you possess and distribute it to the poor, and you shall have treasure in heaven; and come, follow me.' (Luke 18:22). Nicholas used his inheritance to help the needy, the sick, and the suffering; Dylan appears to be following his example in regard to homelessness. Nicholas dedicated his life to serving God, and became a Bishop known for generosity to the needy. He was later exiled and imprisoned, and the anniversary of his death, St Nicholas Day (December 6th), was set apart as a feast day.

Next came 'Do You Hear What I Hear?' (by Regney and Baker, 1962), with the lyrics 'the child sleeping in the night, he will bring us goodness and light'. After that was 'Winter Wonderland' (1934), by Felix Bernard - 'we can build a snowman, then pretend that he is Parson Brown.'

The first markedly Christian inclusion was the carol 'Hark! The Herald Angels Sing', written by Charles Wesley, brother of John, founder of the Methodist movement. It was originally called 'Hymn For Christmas-Day', and was altered slightly by their friend and co-worker George Whitfield, the evangelical preacher who was a part of the 'Great

Awakening' in Britain and North America (1734-1750). Wesley believed in communicating scriptural truth through his songs' lyrics (as, seemingly, does Dylan), and 'Hark The Herald Angels Sing' is no exception. 'Glory' in the first line means 'praise'; to the new-born king who has come to reconcile God and mankind, who have become estranged from God by their sin. 'Peace on earth,' echoes the words of the angels who sang to the shepherds at Bethlehem, 'Glory to God in the highest, and on earth peace among men with whom he is pleased.' (Luke 2:14). All nations are invited to join this 'triumph of the skies' and proclaim along with the army of angels that 'Christ is born in Bethlehem'. This is the promised Messiah who came 'late' in God's salvation plan for mankind, but also at the 'right time'. 'While we were still helpless, at the right time Christ died for the ungodly.' (Romans 5:6).

The virgin birth was predicted by the Jewish Old Testament prophet Isaiah (7:14, KJV), 'A virgin shall conceive, and bear a son, and shall call his name Emmanuel.' The in-bred tendency to sin entered humanity when Adam broke God's command, and was understood to be passed on through the father rather than the mother. For Jesus to be a perfect offering for sin, he had to be without sin himself, hence the necessity of a birth without a human father. Jesus is representing the whole of what Christians call the 'Godhead'; the tri-unity of Father, Son and Holy Spirit. The God who rules from Heaven as Father and is present everywhere at the same time as Spirit also exists in a form that humankind can identify with much more closely - God the Son. The phrase 'late in time' indicates that Christ came in what the Bible refers to as 'the last days'; that is, the era of time between Christ's first and his second coming. Jesus is called the 'incarnate' Son of God, meaning that God chose to come himself as a human baby, 'veiled in flesh', to fully identify with mankind, as 'Emmanuel', from the Hebrew words meaning 'God with us' ('El' - 'God', and 'immanu' - 'with us').

'Prince of Peace' is one of the messianic titles given in Isaiah (9:6), and 'Sun of Righteousness' is found in Malachi (4:2, KJV). 'But unto you that fear my name shall the Sun of righteousness arise with healing in his wings; and you shall go forth, and grow up as calves of the stall.' Jesus is the 'light of the world' (John 8:12), and the 'way, the truth and the life' (John 14:6), and so brings 'light and life to all' to whom he comes. Jesus taking on himself an earthly form meant laying down his glory as God the Son, for example in his omnipresence. His birth, life and death meant the defeat of the power of sin and death over the human race; confirmed by his rising from the dead. The sin penalty that spelt our death was paid for by his death. No wonder the angels who heralded the news to the shepherds praised this new-born 'king of the Jews'.

Bing Crosby recorded 'I'll Be Home For Christmas' in 1943, at a time when many service men and women were separated from home and loved ones by World War II. 'I'll be home for Christmas, if only in my dreams...'

Wartime was the backdrop for the next song too. 'Little Drummer Boy' was composed in 1942 by the American pianist Katherine Davis, under the title 'The Carol Of The Drum', based on a traditional Czech Christmas carol. A poor boy who 'has no gift to bring' asks permission of Mary to play his drum for the infant Jesus. The 'ox and lamb kept time', and afterwards baby Jesus ('the king') smiles at him. 'I played my best for him' would make a good epitaph for any believing musician, Dylan especially.

Dean Martin's 1966 album 'My Kind Of Christmas' featured 'The Christmas Blues' (the lyrics were written by Sammy Cahn and the music by David Holt). Christmas is supposed to be 'a joy of joy', but for many people, often those separated in some way from their family, it is a time of sorrow, depression and, sadly, a higher rate of suicide. As the song puts it, 'Friends, when you're lonely, you'll find that it's only a thing for little girls and little boys.' Taking the 'Christ' out of Christmas leaves only a shell which all the trappings of holly, tinsel and gifts cannot fill.

It was then back to the traditional carols with the Latin 'Adeste fideles, laeti triumphantes, cenite venite in Bethlehem'. 'O Come All Ye Faithful' - 'joyful and triumphant, O come ye, O come ye to Bethlehem.' We are all called to 'come and adore' the one that has been 'born the king of angels' - Christ the Lord. Dylan performs the seasonal classic masterfully, his ageing voice complementing the early eighteenth century composition with its timeless truth.

The album then moves from one of the greatest of the older Christmas songs to one of the best known of the modern era. 'Have Yourself A Merry Little Christmas', a song written in 1944 by Hugh Martin and Ralph Blane. Martin was Judy Garland's pianist, and the song featured in her 1944 MGM musical 'Meet Me In St Louis'. Martin's original line, 'Through the years, we all will be together if the Lord allows', was changed to 'if the fates allow', to remove the religious reference. (Dylan was not the first artist to be pressurized artistically for his faith.) Written to describe a family's enforced move to New York City, it was criticized as being slightly depressing and was partially re-written in 1957 for Frank Sinatra to perform. 'Until then we'll have to muddle through somehow' became 'Hang a shining star upon the highest bough'; the song became a Christmas classic.

If 'Have Yourself A Merry Little Christmas' had once been depressing, Dylan's next track, 'Must Be Santa' (Hal Moore and Bill Fredericks, 1961) was the opposite. Dylan released a video comprising a Christmas party scene of mass dancing to the song, complete with polka-style accordion and a cheery Dylan lighting candles and bearing bottles of wine while mayhem breaks loose. The names of Santa's reindeers are replaced with the names of past US presidents, and the song is played in the style of the polka-rock band 'Brave Combo'. Dylan told Bill Flanagan, 'Somebody sent their record to us for our radio show. They're a regional band out of Texas that takes regular songs and changes the way you think about them.' A great time appears to have been had by all, with the exception of one individual who exits through a closed windowpane, leaving a bemused Dylan on the front steps standing next to Santa himself.

'Silver Bells' is another classic Christmas song, composed by Jay Livingston and Ray Evans and sung by Bing Crosby and Carol Richards (October 1950). 'Children laughing, people passing, meeting smile after smile. And on every street corner you'll hear silver bells' paints an urban picture of Christmas which is often simply the product of people's imagination. The reality may be closer to people rushing about completely self-absorbed, but because lonely people think that everyone else is having a good time the picture of Christmas bliss serves to add to their feeling of melancholy. Flanagan asked whether Dylan missed Christmas in Minnesota on moving to New York; apparently Dylan 'Didn't think about it that much. I didn't bring the past with me when I came to New York. Nothing back there would play any part in where I was going.'

A sixteenth century English carol (originally called 'The First Nowell'; the old English form of 'Noel', the French word for 'Christmas') recounts the angel army announcing Christ's birth to the shepherds, described in Luke's gospel chapter 2. [lxiii] Jesus is believed to have been born at the Feast of Tabernacles. ('The Word became flesh, and tabernacled among us.' John 1:14). At that time of year it is warm enough in Israel for shepherds to be in fields at night (the 'cold' not being quite as 'deep' as in England).

The 'star' that announced Jesus' birth to the wise men in the east was very likely a planetary conjunction of Jupiter and Saturn, one which is believed to have occurred in 6BC. All of the gifts that the wise men brought were very valuable; gold as for a king, frankincense as for a priest (or for God) and myrrh for its anti-septic, perfume and embalming uses, signifying Christ's humanity and death. These gifts, offered presumably in a kingly quantity as well as quality by the wise men, would have made Mary and Joseph wealthy. King Herod (who slew the

---

[lxiii] Luke 2:8-14: 'There were shepherds staying out in the fields and keeping watch over their flock by night. And an angel of the Lord suddenly stood before them, and the glory of the Lord shone around them; and they were terribly frightened. But the angel said to them, "Do not be afraid; for behold, I bring you good news of great joy which will be for all the people; for today in the city of David there has been born for you a Saviour, who is Christ the Lord. This will be a sign for you: you will find a baby wrapped in cloths and lying in a manger." And suddenly there appeared with the angel a multitude of the heavenly host praising God and saying, "Glory to God in the highest, and on earth peace among men with whom he is pleased".

male babies of Bethlehem under four years of age) died in 4BC), another way of dating Jesus' birth to 6BC. [87]

'Christmas Island' (Lyle Moraine, 1946), is a short secular song about the small Australian ruled island in the Indian Ocean given its name by an East India Company ship's captain who passed it on Christmas Day 1643. Dylan has a history of sailing in the Caribbean; the song's line about staying up 'late like the islanders do' may have appealed to him!

'The Christmas Song', (also known as 'Chestnuts Roasting On An Open Fire'), by Mel Tormé and Bob Wells (1944), was made famous by US jazz pianist Nathaniel Adams Coles (Nat 'King' Cole) in his recording in 1946. Dylan included the original version's lines, 'All through the year we waited, waited through spring and fall, to hear silver bells ringing, see winter time bringing, the happiest season of all.' As Dylan explained to Flanagan, he 'figured the guy who wrote it put it in there deliberately. It definitely creates tension; predicts what you are about to hear.'

Always one with an eye to the importance of the last song on an album, Dylan picked 'O Little Town Of Bethlehem', concluding with the words 'Where meek souls will receive him, still the dear Christ enter in. Amen.' Bethlehem was the ancestral home of King David (1 Samuel 17:12), and it was there that the Hebrew prophet Micah (5:2) had said that the Messiah would be born. Joseph, the adoptive father of Jesus, had to return there for the census decreed by Caesar Augustus, and took his betrothed and pregnant wife-to-be Mary with him. Joseph would not have had to search for an 'inn'; rather, he would have gone to his father's house, which would have been hosting other returning members of the family as well. Consequently the guest-room (and not 'inn' as commonly translated) was full, and so Mary delivered the infant Jesus in the family stable, [lxiv] where fear met hope and hope won. ('The hopes and fears of all the years are met in thee tonight.')

Angels are said to have 'wondered' at such love that produced the miracle of the Incarnation (God himself birthed on earth), just as Dylan

lxiv See Dr Bradford's 'The Jesus Discovery'. ISBN 9780956479808 himself does. ('I think of you, and I wonder', 'Love Sick' from 'Time Out Of Mind.') This 'gift' of the baby Jesus is given 'silently', with only a few people being aware of the significance (the shepherds and later the wise men). But where the 'meek' (those willing to humble their pride and reach out in trust and faith) will receive him, this Jesus enters into human beings' lives, heart and soul, as Dylan himself had experienced.

When Flanagan asked Dylan how he liked to spend the week between Christmas and New Year, Dylan responded, 'Doing nothing; maybe reflecting on things.' 'Reflecting' is shorthand for prayer and meditation; a spiritual reflection on God's purposes. The feast of the Incarnation clearly means a lot to Dylan. When told by Flanagan that the Chicago Tribune felt the record needed more irreverence, Dylan responded, 'That's an irresponsible statement... Isn't there enough irreverence in the world? Who would need more? Especially at Christmas time.'

Referring to the differing, and some skeptical, reactions to the album, Dylan remarked: 'Even at this point in time they still don't know what to make of me.' Flanagan's opinion is that 'Christmas In The Heart' 'sounds to me like one of the most sincere records you've ever made.' One would have to agree with Flanagan...

Chapter 16

Jewish, Christian or What?

"I don't have a strong Jewish tradition. If anything I'm a pagan Jew. Existentialist Jew, Buddhist Jew... I don't know what these things mean. Pure Jew? I don't know, I doubt it." (Philip Fleishman, February 1978).

"You were also interested in Judaism at one point. You visited Israel and the Wailing Wall in Jerusalem. Do you feel that your interests at that time are compatible with your present beliefs?" "There's really no difference between any of it in my mind. Some people say they're Jews and they never go to a synagogue or anything. I know some gangsters who say they're Jews. I don't know what that's got to do with anything. Judaism is really the Laws of Moses. If you follow the Laws of Moses you're automatically a Jew, I would think." (Neil Spencer, August 1981).

After having been somewhat dismissive of 'religion' in the interviews of his early days, Dylan's encounter with Jesus as Messiah caused him to re-examine his Jewish roots. He has frequently said that his blue eyes betray Semitic origins that may not be 100% Jewish. "I don't know how Jewish I am. See, with these blue eyes, which are Russian. You know, back in the 1700s, 1800s; I know I have different blood in me." "What sort of blood?" "Cossack blood. I don't know how anyone could escape it, anyone of my family that lived back then." [88] Whatever the DNA profile, there is a sense of 'once a Jew, always a Jew'. A spiritual meeting with the God of Israel changed Dylan, his life and his music. His music would later show that the Jewish and the Christian faiths were linked by the most important person of all, Jesus of Nazareth. Because the majority of the public are unaware of the spiritual reality that is Messianic Judaism, Dylan's faith would be an enigma - just like the rest of him.

The 'Infidels' album was a step in this direction towards his faith roots. The cover photo of Dylan was taken by his ex-wife Sara during a visit to Israel in 1983 as a vacation with Jesse and grandmother Beatty. Jesse was apparently overdue for the ceremony of bar-mitzvah, the Jewish rite of passage to adulthood, and these could be arranged quickly and easily in Israel. Dylan flew out to join them for the ceremony, got described by a Rabbi as 'a confused Jew', and was photographed praying at the Wailing Wall, the only surviving remnant of the Second Temple as rebuilt by King Herod. Tellingly, Dylan's comment was, 'We're talking about Jewish roots. I ain't looking for them in synagogues.' [89]

Keeping people guessing is a Dylan specialty. Enigma and mystery are part of what keeps the public interested and Dylan is well-practiced in both, although a closer look at his interviews and lyrics tell a clearer story.

"When you meet up with Orthodox *[Jewish]* people, can you sit down with them and say, 'Well, you should really check out Christianity?'" "Well, yeah, if somebody asks me, I'll tell 'em. But, you know, I'm not gonna just offer my opinion. I'm more about playing music, you know?" (To Kurt Loder, March 1984, New York).

"Bob, are you Christian or Jewish?" "Well, that's hard to say." "Some more?" "It's a long story." "Well, I'd like to know it." "It'd take too long to tell you." (May 1984, Hamburg, Germany).

"Why was there a confusion for a couple of years and probably still going on in some part of the world, and in this country particularly, about whether or not you're a born-again Christian or a practicing Jew, or what the hell are you?" "Hmm. Well, people are confused about everything these days. You know, they're confused about what kind of car they drive. They just don't know what they want to do." "Why do you think people have become so confused about you and religion?" "Well, probably because I'm on people's minds and religion's on people's minds, so they put two and two together, I don't know... I had to do those *[gospel]* albums. They were very necessary and important for me to do." "Why was that?" "Because people needed to hear them." "At that time?" "Oh yeah." "So you think you were reflecting a feeling that was abroad in this country by picking up religion as a subject matter?" "Oh, we have to be very careful when talking about religion you know, because religion is more than just church." "And what's yours?" "Mine has to do with playing the guitar." (To George Negus, January 1986, Malibu, California).

"Bob, are you Jewish again on this tour?" "Oh, I'm Jewish when I have to be." "When do you have to be?" "Every so often, you know." "Are you a Christian on this tour?" "Part of the time, yeah." (April 1986, Los Angeles, California).

After all of the well-practiced evasiveness, this is a 100% honest answer! Any Christian is at best only truly Christian (in behaviour) 'part of the time' and as a Messianic Jew, Dylan is no different. A visit to the synagogue for a bar-mitzvah, or appearing at a fund raiser for the Hassidic movement Chabad's telethon (for example at Los Angeles in November 1989), as well as Yom Kippur services run by Chabad are occasions when he 'has to be Jewish', because that is who he is by his DNA and his spiritual roots. Dylan is about bridge-building, not causing needless offense. For example, for the August 1986 Chabad annual fund-raiser, Dylan, (with Tom Petty) sang, (by satellite link) the Hank William's gospel number 'Thank God'. Dylan sang: 'There's a road that's straight and narrow, that the saints have travelled on, paved with all the tribulations of the martyrs that have gone, if you're grateful for their victory and for showing us the way, then give thanks for all your blessings, get on your knees and pray. Thank God for every mountain and each sea, thank God for every flower and each tree, thank God for giving life to you and me, wherever you may be, thank God. In this world of grief and sorrow, filled with selfishness and greed, there remains the glory fountain to supply your every need. You can find it in the temple, with a welcome on the door, but be sure to count your blessings, before you ask for more. Thank God for every flower and each tree, thank God for every mountain and the sea, thank God for giving life to you and me, wherever you may be, thank God.'

Aside from transposing the words of the chorus, Dylan sensitively omitted William's final verse: 'Be forgiving to the wayward like the Master told us to, when he said, "Forgive them, Father, for they know not what they do." They would change their way of living, if they could but understand, so remember they're your brothers, they need a helping hand.' That is being sensitive to not cause unnecessary offense, while at the same time, telling it plain.

Afterwards Dylan praised the work of Chabad among drug addicts and encouraged listeners to support them financially. Any Messianic Jew will resonate with deep rooted faith and spirituality in fellow Jews, even ones that have yet to recognize in Jesus the one who fulfils all the Old Testament prophetic scriptures concerning the Messiah as both a king and the suffering servant of Israel and the other nations.

Messianic Judaism appears to have begun to form in Dylan's mind early on in his faith journey; indeed it is the logical position for any Jew that commits themselves to Y'shua as Saviour. In July 1981, Dylan told Neil Spencer (NS), "The only one who can overcome all, that is the great Creator himself. If you can get his help you can overcome it. To do that you must know something about the nature of the Creator. What Jesus does for an ignorant man like myself is to make the qualities and characteristics of God more believable to me, 'cause I can't beat the devil. Only God can. He already has. Satan's working everywhere. You're faced with him constantly. If you can't see him he's inside you making you feel a certain way. He's feeding you envy and jealousy; he's feeding you oppression, hatred..."

NS: "Do you feel the only way to know the Creator is through Christ?"

BD: "I feel the only way... let me see. Of course you can look on the desert and wake up to the sun and the sand and the beauty of the stars and know there is a higher being, and worship that Creator. But being thrown into the cities, you're faced more with man than with God. We're dealing here with man, you know, and in order to know where man's at, you have to know what God would do if he was man. I'm trying to explain to you in intellectual mental terms, when it actually is more of a spiritual understanding than something which is open to debate."

NS: "You can't teach people things they don't experience for themselves..."

BD: "Most people think that if God became a man he would go up on a mountain and raise his sword and show his anger and his wrath or his love and compassion in one blow. And that's what people expected the

235

Messiah to be; someone with similar characteristics, someone to set things straight, and here comes a Messiah who doesn't measure up to those characteristics and causes a lot of problems."

NS: "Someone who put the responsibility back on us?"

BD: "Right."

NS: "From your songs like 'Dead Man' and 'When He Returns', it's obvious you believe the second coming is likely in our lifetime."

BD: "Possibly. Possibly at any moment. It could be in our lifetimes. It could be a long time. This earth supposedly has a certain number of years which I think is 7,000 years. 7,000 or 6,000. We're in the last cycle of it now. Going back to the first century there's like 3000 years before that and 4000 after it, one of the two, the last thousand would be the millennium years. I think that everything that's happened is like a preview of what's going to happen."

NS: "How strict is your interpretation of Christianity? The original Christians seem to have a different faith and belief that got lost."

BD: "I'm not that much of a historian about Christianity. I know it's been changed over the years but I go strictly according to the gospels."

And as Dylan later told Scott Cohen, [90] "All that exists is spirit, before, now and forever more. The messianic thing has to do with this world, the flesh world, and you've got to pass through this to get to that. The messianic thing has to do with the world of mankind, like it is. This world is scheduled to go for 7,000 years *[for the seven days of creation. The rabbis taught that 'the world is to exist six thousand years. In the first two thousand there was desolation; two thousand years the Torah flourished; and the next two thousand years is the Messianic era.']* [91] Six thousand years of this, where man has his way, and one thousand years when God has his way. Just like a week. Six days work, one day rest. The last thousand years is called the Messianic Age. Messiah will rule. He is, was, and will be about God, doing God's business. Drought, famine, war, murder, theft, earthquake, and all other evil things will be no more. No more disease. That's all of this world. What's gonna happen is this: you know when things change, people usually know, like in a revolution, people know before it happens who's coming in and who's going out. All the Somozas and Batistas will be on their way out, grabbing their stuff and whatever, but you can forget about them. They won't be going anywhere. It's the people who live under tyranny and oppression, the plain, simple people that count, like the multitude of sheep. They'll see that God is coming. Somebody representing him will be on the scene. Not some crackpot lawyer or politician with the mark of the beast, but somebody who makes them feel holy. People don't know how to feel holy. They don't know what it's about or what's right. They don't know what God wants of them. They'll want to know what to do and how to act. Just like you want to know how to please any ruler. They don't teach that stuff like they do math, medicine, and carpentry, but now there will be a tremendous calling for it. There will be a run on godliness, just like now there's a run on refrigerators, headphones, and fishing gear. It's going to be a matter of survival. People are going to be running to find out about God, and who are they going to run to? They're gonna run to the Jews, because the Jews wrote the book, and you know what? The Jews ain't gonna know. They're too busy in the fur business and in the pawnshops and in sending their kids to some atheist school. They're too busy doing all that stuff to know. People who believe in the coming of the Messiah live their lives right now as if he was here. That's my idea of it, anyway. I know people are going to say to themselves, "What the f**k is this guy talking about?" But it's all there in black and white, the written and unwritten word. I don't have to defend this. The scriptures back me up. I didn't ask to know this stuff. It just came to me at different times from experiences throughout my life. Other than that, I'm just a rock 'n roller, folk poet, gospel-blues-protest guitar player. Did I say that right?" (California, September 1985).

The concept of a one thousand year period (millennium) when Christ will reign on earth (or, as Dylan puts it, 'When God has his way') is found in the book of Revelation. 'I saw the souls of those who had been beheaded because of their testimony of Jesus and because of the word of God, and those who had not worshiped the beast or his image, and had not received the mark on their forehead and on their hand; and they came to life and reigned with Christ for a thousand years.' (Revelation 20:4).

Messiah would have to be called 'a hero' by any Jew. Judas Maccabeus became a hero to the Jewish people when he drove the Greeks out of Israel in 165 BC, and purified the Temple in Jerusalem where the Greeks had sacrificed pigs on the altar. The occasion is still celebrated today at the festival of Hanukkah. In 1986 one of Dylan's defining faith songs was very much still on his concert set lists, often as an encore. Sydney Australia on February 11 was one such occasion. "It's about that time of the evening again when we have to bid each other adieu. But before I get out of here I gotta sing you all this one song. This is a song about my hero. Everybody got heroes, right? For lots of people Mohammed Ali's a hero, right? Yeah. And Albert Einstein, he sure was a hero. I guess you could say even Clark Gable was a hero. Michael Jackson, he's a hero, right? Bruce Springsteen. I care nothing about them people though. None of those people are my heroes; they don't mean nothing to me. I'm sorry but that's the truth. I wanna sing a song about my hero." [92] And then he played 'In The Garden' - 'Did they know that he was the Son of God, did they know that he was Lord?'

Perhaps the Sydney crowds needed to hear this because the following night's introduction was, "It's that time of the night when we must part company. Anyway I wanna sing you a song about my hero. Everybody's got a hero, right? You know back in the States Ronald Reagan is a big hero to a lot of people. Sylvester Stallone, he's also a hero. Ever heard of him? Or over here maybe Mad Max is a hero? Yeah, we got a lot of heroes over in the United States at the moment. Michael Jackson, he's one of the biggest. And my good friend Bruce Springsteen. He's turned into quite a hero these days. I'll tell you something. I don't care nothing about none of these people. I got a different hero. He might have lived a long time ago, but you know what was good yesterday is still good today. He's the same yesterday, today and tomorrow. I don't know if these current heroes are gonna be." (Hebrews 13:8: 'Jesus Christ is the same yesterday and today and forever.') Later that tour, in Vancouver, Canada, he would say, "I wanna dedicate this next song to all the people with the courage to have faith in something that never falters and never fails." [93] These are odd comments for someone in their 'post-Christian' phase to be making.

Even odder (for someone who has supposedly 'renounced' faith in his 'hero') was Dylan's concert for the Pope John-Paul II at the Vatican on September 27, 1997, at the 23rd Italian Eucharistic Congress. Dylan played 'Knocking On Heaven's Door', 'A Hard Rain's A-Gonna Fall' and 'Forever Young'. The Pope even brought Dylan's lyrics into his homily, saying, "You say the answer is blowing in the wind, my friend. So it is, but it is not the wind that blows things away, it is the breath and life of the Holy Spirit, the voice that calls and says, 'Come!'" The Pope added: "You ask me how many roads a man must walk down before he becomes a man. I answer: there is only one road for man, and it is the road of Jesus Christ, who said, 'I am the Way and the Life.'" [94] After playing, Dylan went up the stairs of the dais to where the Pope was sitting, removing his trademark cowboy hat on the way, and kneeling before the Pope, exchanged a few private words as they clasped hands. The organizer of the concert, Cardinal Ernesto Vecchi, said that Dylan had been invited because he is the "representative of the best type of rock" and "he has a spiritual nature." [95] And presumably also because John-Paul II was something of a fan, unlike his successor Benedict, who has said that he had opposed the concert taking place. [96]

Another odd Dylan happening occurred in April 2004. When the exclusive lingerie firm 'Victoria's Secret' used Dylan's song 'Love Sick' for its commercial in 2003, no one ever expected Dylan to show up in it. Not noted for selling out, Dylan had humourously remarked back in 1965 that the only commercial he would get involved in was one for ladies' undergarments. In 2004 their 'Angel In Venice' commercial featured the sight of Dylan interacting with a scantily clad young woman in a Venetian palazzo, again to the tune of 'Love Sick', doing wonders for 'Victoria's Secret' and their product recognition. What everybody missed amid the clamour to accuse Dylan of gross artistic sell-out was the connection between this and his decision to perform for the Pope back in 1997. The supermodel that Dylan was featured with in the commercial was the Brazilian Adriana Lima, a devout Catholic who in April 2006 told GQ magazine that she was a virgin. 'Sex is for after marriage. They have to respect that this is my choice. If there's no respect, that means they don't want me.' [97] She has been described as 'very strong on family and on religion', and her work-break reading as 'a little book from the Bible... she reads - it's kind of sweet.' [98] Of all the models in all the world...

Chapter 17

Concert Set List Material

Dylan, now aged 70, has toured more than any other artist. His 'Never Ending Tour' began in June 1988, although it is a term that Dylan rejects. 'There was a 'Never Ending Tour' but it ended in 1991 with the departure of guitarist G. E. Smith. That one's long gone but there have been many others since.' [99] In 2009 he told 'Rolling Stone' magazine "These days, people are lucky to have a job. Any job. So critics might be uncomfortable with my working so much. Anybody with a trade can work as long as they want. A carpenter, an electrician. They don't necessarily need to retire." [100]

For observers of Dylan's art, his 100 or so shows a year are a great way of noting the songs in his catalogue that Dylan himself feels are important. He plays the songs he wants to play, and not simply the songs that fans expect to hear. He also takes the opportunity to re-work lyrics, for example changing 'from New Orleans to Jerusalem' to 'from New Orleans to New Jerusalem' in 'Blind Willie McTell'. Set lists tell a story, and I am grateful to Dylan-philes such as Bill Pagel [101] for their painstaking documentation of set list material over many years. So what do the last five calendar years have to tell us?

In 2010 the most performed song was 'Thunder On The Mountain' with 101 appearances, followed by the perennial classic 'Like A Rolling Stone' and 'Ballad Of A Thin Man' at 100, then 'Highway 61 Re-Visited' at 99. 'Jolene' (a newer song from 2009) was next at 85, with 'Just Like A Woman' at 71.

In 2009, 'Like A Rolling Stone' came top at 97, then 'All Along The Watchtower' with 96, 'Highway 61 Re-Visited' with 93, and 'Thunder On The Mountain' with 80. Then came 'Jolene' (released that year) with 61, then 'Spirit On The Water' with 54.

In 2008, 'Highway 61 Re-Visited' was top at 92, then 'Thunder On The Mountain' with 90, 'Like A Rolling Stone' with 79, 'Summer Days' with 70, and 'The Levees Gonna Break' and 'Rollin' And Tumblin'' both with 53.

In 2007, 'Thunder On The Mountain' was once again top with 98 performances. Then came 'Highway 61 Re-Visited' with 92, 'Summer Days' with 89, 'Spirit On The Water' with 87, 'All Along The Watchtower' with 71 and 'Rollin' And Tumblin'' with 68. 'Like A Rolling Stone' was way down the performance list at 43 appearances.

In 2006, the year that 'Modern Times' was released, 'Thunder On The Mountain' was played at every concert that year following its inaugural performance in October, for which reason I am placing it joint top for popularity in that year alongside 'Like A Rolling Stone' on 98 (also a 100% rating). After them was 'All Along The Watchtower' with 91, then 'Highway 61 Re-Visited' with 84, 'Summer Days' with 77 and 'Maggie's Farm' with 59.

'Highway 61 Re-Visited' and 'Thunder On The Mountain' therefore emerge as Dylan's two most performed songs over the last 4 complete calendar years with 376 and 369 appearances respectively. By comparison, the somewhat inevitable classic 'Like A Rolling Stone' comes a poor third at 319, followed by 'All Along The Watchtower' at 277. This is very fitting considering that 'Highway 61 Re-Visited' is a somewhat Old Testament piece ('God said to Abraham, "Kill me your son."') about the test Abraham underwent in (almost) sacrificing Isaac on Mount Moriah (a prefigurement of the sacrifice of Christ). While 'Thunder On The Mountain' is just about as Messianic/Christian a song as you could get. ('Some sweet day I'll stand beside my king.') Two covenants, two mountains; and both clearly very important songs to Dylan personally, being central to his live shows over the past 4-5 years.

Dylan has frequently chosen to open his sets with material that is not of his own composition. A popular choice between 1999 and 2002 was the traditional bluegrass number 'Hallelujah I'm Ready To Go', popularized by Bill Monroe, the Stanley Brothers and later by Ricky Skagg. The title is particularly pertinent given Dylan's brush with a fungal (Histoplasmosis) derived pericarditis (from "accidentally inhaling a bunch of stuff that was out on one of the rivers by where I live.") [102] This lead to the often-humourous Dylan remarking, "I'm just glad to be feeling better. I really thought I'd be seeing Elvis soon." [103]

Dylan sang, "Hallelujah, I'm ready, I can hear the voices singing soft and low. I'm ready, Hallelujah. Hallelujah, I'm ready to go. Dark was the night not a star was in sight, on a highway heading down below. I let my Saviour in and he saved my soul from sin, Hallelujah, I'm ready to go. Hallelujah, I'm ready, I can hear the voices singing soft and low. I'm ready, Hallelujah. Hallelujah, I'm ready to go. Sinner don't wait before it's too late, he's a wonderful Saviour to know. Well, I fell on my knees and he answered all my pleas, Hallelujah, I'm ready to go."

Another such opening number was the gospel song 'I Am The Man, Thomas' (Ralph Stanley and Larry Sparks) which Dylan performed it on 59 occasions during 1999 and 2002. 'I am the Man, Thomas, I am the Man. Look at these nail scars I carry in my hand. They drove me up the hill, Thomas, I am the Man. They made me carry the cross, Thomas, I am the Man. I am the Man, Thomas, I am the Man. Look at these nail scars I carry in my hand. They pierced my side with swords, Thomas, I am the Man. They drove me up the hill, Thomas, I am the Man. They laid me in the tomb, Thomas, I am the Man. In three days I rose, Thomas, I am the Man. The song is based on the account of Jesus' resurrection appearance to his disciple Thomas who could not bring himself to believe that Jesus was alive again, having been absent when Jesus has earlier appeared to his disciples. [lxv]

[lxv] John 20:24-29: 'Thomas, one of the twelve, called Didymus, was not with them when Jesus came. So the other disciples were saying to him, "We have seen the Lord!" But he said to them, "Unless I see in his hands the imprint of the nails, and put my finger into the place of the nails, and put my hand into his side, I will not believe." After eight days his disciples were again inside, and Thomas with them. Jesus came, the doors having been shut, and stood in their midst and said, "Peace be with you." Then he said to Thomas, "Reach here with your finger, and see my hands; and reach here your hand and put it into my side; and do not be unbelieving, but believing," Thomas answered and said to him, "My Lord and my God!" Jesus said to him, "Because you have seen me, have you believed? Blessed are they who did not see, and yet believed."'

More recently there has been a notable change of opening number. From November 17th 2010 onwards, Dylan has opened every one of the 25 concerts to the time of writing with either 'Gotta Serve Somebody' or, more commonly, 'Gonna Change My Way Of Thinking'. The latter song had gone an astonishing 29 years without being performed in concert. When it finally re-emerged on October 4th 2009 in Seattle, Washington, it was the version from 'Gotta Serve Somebody - The Gospel Songs Of Bob Dylan', a tribute gospel album released by Sony/Columbia in 2003 and featuring gospel singers performing some of Dylan's material from the period 1979-1981.

Dylan not only appeared on the album himself, alongside an old flame in the form of the gospel artist Mavis Staples, but also completely re-wrote the material. The new lines are extremely telling; the more so for Dylan choosing the version as the song to open many of his shows with since. Dylan sings, 'Jesus is coming, coming back to gather his jewels', alongside a jokey line about the rule of gold replacing 'The Golden Rule.' ('Do unto others as you would have them do unto you.' Luke 6:31). Dylan sings that he is 'sitting at the welcome table.' 'Eating at the welcome table' is a line from the traditional gospel piece, 'Down To The River Jordan'. 'I'm gonna eat at the welcome table, oh yes, I'm gonna eat at the welcome table, some of these days. Hallelujah, I'm gonna eat at the welcome table, some of these days.'

The song re-affirms that Dylan is now experiencing the sun shining on him (probably after the darkness and cold of depression) and that the ubiquitous train track is running one way only (presumably heaven-bound). We learn that he is emerging from 'the dark woods' (surely of depression) before being treated to a classic Dylanesque line about 'jumping on the monkey's back'; where Dylan takes the concept of having 'a monkey on his back' (presumably meaning depression) and reverses it with typical humour.

The 'country dance' obligingly provides the rhyme for 'pray for guidance', which Dylan encourages us to do on a daily basis, along with the familiar theme of giving yourself, again daily, 'another chance', presumably at redemption (shades of the 'take pity on yourself' from 'Thunder On The Mountain'). The daily nature of 'another chance' mirrors the Hebrew prophet Jeremiah's words of encouragement to the

Israelites when they were led into captivity in Babylon circa 586BC. 'The Lord's lovingkindnesses indeed never cease, for his compassions never fail. They are new every morning.' (Lamentations 3:22-23). The 'storms' of life have taught Dylan a lesson - he has no true 'friend' but the Lord Jesus Christ. On the subject of friends, (and I am obliged to the excellent Markus Prieur and his 'Not Dark Yet' website for hosting the mp3's - surely Dylan approved) a careful listen to recent concert performances of this song reveals Dylan changing the lyric from the original 'Gonna put my best foot forward' to the even more telling closing line, 'Put my best friend forward'.

Such was certainly the case at the Feis Festival in London's Finsbury Park on June 18th 2011; the time of this book's final editing. We personally witnessed from close-range an up-beat, almost jubilant Dylan deliver the this opening song's lines with gusto, in a show that also contained the perennial 'Thunder On The Mountain' as the penultimate pre-encore song, after which the 70 year-old Dylan jogged off-stage. 'Feel like a fighting rooster, feel better than I ever felt' ('Cry A While', 'Love And Theft') seems like a fair reflection, given his ability to still play guitar fluidly and with no signs of small joint arthritis or stiffness.

Final words must belong to Mr Dylan.

"When you look ahead now, do you still see a 'Slow Train Coming'?"
"When I look ahead now, it's picked up quite a bit of speed. In fact, it's going like a freight train now." [104]

Endnotes

1 May 13 2011, BobDylan.com

2 Scott Cohen, 'Spin', September 1985

3 Mark Neuman, Washington Post.com

4 Cynthia Gooding, WBAI, New York, 1962

5 'East Village Voice', January 19, 1971

6 'Christianity Today' Magazine, December 19, 2005

7 'Sing Out!' October/November, 1962

8 Andrew Slater, president of Capitol Records and formerly Jacob Dylan's Wallflowers' band's manager, New York Times, May 8, 2005

9 'Bob Dylan: Behind the Shades Revisited', by Clinton Heylin

10 Joel Gilbert's '1975 - 1981: Rolling Thunder and the Gospel Years'

11 Karen Hughes, May 21, 1980, 'Star', (New Zealand)

12 Joel Gilbert's '1975 - 1981: Rolling Thunder and the Gospel Years'

13 Joel Gilbert's '1975 - 1981: Rolling Thunder and the Gospel Years'

14 Karen Hughes, 'The Dominion', Wellington, New Zealand, May 21, 1980

15 'Not Like a Rolling Stone Interview.' Spin, Volume One Number Eight, December 1985

16 Joel Gilbert's '1975 - 1981: Rolling Thunder and the Gospel Years'

17 Joel Gilbert's '1975 - 1981: Rolling Thunder and the Gospel Years'

18 Joel Gilbert's '1975 - 1981: Rolling Thunder and the Gospel Years'

19 'Rolling Stone' Issue 478/479, July 17, 1986

20 Bruce Heiman, Hollywood, California. December, 1979.

21 Joel Gilbert's '1975 - 1981: Rolling Thunder and the Gospel Years'

22 'Not Like a Rolling Stone Interview' Spin, Volume One Number Eight, December 1985

23 The Observer, Sunday January 20, 2008

24 Cameron Crowe interview, 'Biograph' album

25 Joel Gilbert's '1975 - 1981: Rolling Thunder and the Gospel Years'

26 John Pareles, New York Times, September 28, 1997

27 Tony Wright, responsible for the cover art for 'Saved', Clinton Heylin 'Behind the Shades Revisited', page 524

28 Kurt Loder 'Rolling Stone' Magazine, June 21, 1984

29 Clinton Heylin 'Still On The Road', Constable, page 260

30 James Boswell 'The Life of Johnson', (entry for Friday, April 7, 1775)

31 Kurt Loder 'Rolling Stone', June 21, 1984

32 The Guardian, London, October 27, 2005

33 The Times, September 8, 2007

34 Clinton Heylin 'Still On The Road', Constable, page 256

35 Bowling, David, 'Blogcritics Magazine', October 4, 2008

36 Kurt Loder, 'Rolling Stone' Magazine, June 21, 1984

37 Kurt Loder, 'Rolling Stone' Magazine, June 21, 1984

38 Mark Blake, 'Dylan - Visions, Portraits and Back Pages', page 86

39 Kurt Loder, 'Rolling Stone' Magazine, June 21, 1984

40 May 13, 1981: Pope John Paul II was shot and wounded as he drove through crowds in St Peter's Square in Vatican City by the Turkish Muslim Mehmet Ali Agca. The Pope subsequently visited him in prison and forgave him

41 Dave Herman, London, July 2, 1981

[42] Bill Flanagan, New York, March, 1985

[43] Dave Herman, London, July 2, 1981

[44] Vine's Expository Dictionary

[45] From Shunem, a town in the Hebrew territory of Issachar near Mount Tabor

[46] Simon Napier-Bell recalling CBS executive Dick Katz, The Observer, Sunday January 20, 2008

[47] Karen Hughes, May 21, 1980, in the New Zealand newspaper 'The Dominion', August 2, 1980

[48] Bill Flanagan, New York, March, 1985

[49] 1985 interview on the ABC - TV show 20/20

[50] Jon Bream, Minneapolis Star Tribune, May 23, 2008

[51] Chicago Sun Times, November 17, 1985

[52] Mikal Gilmore, 'Rolling Stone' Magazine, July 17, 1986

[53] Simon Sebag, 'Speeches that Changed the World: The Stories and Transcripts of the Moments that Made History.' Quercus, London, 2006

[54] carolbayersager.com

[55] Bob Dylan, 'Chronicles', page 176

[56] 'War... is a business. If you look at it that way you can come to terms with it.' (Bob Dylan to Robert Hilburn, San Francisco, California, November, 1980)

[57] Clinton Heylin 'Still On The Road', Constable, page 371

[58] Clinton Heylin 'Still on the Road', Constable, page 384

[59] The Guardian, Saturday June 14, 2003

[60] Gino Castaldo, 'La Repubblica', Italy, June 24, 1993

[61] 'According To Matthew', Dr A.T. Bradford, Templehouse Publishing, 2010. ISBN 9780956479839

[62] Biographers Wayne Federman and Marshall Terrill, 'Pete Maravich: The Authorised Biography Of Pistol Pete', by 'Focus on the Family'

[63] Attri and Nagarkar, The Journal of Laryngology & Otology (2010), 124: 919-921

[64] The Telegraph (London), April 13, 2001

[65] Bob Dylan to Jon Pareles, California, September, 1997.

[66] C Nehring, Atlantic Monthly, August 8, 2006

[67] Islamic terrorists hijacked planes and destroyed New York's Twin World Trade Towers

[68] Dave Herman, The White House Hotel, London, England, July 2, 1981. Broadcast by WNEW-FM Radio, New York, July 27, 1981

[69] Credit to Chris Johnson for detecting the textual source

[70] 'The Jesus Discovery', Templehouse Publishing, 2010. ISBN 9780956479808

[71] Virgil, Aeneid 6. 851- 853

[72] Palmer, Robert 'Deep Blues' (Viking Press, New York, 1995)

[73] Thedeltablues.wordpress.com

[74] 'Mother Goose', Children's Songs And Nursery Rhymes, James Miller, 1869

[75] CBS '60 Minute Interview', Ed Bradley, June, 2006

[76] Jonathan Lethem, 'Rolling Stone', September 7, 2006

[77] The Daily Mail, December, 2008

[78] 'Tell Tale Signs' album sleeve notes

[79] RightWingBob.com

[80] "It is the Lord's Day; my wish is fulfilled. I have always desired to die on Sunday." J. Haines, 'America's Civil War', 2006.

[81] Interview with Bill Flanagan, bobdylan.com

[82] Interview with Bill Flanagan, bobdylan.com

[83] Interview with Bill Flanagan, bobdylan.com

[84] Daily Telegraph, August 27, 2009

[85] For example, Lawrence J Epstein ('Best American Poetry') describes 'a good-hearted singer content to be a loyal citizen in the Land of the Great American Songbook.'

[86] Bill Flanagan Interview, 'North American Street Newspaper Association', November, 2009

[87] According To Matthew', Dr A.T. Bradford, Templehouse Publishing, 2010. ISBN 9780956479839

[88] Craig McGregor, March, 1978

[89] Brian Hinton, Discoogle.com

[90] Scott Cohen, California, September, 1985

[91] Babylonian Talmud: Tractate Sanhedrin Folio 97a

[92] Thanks to Olof Björner for his invaluable 'Bobwords' concert introductions at www.bjorner.com

[93] Both quotes courtesy of 'Bobwords' concert introductions at www.bjorner.com

[94] www.vatican.va/holy_father/john_paul_ii

[95] New York Times, August 27, 1997

[96] The Daily Telegraph, London, March 8, 2007

[97] GQ Magazine, March, 2006

[98] 'Showbiz Tonight' June 17, 2005

[99] 'World Gone Wrong' album notes

[100] 'Rolling Stone' August 30, 2009

[101] www.Boblinks.com

[102] 'Guitar World' March, 1999

[103] Sony Music Press Release, June 2, 1997

[104] John Dolen, September, 1995, Fort Lauderdale, Florida

CPSIA information can be obtained at www.ICGtesting.com
Printed in the USA
269086BV00006B/60/P